The Region's Favourite

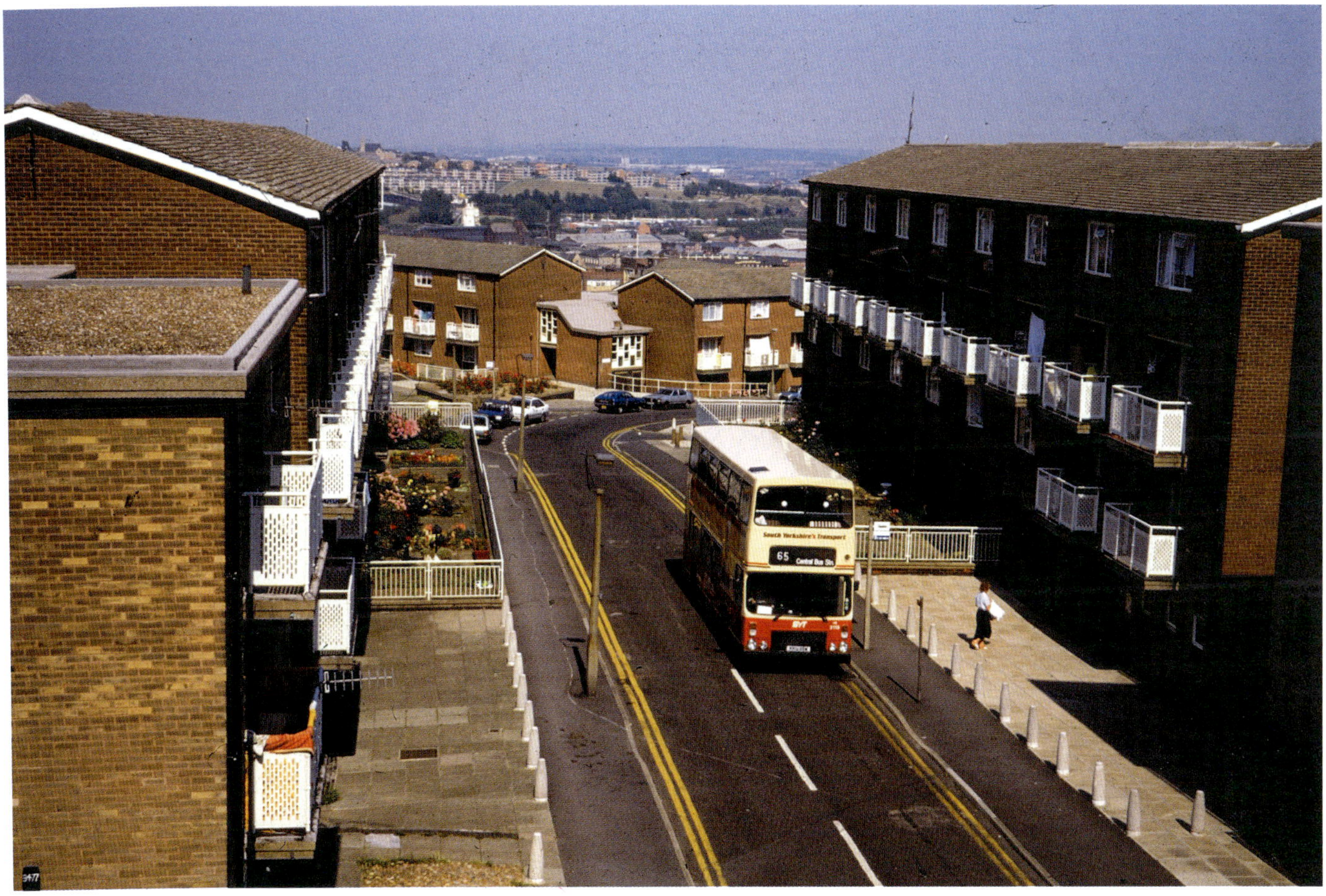

Neil Hudson | Gary Nolan | Darren Sentance

ISBN 978-1-909091-33-7

Published 2021

Published by The Omnibus Society

Designed by Neil Hudson

Copyright

Neil Hudson,

Gary Nolan & Darren Sentance

Front Cover

After the ESOP, quality was going to be the key to success, and in the summer of 1995, 30 Volvo B6 and 25 Volvo B10Ms entered the fleet.

Posed at the exit door of Rotherham garage, 427 and 717 look fresh in the sweltering summer of that year.

Overleaf

Nothing lasts forever, and nearly everything in this shot has now gone. In the summer of 1990, Dennis Dominator 2115 sets down a passenger in the Bramwell Gardens estate on the 'around the houses' service 65 from Oughtibridge to Sheffield city centre. This service was known to drivers as the 'Mountain Goat', due to the number of hills encountered on its journey.

The estate has been redeveloped, and the bus is long since razor blades.

We'd like to dedicate this book to the staff, past and present, who made it such a great company to work for, and without their professional attitudes and determination to keep the show on the road, this story wouldn't exist.

Contents

Introduction		4
Foreword		5
Chapter 1	From PTE to SYT	6
Chapter 2	1986 & 1987	24
Chapter 3	1988	44
Chapter 4	1989	58
Chapter 5	1990	78
Chapter 6	1991	96
Chapter 7	1992	110
Chapter 8	1993	120
Chapter 9	1994	132
Chapter 10	1995	148
Chapter 11	1996	164
Chapter 12	1997	184
Chapter 13	1998	198
Chapter 14	The Service Fleet	210
Chapter 15	Blinds	218
Chapter 16	The Garages	234
Chapter 17	The Fleet	252

Introduction

Neil Hudson

Gary Nolan

Darren Sentence

May 2021

There are, apparently, more acres in Yorkshire than there are words in the Bible. Even if that's not true, it's a big place. From Middlesbrough and Sedbergh in the north; Scarborough and Hull in the east; Bawtry and Sheffield in the south and Saddleworth and Barnoldswick in the west, it's a county united by stubbornness and kind hearts. If it carried on for just twelve miles to the west, it would straddle the country from coast to coast.

The 1972 Local Government Act set about replacing the traditional County, County Borough and City areas with simpler authorities, linked to where people got their local services from. Yorkshire, split into three 'Ridings' (an old Norse term for thirds) was to be carved up, with two new 'Metropolitan' counties, in the south and west (you can never get rid of the Ridings and they still exist today).

These two new areas of Local Government, were also to have bestowed upon them, regional transport bodies called 'Passenger Transport Executives'. These weren't new, having been ushered in through the 1968 Transport Act, but South Yorkshire was to become the most radical.

The County Council set about a policy of social inclusion, before that term had been invented, making public transport the central plank to all planning decisions throughout the region. The former municipal bus undertakings in Sheffield, Rotherham and Doncaster were rolled together to be the operational wing of this new organisation.

The most noticeable plank of the policy was cheap fares. Fares remained at the level set by Doncaster in 1973, and this was then applied across the county. The PTE also set about aggressively buying up any independent operators that wished to sell, and even had sights on Yorkshire Traction.

By 1981 the policy had been copied by the GLC in London, but had been challenged in the courts. That case was lost, threatening the policies in South Yorkshire. By 1984, the Conservative controlled Government of the day, decided that the Transport Executives (which were mainly controlled by Labour councillors) were too expensive, and in general, the world of bus operation needed shaking up.

Two pieces of legislation were laid out in Parliament. One abolished the Metropolitan Counties, replacing them with unitary authorities in April 1986. The second, the 1985 Transport Act, deregulated the bus market in October of the same year, meaning anybody who could provide a service, would be allowed to do so, outwith London and Northern Ireland. Central planning and cheap fares were in the bin, and in the space of six months, twelve years of policy making had been thrown away. That's where our story starts. It's a roller coaster ride, with ups and downs, triumphs and tragedies, but all performed under the steely resolve to provide a high quality, value for money bus service for the people of South Yorkshire and beyond.

It couldn't have been written without the help of former and current employees of SYT, Mainline and First, who have assisted with photographs, archive and rattling our brains with memories of the past.

As well as the authors' photographic efforts, we'd like to thank Richard Simons, Andy Metcalfe, Jamie Scott, Ian Fretwell, Allan Needham, Richard Barnes, Lee Whitehead, Julian Shepherd, Paul Jenkins, Luke Farley, Andrew Radford, Paul Fox, Don Penney, Paul Beardsley, Richard Gregory, Roy Wilson, David Stevenson, Simon Middleton, Andrew Jarosz, the late Terry Cooper and James Horten for access to their photos and collections. Where photographs have been taken from collections, all efforts have been made to contact the original photographer.

The official photographs are from the SYT/Mainline archive.

Foreword

J.I. Davies

The public transport system in South Yorkshire from 1974 to the end of the century, attracted much interest from politicians, economists and transport enthusiasts.

Between 1974 and 1986, SYPTE was well known throughout the UK for its innovative bus policies. Whilst its livery of brown and cream (thought to be a mixture of Sheffield and Rotherham's blue with Doncaster's red) rarely met with approval, it was a pioneer.

Once known as the 'People's Republic of South Yorkshire', the County Council pursued an ultra low fares policy which they believed would encourage public transport use, reduce car ownership and limit traffic congestion.

Undoubtedly these three aims were achieved, with very low car ownership, high levels of patronage and very frequent services, but at an enormous cost to the ratepayers. Bus passengers were able to travel from as little as 2p and timetables were not interrupted by queues of cars heading for town and city centre's.

Rolls Royce engines with Voith gearboxes in the double deckers, bendi buses, free town/city centre circular services and special routes with adapted buses for disabled passengers were a few of the many innovative developments pioneered by a forward looking management team, supported by politicians.

However, this massive public subsidy was attracting the attention of the Conservative Government of the day, who were pursuing an overall privatisation policy in industry and public transport. Led by Nicolas Ridley, as Transport Minister, the 1985 Transport Act was devised to break up the current system.

Bus routes were to be operated commercially, and a new licensing system made is easier for new operators to set up and run services as they wished. SYPTE had to set up a new 'arms length' bus company (SYT) to operate in this new environment.

SYT operated commercially viable routes, with all services converted to one person operation and a fleet reduction of many non standard buses. Hundreds of Conductors, Drivers, Engineers and administration staff took advantage of a generous redundancy scheme, and many later turned up later, working for the emerging, competing operators.

The years that followed saw intense competition on the main, busy corridors and new operators winning PTE tenders for the quieter ones.

With fluctuating fortunes, SYT maintained a commercial core network, but the Government continued to pursue its privatisation policy by forcing the PTA to sell off SYT completely. It threatened that a failure to do so would result in its staff being removed form the Local Government Pension Scheme.

Eventually SYT was sold to its staff on an equal basis, with all staff receiving free shares. This became Mainline and its smart red and yellow buses soon became known across the County.

The new company introduced stylish new uniforms and adopted innovative marketing schemes along with a modern fleet.

New team management structures developed enthusiastic operating and engineering staff, and the number of competing operators reduced, either by sell outs or business failure.

However, the new company had been set up with few owned assets, and was reliant on lease arrangements for its buses and properties. Mainline would continue to develop, but the only way to solve the problem of assets was to be part of a bigger group being taken over by FirstGroup in 1998.

This is a story of continuous change brought about by political strategy. Moreover, it reflects the passion and dedication by staff employed at every level to ensure that safe and efficient services would be provided to the people of South Yorkshire.

Chapter 1

From PTE to SYT

Despite many protests, the 1985 Transport Act was going to be implemented in the autumn of 1986. The exact date was still being argued over in the Lords, ranging from September to October, but SYPTE saw the writing on the wall, and was starting to plan for the future in the late spring of 1985.

The legislation, which followed on from that, scrapping the Metropolitan Counties, gave instructions on how the former PTEs (as well as municipal operators) should detach their operating arm from the residual organisation.

In the case of South Yorkshire, the residual PTE would hang on to the ownership of bus stations, be responsible for concessionary fares as well as planning and supporting local rail services. A separate 'OpCo' would be an arm's length operation, owned by a new PTA (PTAs became the new way of controlling PTEs, with members coming from the local authority areas served by it), but with a nominally independent board, with non-executive's, appointed by it.

Plans for South Yorkshire's 'OpCo', were advancing, and the view was established, early on in the process, that it would need a new, bold identity that could make it stand out from any potential competitor.

Initial experiments were conducted using East Bank based Dennis Dominator 2194. The livery consisted of a modified version of the existing PTE livery using a pinkish cream called 'Cameo'. This was matched with a 'Chestnut' brown skirt and red, self-adhesive lining. The existing PTE fleetnames had an additional 's' added to it, to emphisise that it was South Yorkshire's Transport. Doncaster based Dennis 2218 had the 'Chestnut' in the usual style replacing 'Tan', but found no favour either.

Whilst this initial attempt was seen as being poor and too close to the existing livery, the scheme was adapted for a batch of ten Fastline Metrobuses (1941 to 1950) that arrived that summer, and the 'Cameo' was also adopted as a base for the new 'Nipper' (41 to 53), 'Clipper' (2001 to 2010) and 'Fastline Articulated (2011 to 2013) liveries, introduced on Dennis Dominos and Leyland DAB articulated buses, also on delivery.

A more professional approach was required. Some initial customer surveys praised the low fares and high level of service, but gave poor marks for presentation and staff engagement. Advertising agencies were asked to pitch for a complete rebrand of the company, its marketing and customer engagement. A shortlist of two companies were initially asked to provide a further, more detailed presentation of their designs and analysis.

Left

The livery trials on 2194 were too close to the original PTE livery.

The diagrams, by Luke Farley, show how similar they were. If the new company was going to be successful, it would need to be bolder and more distinctive.

2194 is seen on Sheaf Street, Sheffield in the summer of 1985.

First out of the blocks were Hyphen Hayden. This agency had done work for the PTE before, and had, at its helm, a former employee, in the form of Bruce Hugman. He understood the challenge, but the presentation concentrated on a name for the new 'OpCo' of 'Teambus'. It also combined the existing PTE livery, with this new name. Whilst this approach wasn't accepted, it didn't harm the agency, as they continued to do work for the PTE, as well as create new brands for Lincoln, North Western, Northumbria and Yorkshire Rider. Their mapping style also went on to influence designers in the future.

The second agency provided a more revolutionary approach. Bradshaw and Allwood were a small agency based in Leeds, who had done work for WYPTE. Whilst they kept the approach of 'South Yorkshire's Transport', they came up with a new, brighter, bolder livery. In addition to the 'Cameo' and 'Chestnut' colours, a bold use was made of 'Poppy' red, applied in a new style. When newly painted it look fresh and impressive. In addition, they proposed the use of television and billboard advertising to promote the new image.

Wrapping the whole package together was a new slogan. This played on the SYT brand as, 'SYT around South Yorkshire' (the inference being that SYT substituted sit) and a completely new symbol, based on the SYT letters, interlocked to be one single unit (similarities could be drawn to GMPTEs 'M' blem of the time). Instead of being in Helvetica, the new fleetname was in Crillie Bold, a newish typeface that looked modern and contemporary.

Top to bottom

The cameo cream was being used prior to the new livery, as a base for new liveries for 'Nipper', 'Fastline' and 'Clipper'

Buses painted from late summer had been painted in plain cameo with chestnut skirt in readiness for the new image.

The first bus to be painted in the livery was East Bank based Dennis Dominator 2189. This differed slightly from later repaints, as the fleetnames were painted on and it lacked a cameo line on the skirt. This was used in the filming of the television advertisement. A jaunty tune, based on the new slogan, depicted various people using the bus for all sorts of activities. The 30 second slots were played out on Yorkshire Television and Channel Four during November and December 1985.

The new brand was launched ahead of the actual 'OpCo' on 4 November 1985. The main launch was in Rotherham, but smaller events took place in Sheffield and Doncaster. Buses that had been painted since September had been outshopped in 'Cameo' and 'Chestnut', but without fleetnames. In the week before the launch, as many of these vehicles as possible, had the red added, ready for a 'big bang' roll out that morning.

Members of staff, already fearing what was to happen, were informed about setting up of the new 'OpCo', and the fares increases to come, on the abolition of the Metropolitan authorities, through a new 'Transyt' newspaper, although this ended after two editions.

The first buses to be delivered in the new livery, were a batch of 20, Alexander bodied, Dennis Dominators (2451 to 2470) which entered service between November 1985 and January 1986. Incidentally, these were the last buses to enter service with Rolls Royce 'Eagle' engines, which had been standard for the PTE since 1981. In a slight degrading of specification, these buses lost some internal bright work, but gained tactile hand poles to help older people get a better grip when standing or gaining access to seats.

Real work on the 'OpCo' got going in January 1986. The date had now been set for 26 October of that year. 'D' day, was going to see a revolution in the bus industry, outside of London and Northern Ireland, not seen since the 1930s. The work of the PTE had to continue, so a shadow company was set up within the organisation, to manage how the new business was going to function from day one.

Firstly, the new operator had to register the service provision it was planning to operate commercially, no later than 28 February 1986. This was always going to be difficult for a PTE company, especially one which was operating on fares pegged at the same levels charged in 1975. Although a simplification to stages was made in 1984, essentially, the fare that you paid to the driver or conductor, regardless of inflation that had gone on in the intervening years, was the same as had been paid 11 years previously.

No PTE services operated at a profit, even accounting for the subsidy paid by South Yorkshire County Council. Nobody had a real idea what the cost basis was. Today, your smartphone can give you calculations, and connect you to the rest of the world in seconds, in 1986 computers were still in their infancy and it could take days or weeks to actually discover your fares income, as a phalanx of staff ploughed through daily waybills to establish passenger numbers, and balance the days' takings against tickets issued.

Opposite and Above

The new image was launched in a ceremony at All Saints Square in Rotherham, with further unveilings in Sheffield and Doncaster.

Backed up by television advertising, the image was strong and adaptable.

The last new Dennis Dominators, fitted with Rolls Royce engines, were split between Doncaster, Rotherham, East Bank, Halfway and Herries garages.

Seen entering Waterdale in Doncaster, 2454 is seen on the busy, cross town service group, 455 to 457, between Edlington and Rossington in the spring of 1986.

The PTE had been one of the first to introduce new ticketing technology, this being the British designed 'Wayfarer' machine, but it would take until July 1986 to get every bus in the fleet fitted with this equipment, and even then, due to Union issues, the buses in Sheffield were fitted with a remote printer, whilst in Rotherham and Doncaster, they were fitted with an integral unit.

The hard worked Schedules staff had to prepare a pattern of service based on a combination of 'best guess', in conjunction with a computer modelling scenario, developed by the consultancy MVA, which aimed to predict which particular piece of mileage could be covered in a commercial way, and which would need to go out to tender. Whilst this was an important tool, it did lead to portions of routes being abandoned, which should have been commercially operated, as well as under representing the number of passengers that would eventually use the service.

Bus and crew scheduling can be the make or break of a bus company, and the two key factors that a scheduler must consider when producing driver duties, are the efficiency and the workability of his/her schedule. Efficiency reflects upon the operating costs that the company faces and the workability upon staff morale and motivation – two contrasting factors.

Up to deregulation, the creation of bus and crew schedules, was a labour intensive role undertaken by skilled staff, with graph paper and pen. There weren't as many frequent changes, as there are now, reflecting the stability of the service provided.

The tasks were all carried out manually, the starting point being the creation of bus workings from the timetables that were in place. Bus graphs would be drawn, detailing the work each bus carried out throughout the day, with notable times, highlighted where the bus departed and returned to the garage, and when it was at any points at the start or along the route of each trip where drivers could be changed.

If a bus approaches you displaying a WAYFARER notice it indicates the vehicle is fitted with Wayfarer electronic ticket machinery.

Having paid the driver in the usual way please pull the ticket firmly from the machine.

The detail of each bus would then be recorded on a separate report as a bus working or bus duty/running board.

The noting of the relief points is key for the creation of crew duties, as each bus can be split into portions of work. These portions of work can then be assembled to form a duty for each driver.

In addition to the graphs being prepared manually using pencil and rubber on pre printed graph sheets, bus boards and/or duty boards had to be hand written or typed and copies made for distribution to garage offices etc., as well as at least one copy presented to the driver when signing on for their duty. It was a slow process and required a large number of staff over a short period of time and more expense in Rotherham and Doncaster where duty boards handed to drivers, were laminated onto aluminum 'tins' to make them more robust.

Above

The Wayfarer ticket machine had been first introduced by the PTE in 1984, but it took until the summer of 1986 to be used fleetwide.

At Rotherham, Doncaster and Halfway, integral printers were in use, but in Sheffield, remote printing machines were positioned behind the drivers' cab.

In the run up to de-regulation, each District produced their own schedules and followed their own rules (parameters) in the construction of driver duties and rotas. Local Trade Union representatives were involved in the checking of the duties, to ensure they complied with the rules, which were fairly strict, with a number of restrictions over and above the Driver's Hours Regulations that applied. It is fair to say that the duties were inefficient with rest periods between spells of work, paid (known within the industry as clock to clock). In addition, the levels of spare staff to cover for holidays and sickness were high, further reducing the efficiency if no work was available for those additional cover staff.

In Rotherham and Doncaster there were frequently concerns raised by the Trade Union reps about the length of driving spells on short routes - East Denes (111 & 112) in Rotherham and Hyde Park Circulars (173 & 174) in Doncaster, where round trip times were 20 - 25 minutes. The argument was that the number of trips in a three or four hour spell could be tiring and monotonous, however, the reps also recognised that on these services, drivers had three opportunities per hour to have a short leg stretch or toilet break, compared with some of the longer runs.

In Sheffield it was a different matter where the agreements were more rigid and well documented in the 'Green Book'. Bus workings included guaranteed allowances for layover at terminal points, on the basis of the route length, with duties and rosters constructed around 12 week cycles, providing fixed days off over each 12 weeks of work.

Rest day working was rigid with 'starred' (6th and 7th) days, where work was made available, unless the driver contracted out. Overtime before or after the scheduled duty was allocated under the framework of 'and own' meaning overtime *and own* duty, also known as 'suet' (literally paying for your pudding). The week ran Sunday to Saturday, and holiday allocation was fairly standard, compared with the industry norm of having holiday groups across the year, but on a two week holiday a ruling of 'Saturday prior' ensured that by swapping days off in the preceding week the driver had the Saturday off prior to their holiday commencing. With two holiday groups already unavailable for work on each Saturday, this ruling along with higher service frequencies on this busy shopping day, created problems for staff allocators, with the inevitable stacking of buses with lost mileage being recorded.

Conscious that staff savings would need to be made in the new commercial world, and that service changes would likely be more frequent, an investigation into the recently introduced computer scheduling packages being marketed was undertaken. Doncaster was used as a testbed for the use of the software, and two specialists in the market, Wootton Jeffreys and Giro were challenged to produce a full schedule for the Doncaster operation.

Giro, a French- Canadian company had developed their HASTUS system and won the contest as the Wootton Jeffreys solution struggled to recognise the numerous locations used as terminal points including the two Bus Stations and those within the Town Centre.

HASTUS used research, conducted within Montreal University, and developed in a system of modules that could be adapted to how a company scheduled its staff. Modules included vehicle workings, crew workings and even a rota/ keyboard building function.

Above

The new livery quickly spread and suited all vehicle types.

Only one Volvo Ailsa, 374, was fully repainted, and was withdrawn, due to corrosion in April 1986.

The Leyland National fleet was considerably brightened by the new scheme and they became familiar sights in Halifax, Huddersfield and even Manchester.

The Roe bodied Leyland Atlanteans were well proportioned, but the new livery gave them a 'bald' look.

374 is seen arriving on the Manor Estate in Sheffield, 24 is at East Bank garage and 1741 is seen at Hillsborough Park taking part in the 1986 SYTS bus rally.

It would be some time before the Schedules staff were trained, and be capable of, producing the supporting documents direct from the scheduling program, as well as creating the duties. Until that time the duties, bus boards and rosters were still being produced manually before any staff savings could be made. The move away from driver boards being on 'tins' required an alternative, and the best way forward was that they be inserted into plastic wallets, which was a faster process and further reduced the administrative workload.

Conscious of the need to make further savings, there were several attempts to renegotiate the schedules agreements with the Trade Union, and the emphasis in Sheffield was put on removing the 12 week cycle of rostering, and a proposal of flexible rostering was developed, which allocated the weekly work on the basis of what needed to be covered, rather than having a fixed template for the duties to be fitted into. The discussions were fraught, and eventually there was agreement, with caveats on 'and owns', star days and long weekend guarantees.

The next target for cost savings, was to increase the length of each portion (spell of work) on the many cross city services. The legal maximum spell of duty time, prior to a 30 minute break is 5 hours 30 minutes, but the agreement in Sheffield was capped at four hours on cross city services, which depending on the round trip time, could be further restricted. For example, on the busy cross city service 95, the round trip time was 90 minutes, with driver relief opportunities around every 45 minutes on Commercial Street up, on journeys to Walkley, and Commercial Street down on journeys to Intake. That meant that the maximum spell was restricted to around 3 hours 45 minutes, invariably leading to some duties requiring to be made up to the minimum daily paid hours. This was achieved by showing the time required, as make up, to be shown as spare - in most cases the spare time was insufficient for the driver to be used on any productive work.

In a simple tactic of scheduling, a 3 hour 45 spell, then allowing the driver a 12 minute break by dropping back to a later bus for half a trip (45 minutes), the portion of work could be extended to create half a duty. When this was done as the second half of a duty, the drivers were not pleased, and raised the point that it would be better to remain on the original bus to complete the half a trip and finish 12 minutes earlier. It was pleasing to hear the Trade Union reps accept their members point of view, and that was a start of the easing of restrictions which were included as measures within the introduction of the Keyboard 88 revised working arrangements.

There were lengthy debates about the Saturday prior ruling, which continued to cause staffing shortages on summer Saturdays. It was put to the Trade Union reps that the days of everyone going on their holidays to Mablethorpe by charabanc, that only departed each Saturday, were gone, and that in the modern world, most people go abroad and with flights to Lanzarote on Thursdays and to the Balearics on Tuesdays, having the Saturday off prior to the start of holidays was no longer a necessary, or beneficial privilege. The other concern, taken seriously by the reps was the pressure it was putting on their members, who were working on Saturdays, who could well have a bus missing in front of them. Within time, Saturday prior allocation became allocated on request 'opt in' rather than 'opt out' which was a step in the right direction.

Above

Some quite elderly Leyland Leopards received the new SYT livery. These two former Dearneways coaches, were reallocated to East Bank from Rotherham, after the Leyland DAB articulated coaches had been introduced.

1026 and 1028 are pictured on the front apron of the garage in the summer of 1986. 1026 was not fitted with ticket issuing equipment, and was used, with a conductor, on peak hour extras, as well as runs to High Bradfield on service 62.

Both would not survive the first year with the new company.

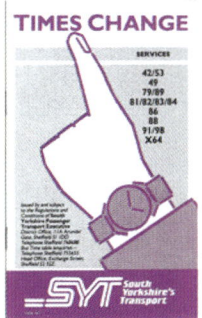

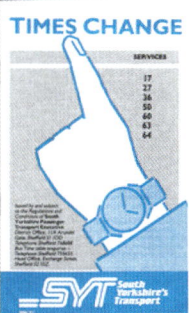

Over a period of a few years and through various pay deals that included small productivity elements, the scheduling parameters became more relaxed and the duties created were more efficient. At the same time, the Trade Union reps still had some responsibility in checking the duties, and now being confident to accept that the computer scheduling software could not create duties outside of the agreement, they were able to spend more time on looking at the duties with a view to making them more workable, without losing efficiency, for their members.

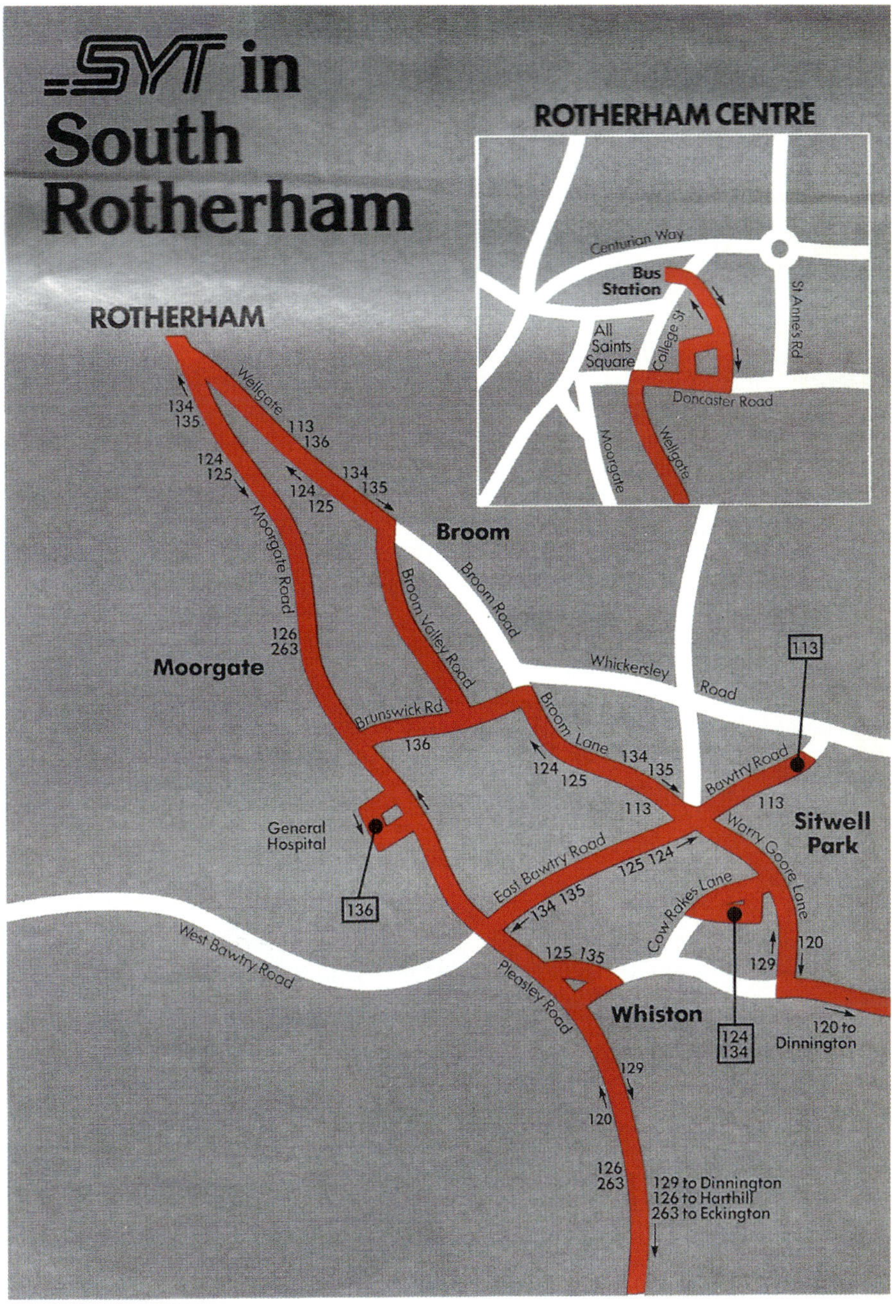

The schedules staff became a small team of talented people and in Sheffield having been split up and working from their own garages at deregulation, came together as a unit initially, at Greenland Road and then Olive Grove. They had a good working relationship with the Trade Union reps and their knowledge and experience were frequently called upon by the Garage Managers to resolve issues relating to duties and rosters.

In the background, with the abolition of the Metropolitan Councils, the fares subsidy came to an end in April 1986. Overnight, a fares increase was implemented that equated to 250%, which naturally had an effect on the number of passengers carried (down by 15%), although this did eventually plateau to about a 10% reduction. This went hand in hand with a reduction in miles operated, and the hard worked schedules staff also had to implement service changes throughout the year.

Rotherham, Doncaster, Dunscroft and Herries Garages were first out of the blocks, with changes implemented in May 1986. Not all the changes were negative. In Rotherham, the opportunity was taken to provide a better service pattern to Brinsworth and Whiston, as well as bringing more services in to Rotherham Bus Station that had operated from College Street and Effingham Street. In the main, services were trimmed at peak hours, and some off peak reductions were made, which included simple things like reducing frequencies from every 10 minutes to every 12, but heavier cuts were made to evening and Sunday frequencies. East Bank, Greenland and Leadmill followed suit in the proceeding months, although Halfway Garage, with its preponderance of mileage outside of the county, and its heavy commitment to schools and British Coal contracts, made no changes at this time.

Above & Below Centre

The promotion for Savercard was mainly by T shape adverts, as seen on 2170 on Centenary Bridge in Rotherham.

Overall adverts. As carried by 2151 in Rotherham bus station, initially referenced Yorkshire Traction and British Rail, but were quickly removed at deregulation.

There wasn't time to analyse these changes, or check if the cuts had been in the right place. Hard worked staff were under pressure to get ready for deregulation. This lead to uneven patterns in some areas, which were corrected in the October, but by then, some valuable customers had been lost.

The increase in fares had been mitigated by the introduction of a period travel pass called 'Savercard'. Initially, this was a PTE product, priced at £15 for a calendar month, but the advertising, again produced by Bradshaw and Allwood, leant heavily on the new SYT image. Use was made of television advertising and the tag line this time was 'Suss out your Savercard'. In furtherance of this promotion, two Metrobuses in Sheffield (1856 and 1857) and two Dominators (2101 in Doncaster and 2151 in Rotherham) were painted in to a modified SYT style livery of brown, red and white with yellow and orange squares, with large pictures of the Savercard ticket on the side.

Initially, the ticket was also available on services of Yorkshire Traction, British Rail as well as any independents or other PTE or NBC companies within the county, but wasn't allowed on SYT buses operating out with the boundary. This situation became even more confusing at deregulation as the product went with SYT and then became operator specific, with minor exceptions on jointly operated routes, as well as being available outside the old county boundary. A recipe for confusion.

Famously, the City Clipper in Sheffield was a high frequency, free, city circle service connecting the somewhat remote Bus and Rail stations with the main shopping areas of Haymarket, High Street, Fargate and the Moor. The new Leyland DAB articulated buses, purchased for the route, that had only entered service in August 1985, had a continental style of boarding and alighting. All three doors were available for boarding, but this caused problems when fares had to be charged. The way around this, was to remove two pairs of seats and install old Videmat, self-service ticket machines, which had last seen use in 1984 and had been stored at Leadmill garage. They had been withdrawn initially due to their unreliability, a tradition they continued when reintroduced. This anomaly was brought to end at deregulation, with all passengers boarding at the front doors and paying the driver in a conventional manner.

Finally, the new 'OpCo' had a name. The prosaic South Yorkshire Transport Limited was registered in 1986, together with a number of other dormant companies, should they be required. In addition, Booth & Fisher Motor services was also retained as a name, and Leyland National 11 at Halfway received a modified version of SYT livery, with the 'Cameo' being replaced by normal cream, and the fleetname modified with Booth and Fisher substituted after the SYT logo. The idea was stillborn, and no further buses were painted in this fashion.

A business plan had to be submitted to the Secretary of State for Transport, prior to the new company formally starting trading, and in pursuance with the Act, the new company also had to make provision for each garage, should the Government require, to be a stand-alone business. This shaped how the company was set up, and as such, a shuffle of mileage and routes would be required to ensure that each garage had a fighting chance of being profitable from day one.— yet another headache for scheduling and administration staff to deal with.

Leading up to deregulation, the PTE had to slim down to a more manageable size, and some 1600 members of staff had to be removed from the payroll. A new redundancy policy, called Policy D, gave enhanced redundancy pay and early retirement to as many staff as possible, initially targeted at those over the age of 50. As the costs of this were borne by the PTE, this gave a slight advantage to the new SYT, as it was not saddled with redundancy costs from day one.

The new board of SYT consisted of existing officers, who transferred over to their new roles. They were:

Peter Sephton – Managing Director

D. Scott Helliwell – Operations Director

Wilf Kemp – Personnel and Engineering Director

Mike Pestereff – Finance Director.

In addition, there were numerous non-executive appointees, drawn from the local authorities of the old Metropolitan County, local Labour Party, T&GWU as well as former NBC supremo Robert Brook.

Backing up this board were two Associate Directors, looking after the day to day running of the business. These were Ian Davies, who looked after Sheffield and Bob Rowe who looked after Rotherham and Doncaster.

As per the Business Plan, and Act of Parliament, each garage had to function as a business within SYT, and each had a Garage Manager, looking after the running of the business at their location. They were:

Iain Duff – Herries

Bill Baldwin – East Bank

Mike Newton – Leadmill

Brian Keith – Greenland

John Swann – Halfway

Malcolm Woodward – Rotherham

Bernard Keane – Doncaster

Colin Fowlston – Dunscroft.

Above & Below Left

The Booth and Fisher name had been eliminated by the late 1970s but plans were made for a restoration.

Bus 11 was repainted using the red and cream from B&F's livery, but it was so close to the new SYT colours, it wasn't perpetuated. The B&F fleetname was eventually removed.

The Leyland DAB artics for the City Clipper had three doors, which were originally for boarding and alighting.

2009 shows this to great effect turning from Pinstone Street into Furnival Gate in Sheffield, an area which is being completely redeveloped.

Right

The former PTE Training Centre at Meadowhall was selected as the new Head Office.

Built on the former site of densely packed terrace housing, the building had been purchased in 1979.

In the bottom right of the picture, early earthworks are in hand to remodel the former Hadfields Steelworks into the site of Meadowhall.

Some of these individuals had wide ranging experience of operating buses and budgets on a day to day basis, some didn't. They were responsible not just for the operations within their garage, but also engineering and finance.

Backing this up was a wide ranging central engineering and central support function which dealt with marketing etc., as well as company policy and giving an overall coherence to how the company was perceived to the wider public at large. Each garage had its own scheduling team, and eventually went on to devise its own service provision.

New entrants to the company were Tom Young from Midland Red North, who came in as Commercial Manager and Jeff Gazzard as Marketing Manager. It was felt the new SYT needed a harder commercial edge, and people with backgrounds outwith the normal operational remit were ideal for the future success of the company.

This new trimmed down company needed fewer vehicles and premises. It was easy to detach non-operational premises/vehicles and leave them with the PTE. Bus stations, and route equipment were going to be their responsibility, and their upkeep and management were retained by them. However, the responsibility for Travel Shops remained with SYT, and the staff for these transferred, leaving the PTE to set up their own departments for such matters, as well as the issuing of concessionary passes and timetables for tendered services.

The PTE had been based at the former Sheffield Transport head office in Exchange Street. It had, next door, the huge Castlegate canteen and Social Club facility. Ideally, as they were physically linked, that would have become the new headquarters of SYT, but that wasn't to be. The new SYT had to find a new base to call home, and that was to be the former PTE Training Centre at Amos Road, Meadowhall.

A squat, 1970s built structure, it had been home to the PTEs Training School and Apprentices since 1980. It was in no shape to become a head office for a company and building work started to turn it in to an office and stores facility, but this wasn't complete until spring 1987. In the meantime, displaced SYT staff were dispersed to Rotherham, Central Works as well as some temporarily remaining in Exchange Street. Driver training went back to Greenland, where it had come from, although based in Portakabins this time and apprentice training, in a much reduced form, continued at Meadowhall.

When it came to operational premises, it was clear there would need to be some trimming performed. Strong board opposition came to closing any operational garages, so, all the former PTE garages passed to SYT.

In Sheffield, there were three substantial structures that had been built since World War 2. Herries, Greenland and East Bank had been built in 1952, 1959 and 1961 respectively, and all had been modernised or extended in the proceeding decade. This came in the form of providing additional pit capacity at each garage, capable of performing MOT prep work; the provision of MOT test facilities and a huge extension at Greenland; creation of a new engineering extension at Herries and a parcel of land beside the garage (commonly known as the dairy park) to permit an increase in the number of vehicles allocated; enormous earthworks at East Bank which underpinned the foundations at the rear of the building as well as providing external parking for 80 vehicles.

Leadmill was the odd one out. Built in the 1913 as Shoreham Street tram depot, it had an extension added prewar to accommodate buses in the adjacent Leadmill Road. Both parts had been combined and modernised in 1960 when trams had been withdrawn, but it was a strange triangular shape, with limited engineering facilities, which compared to other garages were primitive, at best. As the terraced houses surrounding the garage had been demolished during the 1960s for a planned, but never implemented urban motorway, additional land was obtained for parking on Fornam Street and a former engineering works across the road had also been obtained. Woeful it may have been, but it was handily beside the Central Bus Station and main rail station, and also held Sheffield District's cash handling, ticket machine repair shop, lost property and clothing store facilities. It was also known to have the best canteen and was an extremely friendly garage. It had been considered for replacement in the 1970s, but sufficient land couldn't be obtained.

However, Central Works, not more than a mile away, had been heavily rebuilt in the previous decade, and had gained a brand new £2 million roof in 1984. Serious consideration was given to closing Leadmill and moving the allocation in to Central Works. At the end of the deliberations, Central Works closed, Leadmill survived, although Computer Services remained at Central Works for some years afterwards.

The main functions of Central Works were distributed to the garages, although unit repair (engine and gearbox repairs and refurbishments) went to the former paint shop at Rutland Way (that facility moving into part of the extension at Greenland, in addition to the glass fibre and trimming shop from Central Works) and the former blacksmiths shop went to Herries. Office staff decamped to garages, or Meadowhall when it was eventually finished.

Above

Overall adverts continued to be a valuable source of revenue, as well as adding colour to the streets.

2176 and 2234 were repainted in a mainly yellow scheme for National Deposit Friendly Society, 2198 was painted in an imaginative scheme for Independent Express Parcels and 2358 was painted in a very pleasing overall blue for National & Provincial.

These schemes generally lasted for 12 or more months, with the advertiser funding the repainting costs at the end of the contract.

2176 is seen in Norfolk Park, 2198 outside Herries garage and 2358 is pictured on the approach apron at East Bank garage, all in Sheffield.

Above

The scale of the new engineering facilities at Rotherham can be gauged in this view.

In the far distance can be seen the bodyshop, and behind the photographer were further bays and pits.

Very modern, but to a newly commercial company, the shear cost of rates and heating the property, would be difficult to bare.

In Sheffield city centre, the former area office on Arundel Gate was closed with radio control moving to individual garages. Canteen facilities existed at Castlegate, Central Bus Station as well as an office located in the former Inspector Centre in George Street. Two enquiry offices were rebadged as Travel Shops located within the Castle Square (hole in the road) underpass system and at Central Bus Station. Bridge Street bus station closed for business, it being remote from where passengers wanted to go.

Halfway, although within Sheffield, was allocated to Rotherham for engineering purposes. The former Booth and Fisher garage on Station Road had been heavily refurbished with a new wash, floor, roof and extension across the road on Old Lane that held additional MT pits. There was also a parcel of land across from the main administration building that could house overspill buses or company vehicles. Although having been with the PTE for ten years, it still had the atmosphere of a small independent.

Rotherham had been furnished with a brand new garage in 1982 to replace the former premises on Rawmarsh Road. An enormous facility, capable of holding 150 buses under cover, it had been built on a design first implemented for Greater Manchester's facility at Tameside in Ashton. With copious engineering facilities, two bus washes as well as stores and a brake lining shop, it was possible to do many 'big' jobs within its walls. There were also modern office facilities, a canteen (that was never used) and sunken gardens. It was a very nice building to work in, although woefully over provided for. In Rotherham town centre, facilities were provided in the Ceres Building on Frederick Street. This is where the formative SYT Marketing decamped to until they moved to Meadowhall. As well as canteen, signing on and cashing in facilities, it also held the company's Travel Shop in the town. The canteen in Rotherham was a foreboding place, filled with ex miners, who were uniquely militant. Not a place to enter if you were of a delicate persuasion.

Doncaster had a grand building on Leicester Avenue, opposite the world famous racecourse. Inside the entrance door was a palatial staircase which lead to somewhat threadbare, but functional offices. A new engineering block had been added in 1984 As well as MT work, full painting and trimming facilities were provided. In its many nooks and crannies, places could be found to hide preserved vehicles and equipment that many people had forgotten existed. It also held the PTEs experimental Dennis Trolleybus (2450) and its associated electrical facilities. Together with a substantial yard, the garage could easily hold 150 buses.

Within Doncaster town centre, a canteen and office facility was located in modern premises on Duke Street. Accessed from a small courtyard, this was similar in scope to Rotherham, but friendlier. A Travel Shop was located downstairs. A staff car park was available on land at Greyfriars.

Finally, the former T.Severn & Sons facility at Dunscroft, near Thorne, had been retained to absorb the independent operators purchased by the PTE throughout the 1970s. Basically formed out of two sheds, it had smaller engineering facilities, but had an enormous amount of hard and soft standing that could be used for operational or non-operational vehicles.

In the months leading up to deregulation, the new SYT had been blessed with receiving two final batches of new buses. A batch of ten Metrobuses (1951 to 1960) had arrived in June and July, in a new variant of the SYT livery for Fastline services. Initially for Greenland and Leadmill, some of the Gardner, turbocharged, engined buses had been sent to Rotherham to work on the 277/8 and X36 services to Doncaster and Barnsley to gain knowledge of high speed running. They had a new interior of light beige panels and dark brown moquette, enlivened by orange and red stripes.

In September and October 1986, the final Alexander bodied, Dennis Dominators arrived. These were lengthened by the addition of a small bay in the middle of the bus, and were also fitted with a turbo charged Gardner engine. The first 15 (2471 to 2485) arrived in the revised Fastline scheme, and were set to work at Rotherham, Halfway and East Bank (replacing the Metrobus variants on trips to Leeds, as they had a disturbing ability, at speed, to become unstable on motorway work in high winds). They had a revised driving cab, which was raised by about six inches. The windscreen was not raised, which led to frequent complaints by taller drivers about the ability to drive comfortably. The last five didn't arrive until after deregulation.

Above and Right

Doncaster had its own paint facilities and were well ahead at deregulation, initially being a bit over zealous with the use of garage codes as seen on 2219.

These weren't located in the modern workshop extension (right), but in the former workshop area of the main garage.

Atlantean 1797, seen at Armthorpe, was painted out of its Doncaster Transport livery, in an effort to get the fleet looking as uniform as possible for the new environment.

The garage was also home to the unique Dennis Dominator Trolleybus. 2450 would not pass to SYT, but would remain with the PTE.

Left and Below

Valuable orders received just prior to deregulation were a further batch of ten, dual purpose seated, MCW Metrobuses and fifteen, long wheelbase, Dennis Dominators.

1951 is seen in an official shot overlooking central Sheffield from Norfolk Park, whilst 2472 is seen outside Doncaster's South Bus Station, already stained from road dirt.

The batch of three Carlyle bodied Ford Transit's were oddities, but were bought after a fact finding trip to Worcester, to see if minibuses had a future in the area. Fitted with manual gearboxes, they never really settled, and were eventually loaned out, although an attempt was made to find private hire work for them.

Three Carlyle bodied Ford Transit minibuses (61 to 63) had also arrived to give experience of this style of operation, prior to deregulation. They were painted in a mini Coachline livery, and were put to work on a new service M10 between Waterthorpe Market (present day site of Crystal Peaks shopping centre) and Mosborough. They were fitted with coach seats in the new moquette pattern, which also extended to the roof and side walls. Being fitted with manual gearboxes, they proved to be less suited to 'stop, start' bus work in a big city, but no automatic option was available.

Above, Right and Below

Olympian 100 had been ordered by Ebdons, but had sat unused for two years when it was purchased by the PTE, at a good price. With staff studying maps in the cab, it looks like a long distance hire has been planned from Doncaster.

Two former Yelloway Tigers were also purchased, with a growing effort to enter the tours and excursion market. 70 and 73 are seen in Blackpool.

Main fleet buses were painted in a promotional Coachline livery, but Herries based 2199, was the only one with SYT fleetnames, and was adorned with its new colours in November 1985.

Coachline also received some investment in the form of the 'Ebdons' Leyland Olympian, which had been in storage for a number of years. Refurbished by SYT, fitted with new seats and numbered 100, it was the first double deck coach operated, although some Dennis Dominators had been painted in Coachline livery for promotional reasons.

Two former Yelloway Leyland Tigers also arrived (70 and 73) fitted with Plaxton paramount 3500 bodywork, to give extra capacity. A policy also started of moving 'ageless' registration plates from older vehicles to Coachline coaches, which was a fad at the time.

By October, the final changes and tender awards were being put in place, enabling the fledgling SYT to become its initial, final form. Initially, tender losses were mainly in Sheffield. The West Riding Group, based in Wakefield, had the former Sheffield United Tours garage on Charlotte Road on its books, across the road from East Bank, and was using that to provide a base for a new offshoot called 'Sheffield & District'. They had been successful in obtaining a number of tenders for schools as well as main services, abandoned by SYT, in addition to services in neighbouring Derbyshire.

East Midland and Richardson's Travel had also obtained tenders, but the imagined battle between SYT and Yorkshire Traction did not materialise at this point. Rotherham's main tender losses were the X36 to Richardson's and some rural work around Stainton to a new entrant, Glyn Pegg. Doncaster did much better, but lost the Inner Circle to Yorkshire Traction, some evening and Sunday work to old established independent Leon Motor Services and pulled out from large areas of north Doncaster (Skellow, Burghwallis, most of Carcroft). In all, SYT would operate about 80% of its pre April 1986 mileage on deregulation day.

In the final weeks before deregulation, a Customer Services section was set up to answer phone calls and deal with customer enquiries. A band of experienced Inspectors from throughout the company were brought to the Frederick Street premises in Rotherham to give advice to a bemused general public. The company also ran some more television adverts, this time produced by Harrogate based advertising agency Copy and Concepts. The thirty second spots reinforced the message that buses hadn't turned into some kind of nightmare (indeed the advert made use of a bus turning in to a vampire and back again) and that your friendly SYT bus would be there to pick you up.

Above and Left

Sheffield & District were an offshoot from NBC owned West Riding. Leyland National 94, seen above, probably won't endear itself to the good folk of Holmesfield, by spelling the village's name wrong on the blind. Pond Hill, Sheffield.

SYT did all they could to reassure existing customers that buses would still operate after 26 October. Freephone numbers were operated and advertised (left) to smooth people's worries.

The horror stories coming out of Glasgow though, left some very worried customers who expected savage cuts to provision.

Left and Below

It was obviously going to take three or four years to get the fleet into the new SYT livery, so an effort was made to get other buses into an 'interim' solution, that at least made the fleet look similar.

The effect was poor, as each garage varied the amount of red/brown and transfers used.

Herries based 1723 is seen on Paternoster Row, Sheffield. Greenland based 1942 is seen on Sheaf Street, also in Sheffield, and Leyland National 10 is seen fresh from the paintshop, entering Halfway garage.

Sadly, due to the chaotic nature of tender awards, publicity to a confused and world weary general public, was patchy, some not being available until after deregulation day, with hastily photocopied sheets being issued for some routes.

Efforts were also made in September and October to reinforce the SYT livery, by applying red and chestnut paint on to buses untreated to a repaint. Referred throughout the company as an 'interim' livery, this wasn't carried out in a uniform fashion, and some buses operated without transfers or some missing, giving the slightly haphazard appearance to much of the fleet. Whilst SYT stickers had been placed over the previous PTE symbol from March, it took until 1989 until the final 'flying duck' (an affectionate name given to the former PTE symbol) was finally removed from the buses.

Saturday 25 October 1986 was a dismal day. The weather gave a sense of foreboding, as it poured down all day. The worst was now known. Staff who were remaining with the new SYT were about to dawn on a brand new era. So, at midnight, it was goodbye to all that, a brave new world was about to begin.

Chapter 2

1986 & 1987

Sunday 26 October 1986 dawned bright and sunny. The clocks had gone back that morning, so, some people enjoyed an extra hour in bed. Not the employees of SYT, however.

If the service planning had been chaotic as deregulation day approached, the engineers were in visible shock. Not only had they had to cope with closing their central workshop and move staff and plant to garages and other locations, but they also had to cope with a general reduction in spare vehicles.

Due to unsatisfactory delivery dates from the likes of British Leyland, the PTE had established a 30% spares margin for engineering use. To give an example, a batch of Daimler Fleetline buses, ordered by Sheffield Transport in 1973 arrived as late as 1977. Industrial action, endemic in the 1970s and a lack of understanding on the part of some suppliers to the needs of operators, meant that buses designed for a 12 year life, were regularly putting in 18 year stretches, due to a lack of spare parts.

Whilst the PTE had found alternatives to British Leyland products as the decade wore on, the engineers guarded their spare allocation with jealousy. Buses could go in to the works for weeks, and simple jobs that could be carried out at garage level, were forced to make the trip to Queens Road.

The new SYT couldn't absorb such a high cost, and made the spare capacity no more that 16%. Garages were now responsible for general servicing, annual test and paint prep and bodywork repairs. Only the most major body repairs required a trip to the specialist facilities that had been set up at Greenland, Rotherham and Doncaster. Garages were now responsible for their own budget, and in the weird way the company had been set up, internal recharges now became the norm for work performed out of your location.

The engineers had been busy that weekend moving vehicles around to get the most optimal allocation of vehicles, reducing the anticipated spare part holding at each location to a minimum. Leadmill became a 100% Metrobus garage. Doncaster lost all its 'oddities' from the Independents taken over by the PTE by absorbing a batch of Alexander bodied Fleetlines (1538 to 1548) from Greenland. Rotherham gained some Voith gear boxed, Roe bodied Atlanteans from Greenland to start removing some Roe bodied Fleetlines which were starting to show their age, prematurely. All remaining Bristol LHSs were transferred to Halfway, primarily for British Coal contracts.

Above

Two types that left the fleet at deregulation were the unique ECW bodied Daimler Fleetlines and the similarly unique McArdle bodied Volvo Ailsas. 826 is at Waingate, Sheffield & 375 is at Central Works.

Left and Below

The former 'Nipper' Bristol LHSs had all migrated to Halfway for use on colliery contracts, or, as seen at Plumbley, occasional service. 1050 was repainted by the garage painter at Halfway, and the proportions are a little bit 'off', but the effect is quite pleasing.

All four Bristols would be out of the fleet by April 1987.

The Dennis Domino fleet was now too big for the available work, and a number went on loan. 49 (below) seen in St. Helens, looks distinctly work stained.

Peak hour augmentation in Sheffield, saw some former Dearneways Leopards restored to service by the end of 1986. 1085 (bottom) has been hastily repainted and is lacking fleetnames or destination blinds for its new role.

The biggest losses were the final ECW and 'DMS' style bodied Daimler Fleetlines in Sheffield, and the last of the 1976 vintage Volvo Ailsas from Doncaster. A number of Leyland Leopards also departed the fleet as services to Halifax, Huddersfield and Manchester had been lost on tender, and there was no longer a need for such vehicles.

The batch of Dennis Dominos at Doncaster were also redundant, and they went on loan to Merseybus to operate a new network of tendered services in St. Helens. When they returned from that contract, they were hired to Yorkshire Rider for tendered services in Leeds and Bradford, to replace similarly bodied Leyland Cubs that had been withdrawn as unsuitable, despite being less than a year old.

The first Sunday of deregulation was quiet. Drivers got use to unfamiliar routes and vehicles, but the chaos that had been predicted (and witnessed in Greater Manchester and Glasgow) was largely absent. The PTE was still busy issuing tenders after deregulation day, some of which were picked up by SYT. Halfway garage had successfully picked up some Worksop town services to Rhodesia, and interworked this with trips on service 264 to provide a coordinated 20 minute service to the west of the town. East Midland, unhappy with this incursion on its territory, swiftly registered them commercially for operation in January, and the tenders were withdrawn.

It was found that some service provision was inadequate. Under the terms of the 1985 Transport Act, services, as registered, should have operated, unaltered until 26 January 1987. Additional journeys could be added at the behest of local authorities, but generally no changes could be made. However, a small number of improvements were permitted in December 1986, mainly in Sheffield on services 20, 22 and 24, with support of the PTE. This alleviated some of the peak hour problems that had manifested themselves. The engineers took the opportunity to reintroduce some of the 'DMS' Fleetlines to Greenland, and Doncaster slipped out the odd Ailsa during November. In addition, a number of Leopards returned to service at East Bank.

Above

The MCW bodied Fleetlines had all been withdrawn by deregulation, but 1515 to 1519 were soon reinstated at Greenland garage. 1511, seen above in Whiston, Rotherham, was reinstated in December 1986, and was used as an engineering float vehicle until the end of 1987.

Competitors were thin on the ground, outwith of tendered services, but a number of new entrants did emerge. Coachcraft, a small Doncaster based coach operator, launched competitive services to Armthorpe and to the Cantley Estate. In the case of Armthorpe, this was filling a hole left by SYT in its deregulation network. Surprisingly, they made a good fist of it, so much so, that SYT had to think long and hard about how to tackle that sort of incursion.

Left

The new competition was mainly with older vehicles. Richardson's started new commercial services from the Dearne towns to Sheffield and Doncaster. Ex NBC Leopards being the choice as seen here in Mexborough.

Coachcraft operated a mixed fleet, but mainly, elderly Bedfords. As can be seen by the load being carried, at Christ Church, they had quickly established a presence in Doncaster, mainly due to SYT's cautious commercial network.

Glyn Pegg captured a tendered service from Rotherham to the quaintly rural village of Stainton on the borders of Maltby (this being the birthplace of Freddie Trueman). Operated with a hired in Ford Transit from Smith's Van Hire, it sadly proved too much of a commitment for him and the tender returned to SYT in December 1986 (although that wasn't the last the company saw of Mr. Pegg). Richardson's coaches had won the former X36 express from Rotherham to Barnsley and had also made inroads in to several works services in Sheffield, as well as the main, 258 service between Sheffield and Thorpe Hesley. Uniquely, they had also gone on to start commercial express services between Sheffield and Doncaster, via the Dearne Valley, which actually added something different to the established pattern, which also included night services. They continued to operate their popular service from Sheffield to Manchester Airport.

In Sheffield, the main competitor was Sheffield & District. It was professional, well resourced, well managed and was to be a thorn in the side of SYT for a number of years. Its General Manager was Mark Fowles, who in later life went on to be the Managing Director for the award winning, Nottingham City Transport. They had recruited from the Policy 'D' pool of former PTE drivers, some of whom had simply walked in to Charlotte Road on receiving their redundancy cheque, to take up exactly the same job on only slightly worse conditions.

A smaller operator, Groves, launched a motley selection of ex Merseyside and WMPTE Daimler Fleetlines, backed up by an even more eclectic selection of single deckers, on to an unsuspecting public of the Shiregreen estate in Sheffield. This estate was well covered by services 47 & 48, but SYT increased frequencies and lowered fares to compete.

The first marketing initiative of the new company got underway in November 1986. Bus Bingo, was a fun way of getting passengers to travel by SYT bus. Each day, a selection of bingo numbers would be posted on buses; passengers being able to match against their own personal bingo card. Prizes were good, ranging from Savercards to £1000 in cash. The initiative ran for three weeks and although was deemed popular, wasn't repeated.

Publicity was a major headache for the company. Even allowing for the chaos caused by late tender awards, the printing and typesetting issues created enormous problems. These were still the days of 'hot metal' and although some printers had gone to a photographic plate production process, the number of typesetting firms that could deal with the large amount of detailed timetables was small.

Initially, the network was chopped into 26 areas, and an area guide produced for each. Surprisingly, they were going to be charged for, at 15p per guide, but such was the ham fisted way that they had been produced, they were given away for the first three weeks. Distribution was via Travel Shops and local libraries, but in addition the Inspectors who had been used on Customer Services duties were retained and pressed in to use, distributing timetables via the company's 'Roadshow' bus. When changes were necessary, individual leaflets were issued, and in general, the books were phased out by the end of 1987.

Right

Former Mk2 Ailsa 430 was converted by SYT's apprentices to a 'Roadshow 'bus, and was used heavily to promote the deregulated service pattern.

Pictured here at the 1986 SYTS Rally in Hillsborough Park.

Below

The first 39 Dodge S56s started to arrive by the end of 1986. Bodied by Reeve Burgess, they were of a larger body type than what went before, with full size windows.

127, seen on a private hire, was one of a few fitted with dual purpose seats and a luggage boot.

Another avenue explored by the fledging company was the ability to use existing workshop facilities to service trucks and private cars. Autoservices was set up by a former Instructor, Alan Hull. It dealt with a whole range of services, right up to MOT using facilities that had been employed training apprentices. Initially located in a bay at Meadowhall, it moved eventually to Greenland.

Doncaster went to some lengths to entice commercial vehicle users to have their vehicles serviced in Leicester Avenue's extensive workshops, and Rotherham willingly took on the task of repairing and refurbishing vehicles for local preservationists.

Minibuses had become an accepted part of bus operation in the deregulated world. SYT was to be no exception and had ordered 39 Reeve Burgess bodied Dodge S56 buses towards the end of 1986, the first arriving just before Christmas of that year. The S56 was a development of a 1960s parcel van, fitted with a Perkins Engine and Allison gearbox. The Reeve Burgess body was less boxy than some other builders' efforts and was reasonably roomy for the 25 seats that were fitted within.

The engineers, however, wanted to order the more 'big bus' like MCW Metrorider. It was of a more robust construction, using quite a lot of parts from Ford, but had air brakes and a proper bus like feel. It had a number of problems. Initially, it was offered with a manual gearbox, which would entail drivers' having to pass a full driving test to operate them (although an automatic gearbox wasn't far away) and the cost was considerably more.

A minibus operating agreement was agreed with the T&GWU, which allowed for buses up to 25 seats to be driven on a lower rate of pay, and was now seen as the new way to enter the world of bus driving. Garages were now instructed to find new and innovative ways to use these new vehicles, the first of which would launch at the second stage of deregulation in January 1987.

The final five, long wheel base, Dennis Dominators (2486 to 2490) arrived before Christmas 1986. Unusually, they came unpainted, fitted with dual emergency exits downstairs, and luggage racks, aft of the rear wheelarch. Additionally, they were fitted with Alexanders revised dash panel. The destination displays, while extant, were to be covered over, as each one went for painting by contractors into a new 'Super Coachline' livery. Based at Leadmill, as was all of the Coachline fleet, they were to be used to increase the variety and type of hire that could be attracted to the company.

Christmas brought a present of tendered services on Christmas Day, Boxing Day and New Year's Day to the company, and with the major surgery performed, it was now time for consolidation, ready to get in to the full effects of deregulation from January.

Mother Nature can be a cruel teacher. January 1987 proved to be one of the coldest on record, with frequent snow showers leading to days of disruption and, for a newly commercial SYT, lost revenue.

Top and Above

The new Dennis Dominators for Coachline work were great motorway performers, but there just wasn't enough work for a fleet of five. 2487 is seen on an excursion in Blackpool.

Built on seven hills, Sheffield is prone to being badly effected by snow fall, regularly bringing the city to a halt. Greenland based Fleetline 1537 has failed in its attempt to get to the terminus of service 52 at Moorsyde Avenue in Crookes, high in the western suburbs of the city, and has successfully blocked the road.

Now when you've got to nip out, nip out with a Little Nipper

YOUR NEW MINI-BUS SERVICE STARTS MONDAY JANUARY 26th

We are proud to announce our latest arrival – the Little Nipper. A fleet of 25 seater mini-buses designed to give you a better service. With wide aisles and bags of leg room to make your trip as comfortable as possible.

It's the fast and friendly way to nip to the shops, nip to mum's and nip to school. In fact you can nip out almost anywhere on a Little Nipper – from High Green and Burncross to Lound Side in Chapeltown. And with Little Nippers every 12 minutes during the day, you're free to nip out whenever you want.

Look out for your new Little Nipper mini-buses coming your way soon!

SYT South Yorkshire's Transport

The first service change of many, was to concentrate on two areas, and both included the first use of Minibuses.

In Sheffield, the tendered services operated by Sheffield & District on the Greengate Lane Circulars (91 & 98), were found to be highly lucrative, so much so, they had given up part of the subsidy for them. This was eating in to the revenue on SYT services 78, 80, X8 and X64. The service pattern was totally revised, generally forming two circular services 77 & 80, reducing the 78 to be peak hour only, and the withdrawal of the X64. Some spoiler trips were also introduced on service 91 in front of S&D journeys.

Minibuses were introduced on two circular services from Chapeltown to High Green and Burncross, both on 12 minute frequencies, but essentially off peak.

The new brand name for these buses was coined as 'Little Nippers'. This had long been used as a generic name for a child in South Yorkshire, and fitted in the with the 'Nipper' narrative that had been used since 1983. What didn't go down so well, especially with staff who had endured the pain of deregulation, was the emergence of former colleagues, on new starter rates, taking minibus driving jobs, after having taken large redundancy payments on Policy 'D', in addition to seeing former colleagues on S&D who had done the same. The new world was baffling and hurtful in equal measure.

Doncaster had decided to use its initial batch of Dodges to tame the competition being issued from Coachcraft, and started a new service in to Armthorpe, as well as an innovative service around a new estate in Edenthorpe. Again, this wasn't without some upset, as drivers in Doncaster took some limited strike action. Again, common sense prevailed, but, the new order of things was going to take some getting used to. Even more upset was Coachcraft, who folded in February 1987, blaming the Little Nipper incursion for their downfall.

Another operator called 'P Singh' who proposed to operate a minibus service between the city centre and Sheffield Lane Top, failed to appear, despite registering the service, and the PTE producing timetable publicity for it. East Bank revised their Shiregreen services to operate via the Moor shopping area from the January change and introducing bargain fares.

Left

Deregulation in the raw at Christ Church, Doncaster. The new Little Nipper network to Armthorpe, which built three services on top of existing service 181, competed head on with Coachcraft's new services.

Within a few weeks of being in operation, Coachcraft threw in the towel, sighting the minibus network being the reason for their demise.

Christ Church was a traditional terminus for services from the north east of the district, but was somewhat remote from the shops.

A cautious optimism was generally being felt within the company, but more revenue was still needed. A general fare increase was applied from March 1987, introducing peak and off peak fares, but at the same time, major changes were made to the Savercard product. Firstly, in addition to the all-encompassing, network wide, ticket, cheaper regional versions were introduced for each area, and additionally an off peak version called 'Shoppacard' was introduced. This came with a bold new marketing package based around 'Saver...' with words such as cash, time, trouble etc. added on to the end of the initial sentence. Television advertising was eschewed as being far too expensive, but large scale use was made of roadside billboards and on bus vinyl.

Whilst this may have been seen as a well-meaning way of increasing ridership, brand loyalty and revenue take, it gave the impression of being over complicated, especially for long suffering road staff, only just starting to recover from deregulation. This also led to the end of the Faresaver experiment on the Stocksbridge group of services in Sheffield.

Below

'Y' type Leyland Leopards 66 & 68 were transferred into Herries to compete with Sheffield & District on service 49 to the Parson Cross estate.

This was a service withdrawn at deregulation, but offered for tender by the PTE, despite replicating most of SYT's profitable 42 & 53 services.

Faresaver was a stored value, magnetic card, developed by Wayfarer Transit Systems, which acted in a similar manner to a payphone phone card. Users could put multiples of £5 up to £20 on to the cards, and then use to pay for single fares using that method. It was introduced in August 1986 on a batch of specially modified Dennis Dominators at Herries, with top up equipment also available in Travel Shops and Stocksbridge library. In the event, the cost of equipping the entire fleet would have been enormous, and with no guaranteed revenue anymore, it was a cost SYT could no longer afford.

Spring came around, and as the weather perked up, so did the competition. The privatisation of the National Bus Company, meant that the West Riding Group, was now privately owned. The Government had, however, detached the Charlotte Road premises, and coach operation from that group, leaving S&D looking for a new home.

S&D found that quite a lot of the tendered work was actually highly profitable. It extended the 91 and 98 across the city to Handsworth, including a new service 94 via a previously unserved estate in Chapeltown. It had also found that the 49 to Wordsworth Avenue was a money earner (so much so that Herries had to put on a competing service using 'Y' type Leopards and eventually double deckers) and was now going to branch out on to one of SYT's most profitable routes, service 60, with a new service 6, operating exactly the same route, but then continuing to Lodge Moor. S&D, finding a new home on the Dore House Industrial Estate in Orgreave, had also been dabbling in coach hire under the Ridings Travel brand.

SIXTY SHUTTLE
YOU CAN'T MISS IT!

SYT responded to this threat in an innovative way. A two pronged defence of this slice of the network (which passed through a large student community, as well as serving one of the UK's largest Teaching Hospitals – The Royal Hallamshire) was by taking a batch of dual doored, Gardner engine MCW Metrobuses (490 to 499), and painting between the decks yellow. Sadly, not all the buses chosen were in SYT livery, some were in interim, but more staff couldn't be spared for preparation, as paint shop staff were busy painting the new Meadowhall offices.

Within this fleet, a new brand name had been coined. 'Sixty Shuttle' was born. The branding didn't cover all the fleet required for the service, as there was heavy peak hour augmentation, but the main daytime service was now highly visible. In addition, a new minibus operated 'Sixty Shuttle Lodge Moor Link' service, operated on top, but extended through to Lodge Moor Hospital. The minibuses operated were the last of the initial batch, but had been fitted with coach seats and had a boot incorporated in to the rear, ideal for private hire for small groups.

MAKING SURE YOU DON'T MISS THE BUS

The Sixty Shuttle is the latest addition to the SYT fleet. It's been introduced to give you the best possible service on our popular route 60. So there'll be lots of these big, bright buses to speed you on your way. Just look out for the familiar SYT double-deckers with the bold red and yellow **SIXTY SHUTTLE** name between the decks. Shuttles run every few minutes at the busiest times. And extra services during rush hour often cut your waiting time to only 3 minutes. They'll take you right into the City Centre whenever you want – and to the Bus and Rail Stations too.

And the new Little Nipper Lodge Moor Link runs every 15 minutes throughout the day – following route 60 and right on to Lodge Moor Hospital.

UNIVERSITY STUDENTS CAN'T MISS IT

The Sixty Shuttle is the quick and easy way to get to University. You can catch a Shuttle or Little Nipper just outside the Halls of Residence. Whenever you're going to the Royal Hallamshire – for work or to visit friends – catch the Sixty Shuttle. And if you're travelling to Lodge Moor Hospital – the Little Nipper Lodge Moor Link takes **you right to the door** during the day.

HOSPITAL STAFF AND VISITORS CAN'T MISS IT

RANMOOR RESIDENTS AND FULWOOD FOLK CAN'T MISS IT

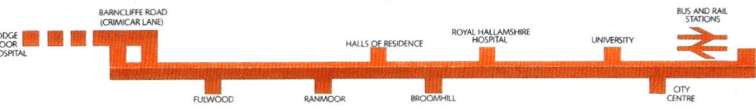

LODGE MOOR HOSPITAL — BARNCLIFFE ROAD (CRIMICAR LANE) — FULWOOD — HALLS OF RESIDENCE — RANMOOR — ROYAL HALLAMSHIRE HOSPITAL — BROOMHILL — UNIVERSITY — BUS AND RAIL STATIONS — CITY CENTRE

SIXTY SHUTTLE TIMETABLE

FROM CITY CENTRE

MONDAY-FRIDAY		
FROM	TO	FREQUENCY
0610	0715	15 minutes
0715	0852	6 minutes
0852	1453	5/10 minutes to Royal Hallamshire
0852	1453	15 minutes to Fulwood
1453	1745	6 minutes
1800	2300/2310	20 minutes
SATURDAY		
0610/0630	0900	30 minutes
0900	1740	10 minutes to Ranmoor
0900	1740	20 minutes to Fulwood
1740	2300/2310	20 minutes
SUNDAY		
0645	1400	30/40 minutes
1400	2300/2310	20 minutes

Certain Shuttles terminate at Nether Green or the Royal Hallamshire Hospital. For full details please call at any SYT Travel Shop.
PLUS Little Nipper Lodge Moor Link. Sheffield to Lodge Moor
MONDAY-SATURDAY 0853 to 1653 every 15 minutes

TO CITY CENTRE

MONDAY-FRIDAY		
FROM	TO	FREQUENCY
0645	0750	15 minutes
0750	0844	6 minutes
0844	0950	12 minutes
0950	1535	15 minutes
1543	1820	6 minutes
1835	2315/2331*	20 minutes
SATURDAY		
0645/0705	0935	30 minutes
0935	1755	10 minutes from Ranmoor
0935	1755	20 minutes from Fulwood
1755	2315/2331*	20 minutes
SUNDAY		
0817	1435	40 minutes
1435	2315/2331*	20 minutes

Certain Shuttles start from Nether Green or the Royal Hallamshire Hospital. * = Runs to Fulwood, Crimicar Lane/Hallamshire Road only. For full details please call at any SYT Travel Shop.
PLUS Little Nipper Lodge Moor Link. Lodge Moor to Sheffield.
MONDAY-SATURDAY 0912 to 1642 every 15 minutes

Left and Below

The 'Sixty Shuttle' branding was eyecatching, and SYT's first foray into the concept. Lodge Moor Link, the minibus element, got a little lost in the Little Nipper brand. Both, however, did a job in dissuading competition.

495 is seen away from home, at the rear of East Bank garage while 135 is entering Sheffield's Central Bus Station, passing the long demolished Sheaf Valley Baths.

The Leyland Lion (bottom) proved a capable performer, but SYT was not in the market for double deck buses, and it returned to Scotland.

It is seen here, whilst on trial in the spring of 1987, in Beighton.

A Leyland Lion was trialed on service 51 for two weeks in the early spring. The Alexander bodied bus was from a cancelled order that was due for Kelvin Scottish, a company that had also over reached itself in the new deregulated market. The underfloor, TL11 engined bus, was 14'9" high, and fitted with dual purpose seats. The bus, whilst successful, was returned to Glasgow, entering service with Clydeside Scottish.

Bus builders generally sent their vehicles to be tried out on service 51. It's a route of distinct contrasts, but noted for its near constant hill climbs to its termini of Lodge Moor and Herdings. The route was known as a 'bus killer' and if your product survived weeks of grueling slog on there, it was good enough for the sales market.

When new, the Fastline double decks, had been fitted with blinds printed on red Tyvek material. Unfortunately, at night, when illuminated, this gave the impression of a red light showing at the front of the vehicle. It's doubtful that any motorist would seriously get confused between a brake light or a strip of light with destinations on it, but a visit from South Yorkshire Police to the company, gave instructions that they were to be altered. In Rotherham, they simply fitted normal blinds in to the boxes, but in Sheffield, a program of fitting blue, fluorescent tubes behind the blinds was instituted, turning the red blinds purple. Some blue lights eventually found their way on to main fleet vehicles.

The splitting of the Charlotte Road premises and associated coaches, under the NBC privatisation plan, was about to cause major issues for SYT. Privatised under the name NTE Coaches, it was sold to the ATL Group, a company which had already bought the established Yelloway coach company in Rochdale, was on its way to buy Crosville and had various coach leasing companies under its control.

They had major plans for the business, and not a lot of it was to do with coaches. The old established Sheffield United Tours business, to which it could trace its past, was taken apart, selling most of the expensive luxury coaches they had, and investing instead, in a fleet of tired looking Leyland Nationals and Bristol REs. It was widely reported that the new owners took a look around the garage and saw that just behind them was the large Norfolk Park estate.

Norfolk Park was a 1960s built estate, mainly of tower block construction, but interspersed with maisonettes and individual houses. In addition, a couple of care homes and student nurse accommodation completed an estate that had been well planned, with a natural bowl of a park alongside. It was a popular estate, but during the 1980s had become difficult to let, but provided good bus territory, being on SYT's busy 70 and 71 circular services.

What SUT (as the new company was now called – it couldn't call itself Sheffield United Tours as that name was now owned by Wallace Arnold) had spotted, was a gap in the market. Whilst the 70/71 were frequent (every 10 minutes), they didn't take people to the shopping areas, but to Flat Street, which despite its name, wasn't flat, and some way away from the shops.

SUT gathered a motley collection of vehicles, painted in a maroon and cream livery, almost identical in style to that of S&D, and operated them every 10 minutes direct from Manor Top (eventually extended to Darnall), through the Norfolk Park estate to Moorfoot, High Street and then looping around the markets and back again. High quality it wasn't, but in a salient lesson to SYT, it took people where they wanted to go, not where the bus company wanted to take them.

Starting in the first week of May, initially they operated free of charge. Yorkshire folk, being thrifty, couldn't resist this, and almost overnight, the 70/71's revenue disappeared. Not just cash, but concession revenue as well, leaving SYT to pick up the crumbs, people who had bought Savercards, and evening and Sunday work. SYT had been caught wrong footed by a nimbler new entrant. More buses were sent into battle (the free offer ended after a week) and long-standing services 23 and 32 were diverted via the estate as services 723/732. This gave a coordinated five-minute frequency, but still didn't take people to where they wanted to go, and this anomaly wasn't put right until November of that year, but by then the damage was done and the competitor was established, going on to start competing on the profitable corridors of Herdings and Hackenthorpe.

Below

The SUT fleet was gathered from far and wide, and the kindest thing that could be said about it, was that it had character.

This former Excelsior Bristol RE was from another company purchased by the ATL Group. It is pictured in the coach bays at Sheffield's Central Bus Station.

The gentleman on the right is dressed in the fashionable garb of the day.

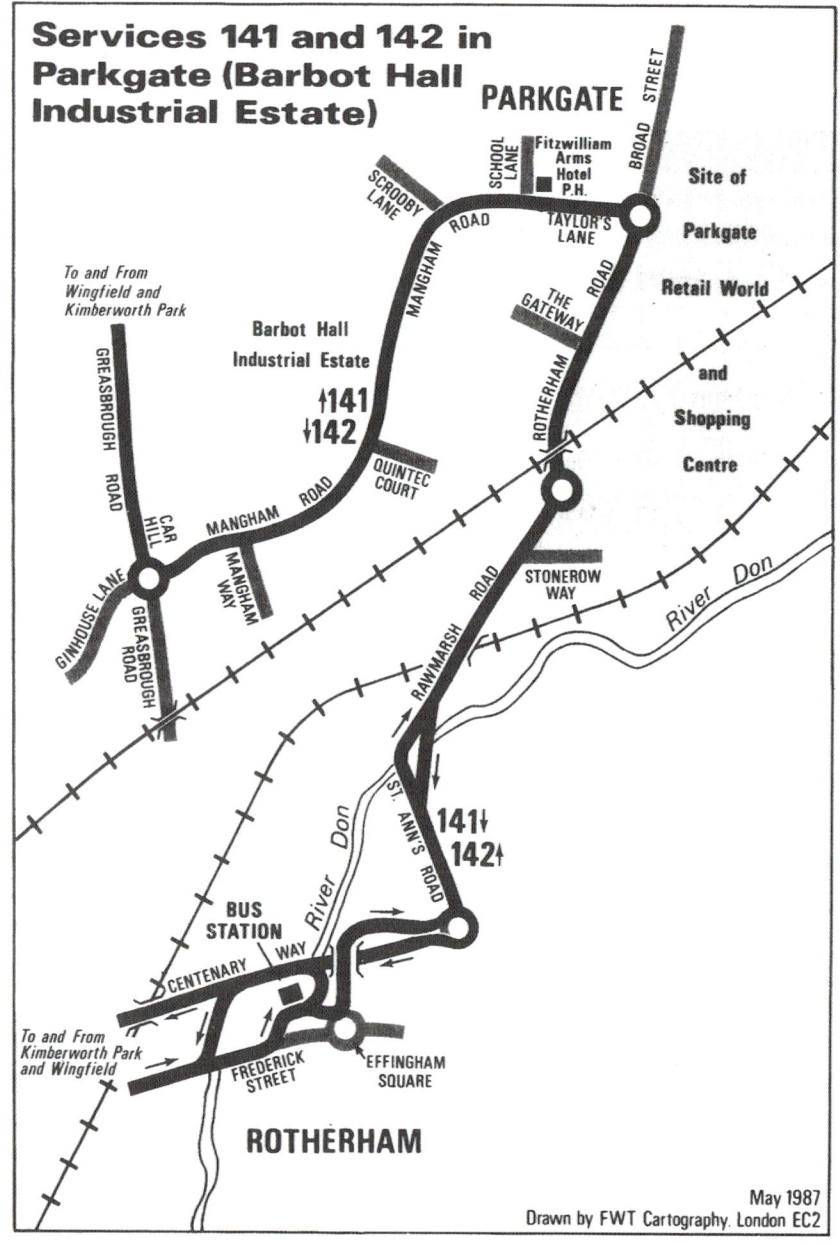

All these competitive battles were eating into the bottom line. The budgets and business plans of the previous years, were now chip wrapping. Whilst Rotherham hadn't been badly hit by competition, the town centre trade had started to be affected by the opening of the Parkgate Shopping Centre. Being located in the traditionally Yorkshire Traction served section of Rotherham, alterations were made to SYT's Kimberworth Park services to serve this new retail hub.

Doncaster seemed to carry on as if deregulation hadn't happened. Most of the town network was intact, the buses were well cared for, but not a penny bean of profit was being made. The Thorne corridor out of Dunscroft Garage was doing well, but major work was eventually going to be needed to the town network to reduce costs.

A further batch of minibuses was ordered to try and oust competitive services, as well as convert some traditional bus services to high frequency operation. More of the Dodge S56/Reeve Burgess combination were ordered, but to a revised specification. Brake life on these buses was terrible, being measured in days, rather than months. A small Telma retarder was retrofitted to the initial batch, and this was now incorporated in future deliveries. This didn't cure all the problems, leading to, in some examples, of brake fade or snatch.

In the summer, the only Leyland Olympian's in the fleet 501/2 were withdrawn and sold to Chesterfield Transport as being non standard. They had been latterly based at East Bank, but with their Hydracyclic gearbox had been problematical for some time and they were seen as being costly to maintain. 501 had been painted in advert for Sheaf Motors at the time of sale, so in order to preserve that contract, Dennis Dominator 2222 was painted in the same style. The fact that the company was advertising the arch rival to bus travel was not lost on some sage observers.

Above

The Dominos used by Yorkshire Rider, were based in Bradford and Leeds. Bus 50, seen in Bradford, was fitted with a farebox for the duration, and is in need of some frontal bodywork attention.

Two big schemes were introduced. The first was at Greenland, where new services were introduced via the Manor estate, replacing double decks on service 92 with a new M26/7 which penetrated the estate further than its predecessor. In a somewhat cruel twist, the evening and Sunday service, initially operated by SYT, went on tender to SUT later that year. Minibuses replaced conventional buses on service 96, a somewhat backwater route around older housing in Darnall, most of which had been demolished in the previous decade and was in the throes of being redeveloped.

Above

Olympians 501 & 502 left the fleet in summer 1987 for Chesterfield Transport.

Non standard, they had managed just over four years service, mainly at Sheffield garages. Their last allocation was East Bank, where 501 is seen in its advert livery.

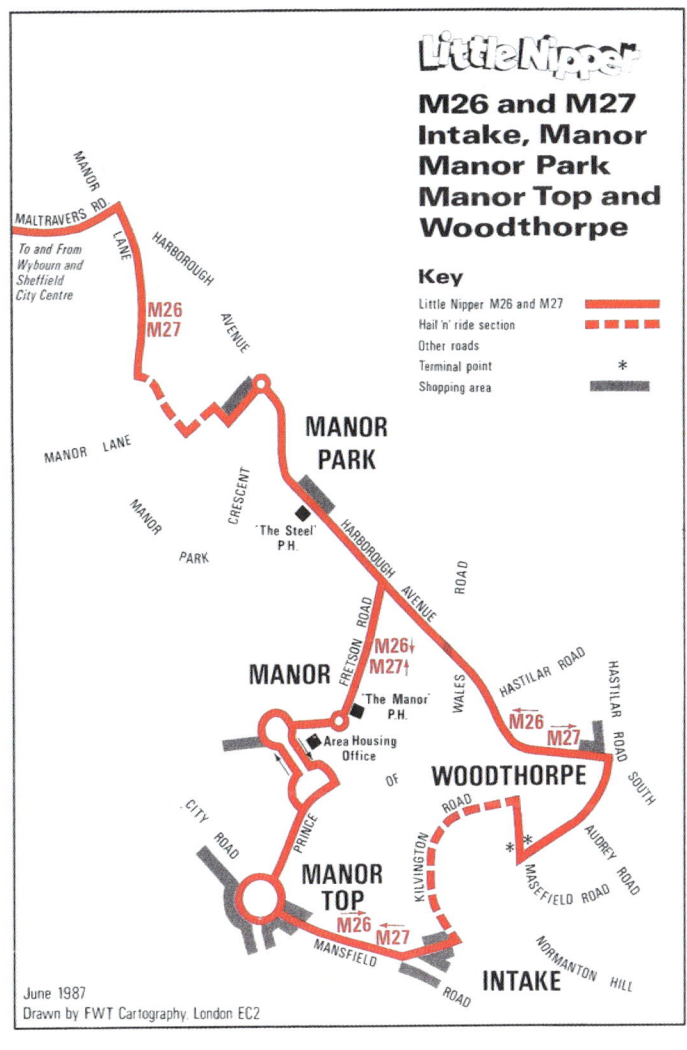

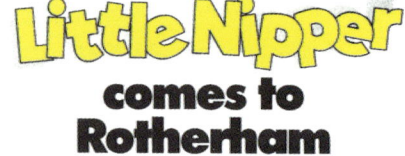

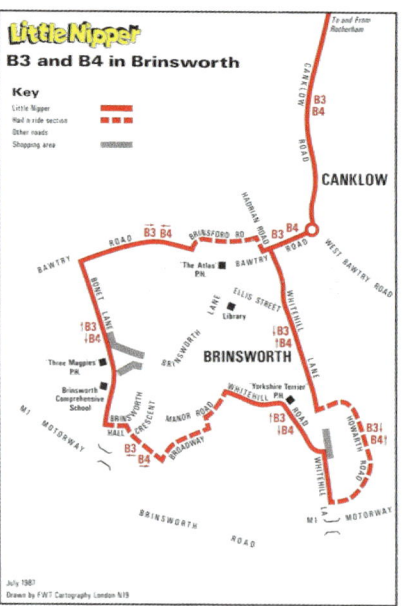

Whilst the buses were new, the uniforms that drivers were wearing could trace their lineage straight back to the 1930's. The former blue serge and 'ice cream seller' summer jackets were swept away with a new uniform in shades of brown, maroon and cream. Drivers could mix and match as required from jumpers, body warmers and ties as suited their own style. Cream shirts were order of the day, but in summer, drivers could wear cream polo shirts. Looking fresh when new, the cream shirts wore badly.

Moves were made to make the customer services part of SYT more professional. A new telephone communications unit was set up within Rotherham garage, where lots of space was available. Called 'Busline' it was manned every day from early until late by Jackie Marshall, Jayne Thornes, Nadine Morritt and Charlene Rowbottom, known with affection as the 'call girls' in those less stringent, politically correct times. In addition applications were invited from the Inspectorate to form a new team that would concentrate on fare evasion and face to face contact. It was estimated up to 5% of revenue was being lost through the peak/off peak distinction not being correctly applied by drivers or being misunderstood by passengers.

Summer had been particularly torrid at Rotherham. It had been recognised for some time that engineering standards were poor, and that corrective action was required. There had been days where the garage, despite it having the best equipped workshop in the company, had failed to meet its PVR (peak vehicle requirement). The fleet looked unkempt, downright filthy, with interiors in the same condition. It had become common practice to deal with graffiti on vinyl seats, on the upper deck, to have the offending scribbles painted over in chestnut or tan paint. Buses were also issued in to service with unpainted panels. Buses had been sent to other garages for work, but the situation came to a head in August.

Above

Rotherham based Atlantean 1624, leans heavily to the offside, with a good load for Whiston and Cowrakes Lane, out of the dark cavern that was Rotherham Bus Station.

Of course, you would have to know where it was going, as the driver has selected the unhelpful 'Circular' on the destination blinds. Whilst technically correct, it did little to help the uninitiated, and would prove a difficult practice to stop.

Similarly at Rotherham, the network of services to Brinsworth and Catcliffe had part of their patronage removed by house clearance in Canklow for a new relief road, and the new minibus services replaced some of the old circular services to try and drum up new passengers. In addition, minibuses were placed in to service on routes to Whiston, an area of surprisingly high car ownership, but also serving the Rotherham District Hospital on the way.

Malcolm Woodward was replaced as Garage Manager by Colin Fowlston, with Malcolm going to Greenland to help out in the battle with SUT. The engineering management at the garage was allowed to depart, and a whole new team was put in place. It is with some credit, that within 12 months, the fleet was restored to an excellent condition.

Some of the new minibus services had been successful in dissuading competition and reducing costs, but some more innovative services had floundered. Herries had introduced a package of services between Kilner Way shopping centre and various estates in the Hillsborough and Parson Cross/ Sheffield Lane Top area. They hadn't done sufficient business to continue, so the buses were reused to provide a competing service from Firth Park to Shiregreen, using previously unserved roads, competing with Groves, eventually extending in to the city centre, operated from East Bank. This eventually caused Groves to exit this part of the network, using their resources to compete on the High Green via Firth Park corridor instead.

In addition the minibus services operating around Chapeltown and High Green were revised to cover more areas in the autumn but eventually these were withdrawn, only to be picked up on tender by SUT, demonstrating that the PTE were either very canny with their tender budget, or the prices received were much less than they had budgeted for. Minibuses were used to SYT's benefit on a number of Sunday and evening tenders where 'big' buses had been previously used.

As September moved in to October, the first set of tenders came up for renewal. All was not well for SYT, losing further work to East Midland who now took a sizeable chunk of the Dinnington evening and Sunday network as well as a sizeable quantity of schools work. Another new entrant, Andrews, a small bus and coach training company also entered the fray winning some schools contract work, to which they attached commercial journeys to make good the driving day.

Meadowhall head office was now fully up and running, and with the exception of Computer Services, Central Works was finally closed and vacated. The unit repair section had settled at Rutland Way and had won a contract to become an aftermarket sales provider to Voith for the north of England.

Above and Left

Looking particularly filthy, Roe bodied Fleetline 1453, exiting Rotherham Bus Station for Blackburn (not Lancashire), does not exactly ooze quality, and the condition of Rotherham's fleet required corrective action in the late summer.

East Midland had always operated into SYT's patch, but was now busy taking work away. Worksop based, Bristol VR 150, works a busy service in from Tickhill to Doncaster, South Bus Station.

Andrews had branched out from PSV tuition to schools work. This very smart, ex Pontypridd AEC is on its way to the smart suburbs of Totley, Sheffield.

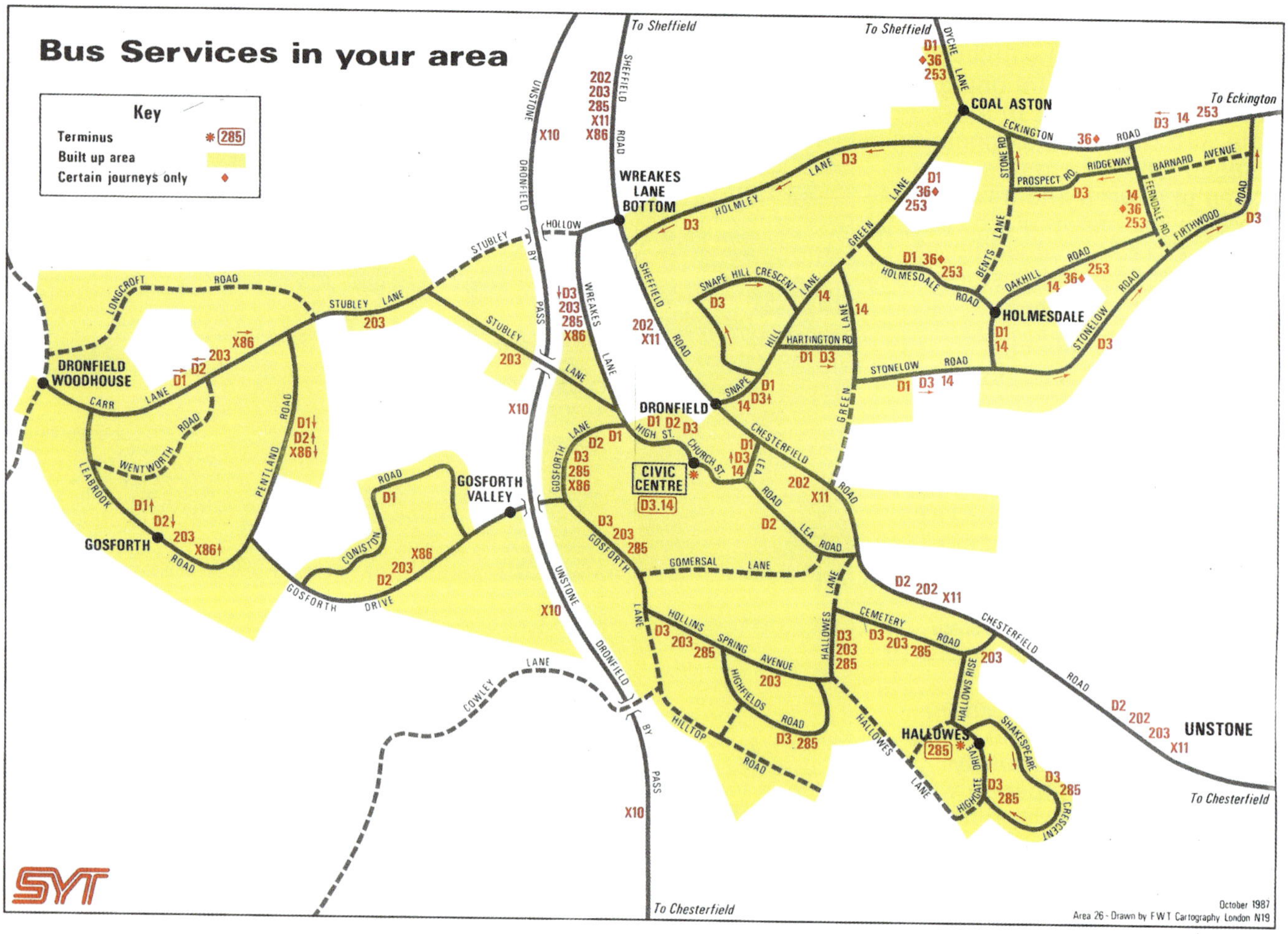

Bus Services in your area

Key
- Terminus ★ [285]
- Built up area (yellow)
- Certain journeys only ◆

October 1987 — Area 26 - Drawn by FWT Cartography London N19

The fluctuations in passenger demand had settled at being 6% less than that initially budgeted for by the end of the autumn period. It was plain to see in tender renewals that the company couldn't compete on an equal footing with its current cost base. Major changes would be required to reduce costs and increase revenue. More minibuses were introduced to tackle costs. This time, the network of services to Dronfield, Gosforth and Coal Aston, operated in conjunction with Chesterfield Transport were radically overhauled.

The huge Gosforth estate, once Europe's largest private housing development, had the misfortune (fortune depending on your outlook) of just being over the border in Derbyshire, although most of its residents looked to Sheffield (when the estate was planned, this part of North East Derbyshire, would have been absorbed into the city) for employment and leisure activities.

A network of services had been built up in previous years, in conjunction with Derbyshire County Council and Chesterfield Transport, which served the estate in a pattern which offered express services between Sheffield and Chesterfield, and slower services between the two, serving Dronfield town centre, as well as the estates on either side. Separate services to Holmesfield, Hallowes and Eckington via Coal Aston, had been absorbed in to the pattern over the years, leading to a broad six buses per hour between Sheffield and the wider estate area, but it wasn't coordinated, with differing stops, routes in to central Sheffield and each separate leg was at a low frequency. A transport coordinators dream, a passengers' nightmare.

Initially at deregulation, the Holmesfield service (286) had been lost on tender to S&D, together with the local 'Quicklink' (503/4/5) services that met trains in the peak hours at Dronfield station. This had an effect of the viability of some services at Halfway garage, as the tenders for the 'Quicklink' services were built around schools services in Dronfield and neighboring Eckington. The former 201 to 204 group of services had been reshuffled in late 1985 with an X11 direct express, between the city and Chesterfield, but with slower off peak variants.

40

Chesterfield Transport had long been unhappy with its share of the operation and indicated it was going to operate an even faster X10 via Dronfield bypass. The estate was very much commuter territory, and outside of the peaks, the services were heavily reliant on concessionary fares holders. Whilst busy, they couldn't be described as money spinners, so a deal was worked out that created a network of minibus services to cater for the estates, leaving Chesterfield Transport to take the express network. SYT also launched a new X86 to Holmesfield to compete against S&D, who had found the 286 route they'd won at deregulation lucrative. Chesterfield Transport had also been particularly unimpressed that SYT had won a tendered service between Dronfield and Chesterfield via Holmesfield, but that was added in to the network as well. SYT retained the former Booth & Fisher service 253.

Initially all was cordial, as it had reduced costs on both sides, and each partner had got what they wanted out of the situation. Savercards were valid on both operators, as was Chesterfield's 'Spire Saver' ticket, but this situation collapsed in to bitter recrimination in 1988, with each operator refusing to take the other's tickets.

An effort was also made to remodel travel patterns between Sheffield and Rotherham. Closure of steelworks, removal of terraced housing and other changes to travel patterns had removed numerous passenger journeys from service 69, a once, every six minutes frequency route, with a need for duplication on top. That was now down to every 12 minutes, which was none too shabby, but on top there was SYT's X91 service to Thurnscoe, Yorkshire Traction's X90 to Mexborough and Richardson's X42 to Doncaster, via Rotherham and the Dearne towns abstracting revenue. In addition, British Rail, in association with the PTE, were busy upgrading the rail route within the Dearne Valley and had opened a new, central railway station, in Rotherham. They were shortly to start replacing 1960s built rolling stock with brand new 'Sprinter' units, giving a much improved product.

Top, Middle and Bottom

Chesterfield had introduced a new livery at deregulation. Roe bodied Fleetline 154, is on service 204, part of a network, which connected Sheffield with Chesterfield, in this case via Coal Aston. The bus is getting ready for the off from Sheffield's Central Bus Station.

As part of the Sheffield to Rotherham corridor change, Rotherham based Leyland DABs 2011 to 2013 were outshopped in this cameo and red livery. To make up the numbers for new service X69, and existing service X91, Leyland National 27 was similarly adorned. Both were photographed at Rotherham garage.

The 'Fastline' logo on the front of bus 2011 was made of reflective vinyl.

Below

The PTE was an early user of the Dennis Dominator. 521, was the second delivered, and was given a Rolls Royce engine after delivery.

The Halfway garage painter has been busy again, but has missed out the between deck stripes, and has made a hash of the transfers, in this attempt, seen outside the 'new' engineering pits.

The bus is on its way to a British Coal contract, on which a lot of the garage's work, had relied on.

The X91 was a remnant of the former Dearneways service that had been snapped up by the PTE in 1981. Brand new articulated coaches had been introduced in 1985 to the route, required because of a low bridge restricting headroom on this busy service, but had seen a falloff in patronage. This had been two fold. A closure of collieries in the area had suppressed travel to major towns and cities as job prospects were weak. Secondly, the introduction of the arctics had affected the service pattern. Traditionally, the service had operated hourly, but with duplicates that ran on top, but ran as X92's that went fast to Rotherham and Sheffield, missing out lots of stops. By only running an arctic every hour, the perception was that the service had got worse and less frequent. Added in to the mix was service 277/278, the long cross county link between Sheffield and Doncaster via Rotherham.

In order to try and compete with the train service, the 277/8 were rebadged as services X77/8, despite having no route or timetable changes. On top of the X91, a coordinated X69 was grafted onto the pattern, every 15 minutes using the arctics and Leyland National 27. These buses were given a slightly revised livery of 'Cameo' with a red skirt and red and brown lines with large Fastline logos on the side.

The reduction in costs could only really be tackled with a reduction in unremunerative mileage and facility consolidation. Frankly, there was too much space for too few vehicles. Looking around the company, of the Sheffield garages, East Bank and Leadmill were profitable, Herries marginal and Greenland was hemorrhaging cash. Rotherham, due to its enormous overheads, by being blessed with an almost brand new garage was also in financial straits. Doncaster seemed locked in to a period of inertia, making very little change to its network, but although the Thorne corridor was good bus territory, reshaping of the town network was required. Halfway, despite being based in a developing area of south east Sheffield was also loss making.

From an outsider's perspective, you would probably look and say that the best way to remove costs, would be to consolidate your smaller locations in to bigger ones removing overheads instantly. But, internal politics came in to play. There had long been disagreements between some Garage Managers and members of the Directorate. These had been festering for some time, but finally came to a head.

It would have been easy to close Dunscroft and move it in to Doncaster, but that would have been inefficient to some degree, requiring a large amount of dead mileage between some of the outer ends of quite long routes and the garage. Until Doncaster could revise its network, this was unviable.

Rotherham, having endured a torrid year, should have been a nailed on closure. It would have been unpalatable to quite a number of the, mainly, Rotherham appointed members of the non-executive board. Negotiations were entered in to with the newly privatised NFC (National Freight Corporation) to take on the building, with Rotherham moving to a smaller location within the town, but at this stage, that idea was stillborn, but would prove to be a noose around the neck of the company for the remainder of its life.

Greenland had not coped well with competition initially, but was fighting back, so much so that it was able to put on a family fun day/Christmas Fayre in December 1987. It had an enthusiastic management team, and was now, effectively a pseudo central works. It simply wasn't practical to close.

Halfway could have been closed, and the routes moved in to Greenland and Rotherham, but, as in the same vein as Dunscroft, some of the contract work it operated would have become unviable, due to the dead mileage that would have to be operated. Whilst the tenders may have been lost or retained, the prevailing thought was that you didn't want another competitor on your doorstep, with lots of off peak buses that could be used on your best routes, between the schools tenders.

Herries was marginal. It had coped well with competitive incursions and was well placed to deal with threats in the north of the city. Similarly, Leadmill, despite being an awkward shape and with limited facilities, had proved quite adept at dealing with competition. That left East Bank.

East Bank had been consistently profitable, operating some of the busiest routes in the network. It had a charismatic leadership team, led by Bill Baldwin. However, his 'go alone' style of management, although winning unending devotion from his staff, had frequently butted heads with members of the Directorate. On hearing that East Bank had been selected for closure, the management team offered to buy the garage from the company; an offer rightly refused. However, by closing the garage in 1988, this would open deep scars, that wouldn't be healed until well in to the next century, and opened the door to further competitive battles.

Negotiations were also opened in to a general package of changes to terms and conditions throughout the workforce, affecting all grades from official staff (administration) to drivers to engineering grades. Savings of around 8 to 10% had to be found by the start of the financial year in April 1988. Christmas 1987 was going to be particularly unpleasant, but was made even more so when the tender package for Christmas was announced, and won, by SUT, A&C Wigmore and Groves.

Negotiations for driving staff accepted that all drivers currently employed, retained their existing standard rate, however, a reduced rate would now be paid for overtime and new starters would be offered a less generous hourly rate. In addition, volunteers would be sought to take a lower rate of pay with a lump sum, paid as compensation, who would then go on to a revised working pattern, called 'Keyboard 88'. However, in a ballot of driving staff, only drivers in Doncaster and Dunscroft accepted the deal, so it was back to the negotiating table. The first months of 1988 were not going to be an enjoyable time for anyone connected with the company.

Above

2358 was the first East Lancs bodied Dominator to receive the new SYT livery, after losing its overall advert.

Pictured on the top park of the doomed East Bank garage, the smoke coming from the exhaust was a tell tale that the bus hadn't been started for a while, and the engineer driving it, is giving it a test drive before releasing it into service.

Chapter 3

1988

Below

Doncaster's town network was remarkably unchanged from the pre-deregulation network, inherited by SYT. This wouldn't be the case by the spring.

2212 is seen at Beckett Road terminus, on a route that would be replaced by minibuses later in the year.

Doncaster district was home to quite a few of these 'broadside' adverts, normally related to home improvements or flower shops.

If the last months of 1987 were terrible for the company, then the next four months leading up to the closure of East Bank were to be challenging, as the process of voluntary redundancy, staff movement, and continuing negotiations over pay and conditions were ongoing.

Driving staff had accepted a revised package of terms and conditions in the first week of January, accepting an increased lump sum payment for staff volunteering, or being placed, on the new 'Keyboard 88' rotas. The Inspectorate and clerical staff also accepted revised terms, which involved working an extra hour each week, in exchange for a freeze on wages for 12 months, effectively offering efficiency savings, and enabling some staff to depart the business. Negotiations with Engineering (commonly known as Inside grades) continued, but this would come to a head in the spring.

As part of the negotiations, the employees asked, that if they were giving up something for the business, shouldn't they get a share of the company in return? The seeds of employee ownership had been planted.

Another fare increase was also imposed from January, raising all fares by 5p. For an area that hadn't experienced a fare increase for 11 years, three in the space of 20 months generated the expected chorus of disapproval from the general public, who rightly complained, they were paying more money, for a materially worse service.

Doncaster and Dunscroft, having accepted the 'Keyboard 88' deal earlier, made a relatively modest package of service and frequency cuts in February, the restructuring of many town services, had to wait until more minibuses were available. The package wasn't all negative; a service to Bessacarr Grange was introduced, serving a new housing estate beside the east coast mainline. Peter Edwards was also appointed as the new Garage Manager at Dunscroft.

They had also been quietly beavering away in the tendered market, and had gained workings on services in to Wakefield and South Elmsall from West Riding. Coupled on to that was a tendered service from Pontefract to Ferrybridge, making inroads to the competitors market.

The entire fleet of Dennis Dominos were now back with the company, and they'd all been reallocated to Greenland, to operate further minibus services like the M41 to Hackenthorpe and the M28/9, an eastern circle service, encompassing parts of Attercliffe, Darnall, Manor and then adding an additional six buses per hour through Norfolk Park. Also converted were the Wybourn circle services 10 and 11, which had only been created the previous June, from double deck operation. Management's plan to get minibus drivers to drive these, painting them in Little Nipper livery in the process, however, fell foul of the minibus agreement, as these buses had 33 seats, so had to be driven by double deck drivers instead.

SYT had won the majority of the tender renewals at the start of the year, winning some back from S&D. However, having found some of the tendered network profitable, to such a degree, that they had invested in brand new Leyland Lynx buses, S&D quickly registered some of these tenders commercially.

Under the 1985 Act, PTEs could award tenders to boost services, where they felt the commercial service couldn't cater for anticipated demand. For example, service 84 to Roscoe Bank, had been registered to operate every 20 minutes throughout the day, coordinated with service 86 to Stannington, to provide a ten minute interval. The PTE thought that service 84 actually required an additional bus per hour, and accordingly put out a tender.

In this case, the additional journey per hour, was won by S&D, but because that didn't fit in to the coordinated service pattern, it meant that the S&D journey actually operated on top of a commercial SYT journey on service 86. This gave S&D valuable additional mileage, which gave them experience of other areas of the city, helping them to expand. The use of frequency enhancement tenders diminished from 1989.

Above

The Optare bodied Dennis Dominos had found a home at Greenland garage, and 45 is seen in the incomplete Crystal Peaks bus station on an M40 back to the city centre.

Sheffield & District had been able to fund some brand new Leyland Lynx from its mix of tendered and commercial operation.

The 27 was an enhancement tender, sitting in the middle of SYT journeys, but only on a Saturday. Barmy.

Clockwise from top left

You pays your money, you paint your wagon. Despite some of the adverts being for SYT's main competitor, the car, valuable revenue couldn't be sneezed at.

146 at Worksop; 1572 at Doncaster South Bus Station; 1869 on London Road, Sheffield; 2188 in Haymarket, Sheffield; 2198 on Pond Hill, Sheffield; 2232 in Church Street, Sheffield and 2271 in Rotherham Bus Station.

Crystal Peaks, a major new retail centre opened at the end of March, located in the Waterthorpe area of the Mosborough townships, in the south east of Sheffield. Most services in the area were diverted to serve the spacious, 8 bay, bus station that was integral to the success of the venture. Further Little Nipper services were added, as the centre grew in popularity. This was promoted by two minibuses being given a very pleasant white, blue and pink livery advertising the centre.

Retail was quite a theme for overall advert buses throughout the year, with 2188 donning a stylish, white based advert for the Orchard Square development in Sheffield, 2198 in a similarly themed white livery for Debenhams and Metrobus 1869 advertising What Shops, also in Sheffield. At the end of the previous year, Rotherham based Dominator 2271, and Herries based 2285 had been blessed with adverts for Children's World at Parkgate. In Doncaster, virtually the entire fleet had rear end adverts for shops in the town or The Star newspaper, and this fad had also spread to Sheffield and Rotherham, with a large number for Brook Shaw Motors and TC Harrison, the direct competitor to the bus, with 2232 being repainted into a advert for the GK Group. Broadside adverts were also applied to 1563 and 1572 in Doncaster advertising Plasvent Windows.

The major event in April was the closure of East Bank garage. This necessitated a major set of service changes that affected the entire company. In order to absorb the services and vehicles, a shuffle of routes between operating centre's was required, with most East Bank routes going to Greenland, Herries and Leadmill, but to make room, Greenland's journeys on services to Beighton, Eckington and Mosborough went to Halfway. Rotherham also acquired parts of services 1, 24 and the 34 group, as well as becoming wholly responsible for service 69 between the town and Sheffield.

The company also took the opportunity to deregister 2 million miles of non-commercial mileage, which was subsequently tendered, and returned to the company on an emergency tender, until August. Buried deep within the package were some minor improvements, including a new X18 service, jointly operated with KHCT, between Sheffield, Doncaster and Hull. Leyland Leopards 16, 18 and 99 were transferred to Doncaster garage to operate it.

There was a reshuffle of vehicles throughout the company. The main highlights being that Greenland got all East Bank's Fleetlines (from the batch 1535 to 1560), the entire batch of East Lancs bodied Dennis Dominators (2351 to 2365) went to Rotherham and Leadmill had to accommodate the Leyland Nationals (22/3) and Leyland Leopard (65) used on the disabled persons network. The unique batch of Northern Counties Dennis Dominators (2311 to 2320) remained at Greenland.

The first of the former 'Super Coachline' Dominators, 2486 and 2487 were repainted in SYT livery, and were allocated to Doncaster with revised Fastline branding for service X77/8. The rest of the batch eventually being allocated to Herries (2488) and Halfway (2489/2490) as the company couldn't justify the expense of having virtually new buses sat, unused for the majority of the time, at Leadmill.

Below

Long before low floor buses, wheelchair passengers were catered for by a special network of services, on selected days, operated by specially adapted buses.

Leopard 65 had been converted in 1986, incorporating a lift into its hind quarters, and had been painted in Coachline livery to appeal to a broader market.

It was moved to Leadmill when East Bank, where it is pictured, closed.

Above

The Northern Counties batch of Dennis Dominators were falling due for their first repaint in 1988.

Purchased at a time when Alexanders were quoting higher costs for their 'R' type bodywork, they incorporated a number of PTE specified parts.

Annoyingly, for the driver, there was a small lip into the cab (which was easy to trip up on) and the handbrake was angled in a slightly odd way, making it more difficult to operate than standard.

2314 is pictured at Crystal Peaks, fairly fresh from the paintshop, but has already required a new panel behind the rear wheel. It hasn't been painted properly, and this was a consequence of the industrial relations issues in engineering at that time.

Leopards 19 and 20 had also been allocated Herries for private hire and received SYT livery, antimacassars, losing fare collection equipment at the same time. When required, they could be loaned to Coachline.

The main vehicle withdrawals from the closure, came from the sale of the batch of 50, 1980 vintage, MCW Metrobuses (450 to 499) to Ensign, Purfleet. These dual door, Gardner engined buses, had seen heavy use throughout the city, with 40 being allocated to East Bank and 10 being allocated to Leadmill. In order to release the buses from Leadmill, single door Metrobuses were drafted in from Greenland. This had the effect of ending the Sixty Shuttle branding, introduced the previous April. This batch of buses, initially purchased by Ensign, attracting a sale price of £18,000 per bus, were then spread far and wide, ending up in diverse locations such as Leicester, London and Hong Kong.

Added to the final withdrawal of Rotherham's last Fleetlines, from the batch 1446 to 1455, the Bristol LHSs, the final 'DMS' Fleetlines (1511, 1515 to 1519) at the end of 1987, and a start made on the 1979 batch of Leyland Nationals (from the batches 5 to 14 and 1059 to 1066), meant the company was almost 100 'conventional' buses lighter, than at the start of deregulation.

As part of the company's restructuring plan, numerous members of staff had left the business. Around 100 drivers had taken voluntary redundancy, but sadly, some members of management and engineering staff had to be made compulsory redundant. In previous restructurings, the company had lost Jeff Gazzard as Marketing Manager, Nick Hill as Computer Services Manager and were now about to lose other key members of the team.

Iain Duff, Garage Manager at Herries left to become Director of Operations at Chesterfield Transport (later, using his local knowledge to submit, and win various tenders in Sheffield); Mike Greenwood, Customer Services Manager went to the FWT Marketing Consultancy; Bill Baldwin, Garage Manager at East Bank took his redundancy, but was back on the bus scene in the August. The most high profile departure was that of D.Scott Helliwell as Operations Director. He left to take up the position of Managing Director of the newly formed Manchester Metrolink company. It was clear that a further reorganisation would be required.

The ongoing discussions with engineering staff to change their terms and conditions were bogged down in recriminations, and the closure of East Bank, and the issue of compulsory redundancy notices had exacerbated the problem. This finally came to a head on 22 April, when the company issued letters to all engineering staff, affectively giving them 12 weeks notice of changes to their terms and conditions. Fire and rehire is nothing new.

Engineering performance had become woeful, with most garages missing their PVR due to go slows and work to rule initiatives, instigated by the Trade Union. From the management perspective, there was a realisation that garages needed to split the operational function away from engineering, and that was now to be worked in to a fully-fledged plan. Engineering was to be reorganised in to three sections; Vehicle Maintenance, Ancillary Services and Engineering Services (effectively getting buses on the road, cleaning, and painting/central engineering). An investigation was also to be undertaken in to separating Autoservices and Central Engineering (Rutland Way) in to a free standing, wholly owned businesses (although this never happened).

In the event, the need for such action was withdrawn, as enough volunteers were found for voluntary redundancy and the workforce agreed to changes in their terms and conditions.

The major upset felt throughout the company, however, would take years to heal, and in some cases, was never fully recovered from.

A new batch of Little Nipper minibuses started to enter service from late spring. Now badged as the Renault S56, these 30 vehicles (190 to 219) had a revised cowl, uprated engine and brakes, and were fitted with a retarder from the start. They were also fitted with Reeve Burgess' newly styled Beaver bodywork. Whilst being slightly boxier than the previous body it replaced, it looked quite modern. This batch was allocated to Greenland, enabling earlier minibuses to be cascaded to Doncaster.

Above

Leopards 19 and 20 were allocated to Herries, primarily for private hire and family and community services contracts. Seen in the back yard at the garage, it appears it has had to be used on service 33.

The new Reeve Burgess Beaver body was unveiled in the spring of 1988, with SYT being one of the first customers.

The batch of 30 were all allocated to Greenland, where bus 214 is pictured, allowing earlier buses to be cascaded.

Clockwise from Top Left

Doncaster's final batch of Fleetlines, ordered originally by the Corporation, were withdrawn in 1988.

As the company was struggling with a backlog on engineering work, some were placed on 'warm' reserve, and were used as float buses between garages. 1569 is performing such a role in Rotherham.

Premier's fleet included this gem (top right) of an Alexander bodied Ailsa. Not operated by SYT, it gave a glimpse as to what SYT's own Ailsas would have looked like, if they had arrived with their specified Alexander bodywork.

To keep the Premier name alive, which had good feelings locally, Atlantean 1648 was repainted into pseudo Premier livery for private hire work.

Sadly, a mix up in the purchasing/sales department, meant this bus was withdrawn and sold, instead of a sister bus, not long after it had received this colour scheme.

Doncaster used the opportunity to convert some high frequency town services to Little Nipper operation, replacing double deck and single deck buses on services 163 (Beckett Road), 172 (Hexthorpe and Clay Lane), 173 (Hyde Park) and enhancing existing Little Nipper services (A1 to A3 Armthorpe; B2 Bessacarr; E1 Edenthorpe), with new services M70 through to M89. This enabled Doncaster's unique batch of East Lancs bodied Leyland Fleetlines (1561 to 1575) to be withdrawn from service. These buses went in to store at East Bank, but some were subsequently used as engineering support buses at Greenland and Rotherham.

Not one to let the grass grow under their feet, Dunscroft garage absorbed the operations and vehicles of Premier Coaches of Stainforth, which SYT had purchased in June. This finally gave SYT the monopoly on the busy routes to the north east of Doncaster, begun in the 1970s by the PTE, to the important catchments of Stainforth, Hatfield, Thorne, Moorends and Goole.

An eclectic selection of vehicles was included in the sale, including a Volvo Ailsa. Whilst all the vehicles received SYT fleet numbers, none entered service, being replaced by surplus vehicles from within the company, with the exception of a pair of Plaxton bodied Bedfords (82 and 87) which were retained in full Premier livery, to start an embryonic coach business. Leyland Atlantean 1648 was transferred to Dunscroft and was painted in Premier livery, to advertise the new coach unit, being replaced later by similarly bodied 1762.

A further fare increase was implemented at the end of June to assist in stabilising the ship. Certainly, there were some signs of optimism that the worst was over.

The competitors hadn't been quiet during this time. SUT had registered further routes, disposing of their ideas about being different, and now simply registering on top of SYT services. They were active in the tendered market, purchasing a batch of MCW Metroriders to compete for minibus tenders. They now had a base in Dinnington, and had set about services to Rotherham, as well as operating around the Kimberworth Park estate. Quality, and reliability was poor, and buses were widely shared throughout the new ATL group, leading to buses appearing in Rochdale and Sheffield in the same livery. A tentative tender win in Leeds had produced an off shoot called 'Airebus', in a blue and cream livery, but poor reliability and quality issues, led to Metro (WYPTE) revoking the tenders, and reissuing them to Yorkshire Rider.

Two Neoplan N416 buses, with Caetano bodywork had entered service with them, being used on competitive journeys on service X77 to Doncaster and on tendered service X39 to Penistone. Exotic they were, but Bill Devlin, the Engineering Manager, who had come to the company from Clydeside Scottish, made them work. Bill later went on to be Engineering Director at Lothian Buses, after a string of senior positions within Stagecoach.

Their best, and probably only real initiative, was a competing service to Leeds using Neoplan Skyliner double deck coaches, released from the company's commitment to Intasun and Fiesta holidays. Painted in a white livery, with large red X32 branding and with welcome hosts, these coaches were placed in front of journeys operated by SYT, West Riding and Yorkshire Traction on the traditional service.

Above

SUT had invested, via the ATL group in small batches of MCW Metroriders, a pair of Neoplan single deckers (both pictured in Sheffield) and had repurposed some former Excelsior and NTE Neoplan double deck coaches for competing services to Leeds (pictured in Barnsley).

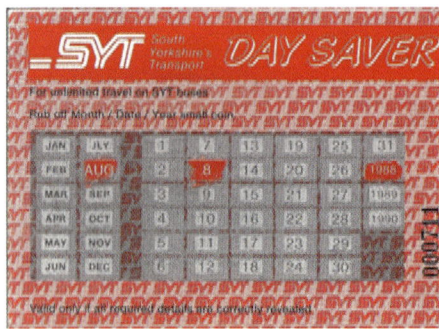

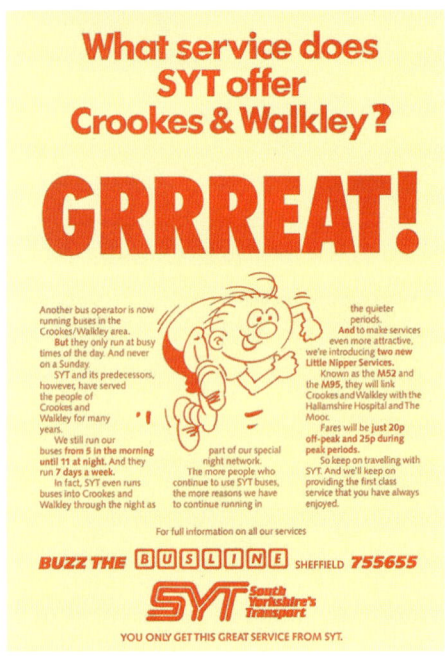

Above Right

Yorkshire Terrier sprang on to the scene in August, with a fleet of secondhand Leyland Nationals, of varying vintage.

This one, pictured on Commercial Street in Sheffield, had originally been in the Midland Red fleet. The blinds appear to be of PTE vintage, and the ticket machines appear to have come from the PTE store as well.

With excellent management, it was a self inflicted wound for SYT.

The traditional operators responded by placing buses five minutes in front of the SUT journeys, which were five minutes in front of the existing departures. Three buses, all departing for Leeds, within 10 minutes, was bizarre. Added in to the mix was cheaper fares. The PTE had to move the competing services in to the former bus park on Harmer Lane, which had become the new overflow bus station. SYT used Fastline Metrobuses and Dominators, West Riding used Olympians and Yorkshire Traction a mix of Metrobuses and Olympians, all of which couldn't match the quality feel of the Neoplans.

The company introduced 'Day Saver', a go anywhere day ticket from the June fare increase. Priced at £1.95, the only places you couldn't use it on were the X18 beyond Armthorpe to Hull and the X32 beyond Barnsley to Leeds. Initially sold as a card that was date stamped, this was replaced with a scratch off card later in the year. However, you still had to travel to a Travel Shop to purchase the ticket. On bus sales would have to wait for a further six years.

The closure of East Bank was fresh in the memory when in August, a new competitor arrived on the scene, in the form of Yorkshire Terrier.

Fronted by Bill Baldwin and the majority of his former management team at East Bank, it initially operated seven Leyland National buses, based at the Keaton Steelworks, right beside Greenland garage. Starting with two routes, the 15 and 16, which were circular routes taking in substantial chunks of busy SYT services 52 and 95 to Crookes and Walkley, differing from them by operating via the Moor shopping area.

SYT initially responded by registering two competing services (M52 and M95), operated by Little Nipper minibuses, from Leadmill garage. By the year end, Yorkshire Terrier had started operating the full length of service 52 and had started a second route, the 25, from Woodhouse to Bradway and were also looking at the Parson Cross and Norfolk Park areas as well. Such was the speed of their expansion, they had to move to the old Central Works site, only recently vacated by SYT.

SYT had always been keen to explore commercial opportunities for engineering and an interesting opportunity came up, with a tender being issued by the Home Office, for the storage and maintenance of the vehicles and associated equipment of the EFS, the Emergency Fire Service, which was basically the Bedford RLHZ 'Green Goddess' Fire engines and associated Land Rovers, Austin Gypsys and Brockhouse trailers. Held in reserve, in case of national emergencies, they were often portrayed as strike breaking vehicles, they would occasionally be drafted into areas suffering flooding, to aid local fire brigades with pumping out etc.

SYT had been invited to tender for this contract in February, with the view of using East Bank, and the company set up a small team to carry out a feasibility study. In April senior members of the team visited the Home Office Storage and Supply Depot at Branston that was currently carrying out the task, that SYT were tendering for. The results were fed back to the team and senior managers at SYT for consideration. In June the Home office invited SYT to tender a price for storing, and pressure testing, 26,880 lengths of 75ft long hose.

By September SYT had requested two Fire engines to help gain more knowledge to submit a tender. The pair (SYH 463 and PGW 410) arrived at East Bank and were subject to inspections, pump testing, brake tests and a full report given back to the home office with some of the defects rectified by SYT staff.

The Home office had strict procedures for storage of its vehicles, all were to be raised off the floor, fuel drained, clutch pedal depressed etc., but in contrast to that a rotating road test and examination regime was to take place with a set number of vehicles being available in an emergency in a matter of hours to cover region two; West and South Yorkshire and parts of Humberside, and region three, to cover Derbyshire, Nottinghamshire, Lincolnshire and Leicester.

By mid-October SYT had viewed an additional building for possible/additional use at Newton Chambers Industrial Estate in Chapeltown, but was found to be in a poor condition and not pursued. Around the same time, the project team were disbanded, with the tender being submitted. Unfortunately all efforts came to nothing, as the contract was eventually awarded to TNT Truckcare in Staffordshire, in July 1991.

In September, a second entrant, also formed by former SYT East Bank staff, this time drivers, entered the fray as Sheafline, operating from the former Tram Sheds on Weedon Street in Tinsley.

They started with a batch of former GMPTE, Park Royal bodied Leyland Atlanteans, operating on key SYT corridors to Totley, Wybourn, Hemsworth, Shirecliffe, Jordanthorpe and Batemoor. While some of these services were direct copies of what was already there, albeit via different combinations of corridors, they did tap in to a hitherto unserved market between Batemoor and the city centre via Chesterfield Road, which quickly gained popularity.

It was not lost, on most people, the significance of these competitors being unleashed by the direct actions of SYT in the previous 12 months.

Above

The Green Goddess has an almost legendary reputation in the UK, and is commonly remembered as the vehicle used when fire services went on strike.

PGW410 was one of two loaned to SYT during 1988, and is seen here at Meadowhall HQ for inspection by the engineering team.

Above

The second new entrant led by former SYT employees in 1988 was Sheafline.

Pictured in Sheffield's Church Street, the buses looked smart, but with no management expertise, they would quickly run into problems.

An open day was held at Greenland garage, the first proper one since 1986. As well as the usual events, visiting buses, bus wash rides and the like, visitors could take a look around the vast engineering facilities to see how their buses were looked after. As Yorkshire Terrier were next door, they cheekily parked a bus beside the fence, inviting people to look around. This was quickly covered over with an SYT bus, parked against it.

Service changes were mainly concerned with tidying up some issues from the East Bank closure, but in August, SYT lost a significant amount of emergency tenders it had been awarded in April, to S&D and SUT. Quite a lot of frequency enhancement tenders had been awarded by the PTE. Significantly, S&D gained a large chunk of Rotherham Sunday work, easily operated from their new base in Handsworth, being less than half a mile away from the Rotherham border. Doncaster won a small package of minibus services in Rossington, but the X18 failed to make the grade, and the operation was given over to KHCT.

Rotherham, who having rescued their engineering performance, found themselves in trouble with the Traffic Commissioner for failing to display the correct destination blinds on certain journeys. This was mainly due to the influx of buses from Sheffield after East Bank closed, and the inability to show Rotherham destinations and vice versa. Whilst new blinds were on order, and some effort had been made to search stores all over the company for old blinds that could be 'chopped' up and inserted in to Rotherham blinds, these didn't arrive until the autumn. The company got away with a formal warning on this occasion.

A package of improvements was also made to Sheffield services 1, 34, 35, and 39, primarily operated by Rotherham, but with some input from Leadmill and Greenland, to improve access to the Flower Estate in Wincobank. The chance was also taken to restructure the timetable to make it easier to understand, and, more importantly, cheaper to operate.

Employee Share Ownership Plans were now being actively discussed throughout the company after the successful sale of near neighbour, Yorkshire Rider, in October, to its employees and management. There was significant interest from the Unions, mainly as a way of preserving jobs, but negotiations would be painful, and take a further five years to reach fruition.

The final reorganisation of the year, saw a rejig of the Directorate and senior management of the company. In engineering, Alan Jones joined the company from London Country North East, as Associate Director of Engineering, under Wilf Kemp.

His remit was to restructure the garage engineering effort after a long, tortuous summer, rebuild morale and make the section more client focused, the client being the operational side of the business. He left the business in the following February, but his legacy was the ability of SYT stores to sell parts to its competitors, a somewhat self-defeating act. In addition, the contra deals with other bus companies, for attending breakdowns out with the normal operating area, came to an end. From now on, attendance at other bus company's breakdowns meant an invoice was produced.

A new Operations Director arrived in the form of Bob Montgomery. A tall Scotsman, he breathed new life into a section of the business seriously questioning how they could cope with so many competitive battles.

He rattled the Union, but gave unswerving loyalty to his staff. He had previously been the Managing Director of Manchester Minibuses (The Bee Line Buzz Company) which had been terrorising GM Buses in south Manchester, Trafford and Stockport, before that, holding a similar role at NBC company Red Bus in north Devon.

Ian Davies continued to be Associate Director Operations looking after Sheffield and Rotherham, with Bob Rowe now acting as Area Manager for Doncaster. Tom Young had left the company for London Forest, and was replaced by Graham Hogg as Commercial Manger, assisted by Steve Arnold as Marketing Manager. Peter Edwards moved from Dunscroft to Herries with Dave Henderson replacing him. This was to be a holding pattern, as further reorganisation was planned for 1989.

Bob Montgomery had a vision for buses. He saw them no differently to running a retail business. The company had goods to sell (seats) and a market to sell them to (customers), which had to be at a price (the fare), which was value for money and was of sufficient quality to bring repeat custom. The notion that a bus company was any different was alien to him.

Above

The X18 had been a speculative venture, in association with KHCT, between Sheffield and Hull. However, it lost 88 pence for every mile it operated (which was a considerable distance between the two cities), and SYT left the route in the autumn.

99 had been painted into this individual livery before its transfer to Doncaster, where it is seen entering the South Bus Station.

The Marshall bodied Atlanteans were ungainly looking machines. The SYT livery brightened them up, but couldn't hide their top heavy appearance.

Recently repainted, Rotherham based, 1835, is seen at a SYTS event in Hillsborough Park, Sheffield.

Bob spent his first few weeks understanding how elements of the operations were managed, by directly speaking to his team. He recognised that too much management time was spent on ensuring that low earning school contracts left the garage each morning and afternoon, whereas very little attention was paid to the routes, like service 52, which were the company's bread and butter.

He looked at SYT overall and saw a company that was trying to do too much. In his eyes, the company should set its stall out differently. SYT should prioritise its routes according to profitability and then simplify the network around that base. It was a forerunner to today's 'Overground' and 'Citi' networks operated by First and Stagecoach, which in later life, he actioned, going on to hold senior positions in both companies. He also recognized that excessive amounts of management time was being spent on low earning school services, that would be more productively targeted at the busier, more profitable, services.

With this in mind, a working party was established to look at all aspects of the company, and create a fully developed commercial plan, that could stem the loss of patronage, find the most efficient use of resources, battle against competition and, ultimately, produce a profitable company that could blossom in the future. At the heart of the matter was should SYT continue to operate all of the mileage it currently did, or should it simply concentrate on a core network, leaving the rest to competitors?

Under its current ownership structure, that was not going to be acceptable, so radical ideas were needed.

Service 52, a long established former tram service, operating between Crookes in the western suburbs of Sheffield, through the city centre to Darnall, Handsworth, Ballifield and Woodhouse in the east, was a heavily trafficked service, running up to every six minutes during the day. As well as serving busy areas of housing, it also served the Children's and Weston Park Hospital's, Sheffield University and its resultant student population at Broomhill.

The 52 had long underpinned the financial performance of Greenland garage, which had been suffering from multiple attacks on its network of services through Norfolk Park, Manor and Woodhouse. It now had three competitors on the 52. Yorkshire Terrier was the main competitor, with SUT and S&D operating more sporadically, the latter only between Woodhouse and the city centre.

One of the first acts of the new working party, was to think of new ways of repelling these competitors and restoring profitability to this important service as well as stabilising the finances of Greenland. What they thought of was a novel plan, which would have been familiar to Bob Montgomery; minibus operation.

Initial computer modelling showed, with the right balance of frequency and driver terms and conditions, an increase of patronage could be expected from current, non-users, as well as seeing off the competition. He was initially unconvinced that this course of action would work in Sheffield. He'd had plenty of experience in his previous post, and whilst minibuses had an effect, the cost base was difficult to get right, and Manchester Minibuses were never profitable, to such a degree, as to finally de-stabilise GM Buses. In fact the opposite had taken place, as they had also taken minibuses in great numbers to see off this incursion.

Below

The SYT livery had evolved over time, mainly to appease the engineering section.

The initial livery on buses with an enclosed engine bustle, meant that part of that was painted cameo. This proved impractical in service, and as can be seen in Luke Farley's illustration below, this was changed to incorporate the whole bustle, on repaint.

To help persuade the board, a number of minibus demonstrators were brought to Meadowhall head office in late November. As well as the existing Renault S56, chassis from Mercedes, MCW, Optare and Talbot were examined, in various lengths and widths. Finally convinced, the approval was given.

Under the terms of the 1985 Act, uniquely, PTA owned companies, could only operate within their existing sphere of operation (until privatised). This was seen as being a way from stopping these companies using their existing resources to fight battles far away from home. In SYT's case, this actually gave it quite a wide area, as its buses had operated as far as Clay Cross and Worksop to the south, Goole to the east, Leeds, Bradford, Huddersfield and Halifax to the north and Manchester to the west.

Wakefield, the home of West Riding, also fell within this category, but it would be an outside source that would approach the company for help, that would prove to be the catalyst for a competitive battle on their doorstep.

Compass Coaches was a small operation based in Wakefield, who were looking to expand. After approaching SYT for the loan of vehicles, a partnership was developed, under the chairmanship of former Premier Coaches owner Bob Wilson. SYT would take a shareholding in the newly named Compass Bus, and would inject expertise into the business by seconding members of management to help get it running. A small fleet of Leyland Leopards and Nationals that were surplus to the needs of SYT were prepared at Herries garage, painted into Compass' yellow and blue livery, backed up by Domino 47 and, occasionally, a Dodge minibus. The three former mini Coachline Ford Transit minibuses were also brought back from hire to Cardiff Bus and sent to help out.

West Riding's two busiest routes were the 110 from Kettlethorpe in the south of Wakefield through to Leeds and the 126/7 to Dewsbury.

Compass targeted these, also using MCW Metrobuses from Leadmill on Saturdays to cope with the loads on the 110, as well as entering the tendered market. This was a wholly unusual approach, but it gave spirit to long suffering staff that the company was fighting back, and wanted to survive and thrive. 1989 was going to be a whirlwind of change that breathed new life in to the company.

Above

The 31 strong batch of Alexander bodied Fleetlines were still giving yeoman service in Doncaster and Sheffield.

1539 is seen on Duke Street, in Doncaster, on the punishingly busy 181 to Armthorpe.

A friend in need is a friend that can hurt your competitor. Compass bus had plenty of Leyland Nationals and Leopards from SYT, but the need for something smaller, was met by Dennis Domino 47, seen here in Dewsbury.

Chapter 4

1989

Above Right

Pictured in 1987 at Firth Park, the vandalism damage on MCW Metrobus 480, was symptomatic of the problems of 'tagging'.

These random squiggles were meaningless to most people, but looked unsightly and gave an air of neglect.

After 1989, the incidences of this reduced, but it would take effective, expensive action to finally overcome.

The year started with an air of cautious optimism. The Directorate had released the first set of accounts for the period October 1986 to April 1988. This showed a loss of £5.5 million, made up of a trading loss of £1.25 million, with the remainder being restructuring and redundancy costs. Whilst significant, it could have been a lot worse. Initial talks had been held with the PTA about an employee buyout, but, at best, the response was lukewarm, despite threatening overtones from the Government about breaking up the company.

Problems were never far away. Vandalism, a perennial problem for all bus operators, had been on the increase, especially in Sheffield and Rotherham for

In the period immediately after deregulation, a spate of 'tagging', essentially graffiti, had become prevalent on the interiors and exteriors of buses, following a trend that had started in London and had spread to Birmingham. This was helped by the easy availability of spray paint and new paint markers.

Apart from being unsightly, it gave an impression, if not quickly removed, that nobody cared and nobody was in control. Some of this graffiti was vulgar and was a real issue in the High Green and Parson Cross areas of Sheffield, so much so, that unaccompanied travel by children, was banned after 2000 hrs. On services 79 and 89.

Effective action with South Yorkshire Police dampened down some of this, but, it kept returning in waves. Six Herries based Dennis Dominators were fitted with CCTV equipment, then in its infancy, to catch these youths in action, but more robust action would be needed.

All night bus services were revised in January 1989, on a part commercial, part tendered basis in Sheffield. Some, hitherto, unserved communities were now blessed with regular departures throughout the night including Dinnington. All night bus journeys, and their tendered early morning twins (frequently referred to as 'fresh air' buses, for their lack of patronage) were operated by a small, dedicated, keyboard of drivers at Leadmill garage.

The first marketing initiative of the year was to offer return fares, under the banner of 'Pay Once, Travel Twice', on services with competition in the High Green, Chapeltown, Low Edges and Bradway areas of Sheffield, in competition with Groves, Yorkshire Terrier, SUT and Andrews, who had moved on to a number of SYT services, between their schools commitments. They had secured the last AEC operated on the Isle of Man, and had commendably restored it to original condition, mainly being used on their journeys on service 24.

The PTE had been busy getting a makeover, and had finally ditched the 'flying duck' for a new yellow and blue 'T' symbol, and restyled themselves as the 'Transport Executive'. Quite what the general public made of this, nobody knows, but with it came a new, all operator, Travelmaster travel card. This followed unsuccessful attempts to persuade SYT to allow the Savercard product to be taken over by them. Savercard had become a well-known product and fostered tremendous loyalty towards the company, entering the local vernacular as a byword for a travel card. The PTE had also been busy setting out its plans for its light rail system, which they reckoned could take 15% of the public transport market.

Following the minibus trials held in the previous year, the company decided to stick with the Renault S56. Earlier variants of the model were now being fitted with revised brake linings to help the instances of fade and overheating which were still occurring, despite the retrofitting of retarders. For the new service 52, 35 new minibuses would be required for PVR, but this is where fate leant a hand.

Lincoln City Transport had adopted an aggressive, expansionist policy after deregulation. They were famous for introducing FX4 taxicabs in their home city under the 'Lincoln Limo' brand, offering door to door travel, and had launched a competitive battle against Lincolnshire Road Car in Scunthorpe under the brand name 'Betta Bus'.

Above and Below

Andrews had initially restricted themselves to tendered work, but to make up the driving day, they had also branched out on to commercial service against SYT.

Looking immaculate, the last AEC Regent delivered to a UK operator, Douglas Corporation, is seen here outside Rotherham Police Station.

Looking less than immaculate (below), despite being virtually brand new, the Betta Bus network in Scunthorpe, wasn't the most inspiring brand.

Lincolnshire's loss was SYT's gain, when this virtually brand new bus, made the move along the M18.

Below and Opposite

The new Eager Beaver image was certainly eye catching. The cartoon figure (below) was depicted on everything from ties (from where this sample comes from) to publicity to vinyls.

The new Northern Counties bodied vehicles were certainly different to what had gone before, but fitted in well with the existing fleet.

The ex Lincoln buses simply required repainting and fitment of ticketing equipment to merge effortlessly into the rest of the existing Beaver batch.

232 is pictured on launch day at Bramall Lane, whilst 249 is pictured at Crookes Junction, Broomhill.

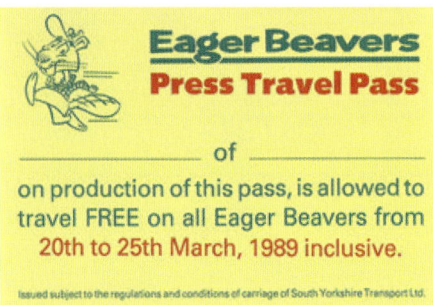

Unfortunately, they had over reached themselves, with both ventures folding by the end of 1988.

This had left Lincoln in the embarrassing situation of having 15 virtually brand new Renault S56 buses with Reeve Burgess bodywork, virtually identical to those operated by SYT, in addition to four similar, but smaller Ford Ivecos, with nothing to do. Not being a company to look a gift horse in the mouth, SYT purchased these vehicles, initially using them for driver training. In addition a batch of 20 Northern Counties bodied S56s, which had been built as dealer stock, were also taken on. A couple of existing 1988 S56s (218 and 219) were also moved from the main fleet to act as spares.

The 'new' service 52 was to operate on a greatly increased frequency (every 3 minutes), with unscheduled extras added as and when required. Over 90 new drivers and engineers were required, and press adverts went out in January. This time, the policy was to recruit people with retail, rather than PCV experience, and then train them how to drive a bus. An emphasis was placed on trying to recruit as many women as possible, as they were under represented within the workforce, and the general feeling was, they gave better customer service.

The unit was going to be quite separate from the main fleet. Two Portakabins were obtained and placed on the top park at Greenland garage. This gained an affectionate name of the 'Beaver Hut'. A separate engineering bay was set up in the garage extension, and fitted with vehicle lifts, to perform essential tasks and regular inspections on these new buses. It would control its own fleet, with its own separate radio channel. The buses on service 52 were the first to be fitted with 'Band III' radio equipment. Cleaning, fueling and overall management control remained with Brian Keith as Garage Manager.

To manage this new unit of staff, applications were invited for a Unit Manager and an Engineering Manager. The two successful applicants were Mike Robertson and Alan Hull. Mike had previously been an Inspector and Alan had been running Autoservices. To perform inspectorate services, a new grade of Leading Driver was created and was filled by ambitious, young employees.

With the buses in place, all that was required was a brand name and livery. Step forward Eager Beavers. In a move which broke away from all conventions regarding bus livery, a new yellow, red and blue livery, in diagonal chunks was married with a black skirt. The cartoon Beaver was produced in full colour on the side of the buses, as well as in promotional material. Timetables were not issued, instead a frequency guide, with first and last times was released to the general public, although later, a functional leaflet was produced.

Drivers were given a new uniform of blue blazer, white shirt, grey trousers and an orangey/red tie, all emblazoned with the Eager Beaver motif. Drivers were also given a standard SYT raincoat and bag.

The effort involved in getting 37 buses painted, vinyled, and fitted out for this new operation was enormous. All sections of the company were involved, but it was a struggle to get enough driving test slots for the required number of staff. As well as the ex-Lincoln S56s, the Ivecos were also used for training, these being deemed unsuitable for use at that time, remaining in the white livery they arrived in.

A promotional launch was undertaken at the home of Sheffield United, Bramall Lane, on 13 March, with services commencing battle with the competition on 20 March. Initially, as you would expect, there were some teething problems, especially bunching, and additional Inspectorate assistance was given to sort this out, but the image was strong, and the turn up and go frequency was a positive boon.

EVERYBODY'S CATCHING EAGER BEAVER FEVER!

Route 52

Starting on **MONDAY MARCH 20th**
Frequent, friendly Eager Beaver minibuses will take over on Route 52. You just can't miss them!

- Crookes
- Broomhill
- City Centre
- Attercliffe
- Darnall
- Handsworth
- Ballifield
- Woodhouse

Have you got it yet?

The new Eager Beavers from South Yorkshire Transport are the most exciting things to happen to buses in years. You'll find them beavering about on the existing Route 52 between Crookes, the City Centre and Woodhouse, and you just can't miss them. They're faster, friendlier and more frequent than anything else on the road and they're part of SYT's commitment to improving the way you travel.

BEAVERS DO IT FASTER!
These nippy little minibuses can beaver in and out of the traffic, running rings round old fashioned buses. You'll find you get where you want to go much more quickly.

BEAVERS DO IT MORE OFTEN!
They'll be running from 5am until 1am, seven days a week.

And they'll be going your way, literally, every couple of minutes of the day. It means you'll never have to wait for a bus ever again.

BEAVERS DO IT IN STYLE!
The buses are the last word in modern transport design. They're spacious, comfortable, warm and beautifully clean.

BEAVERS DO IT THE FRIENDLIEST WAY!
Eager Beavers are lovely and cosy and you'll find yourself travelling with new friends every journey. You'll find the drivers really caring, courteous and considerate too.

WHERE CAN I CATCH A BEAVER?
On the following sections of the route, just pick a safe spot away from road junctions, parked cars or pedestrian crossings and our drivers will stop to let you get ON or OFF the bus.
BETWEEN CROOKES TERMINUS AND THE PUNCHBOWL.
BETWEEN WOODHOUSE TERMINUS AND BEAVER HILL ROAD/JUNCTION A57.
On other sections of the route, for your safety and the convenience of other road users, our drivers will only stop at normal bus stops.

HOW FREQUENT ARE BEAVERS?

MONDAY TO FRIDAY			SATURDAY			SUNDAY		
5.15am until 6.05am EVERY **20 MINS.**	6.05am – 11.05pm EVERY **3-5 MINS.**	11.05pm until 11.45pm EVERY **10 MINS.**	5.10am until 7.40am EVERY **20 MINS.**	7.40am – 11.05pm EVERY **3-5 MINS.**	11.05pm until 11.45pm EVERY **10 MINS.**	5.05am until 6.05am EVERY **30 MINS.**	6.05am until 11.05am EVERY **20 MINS.**	11.05am until 11.45pm EVERY **10 MINS.**

WE BEAVER THIS-A-WAY AS USUAL...

CROOKES, Heavygate Ave, Heavygate Rd, Northfield Road, Crookes, Crookes Road,	**BROOMHILL,** Whitham Road, Western Bank, Brook Hill, Upper Hanover Street,	Glossop Road, West Street, Church Street, **HIGH STREET,** Castle Square, High Street,	Haymarket, Waingate, Lady's Bridge, Wicker, Savile St, Attercliffe Rd.	**ATTERCLIFFE,** Staniforth Road, **DARNALL,** Main Road, Handsworth Rd,	Retford Road, **BALLIFIELD,** Beaver Hill Rd, Badger Road, Station Road,
				HANDSWORTH,	**WOODHOUSE.**

There are certain earlier and later Beavers funded by South Yorkshire P.T.E. to give customers a complete service – please ask your driver or call the Beaver Line.

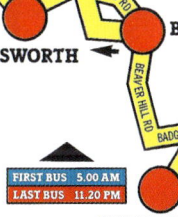

For more information Call the BeaverLine 755655

Above

The PTE had taken a long time to settle on a standard bus, and was inclined to take in waifs and strays that had been ordered by other operators, but not delivered.

323, pictured at the old Belle Vue ground of Doncaster Rovers, had originally been ordered by a Lancashire independent, and after migrating from Sheffield, had found a home at Dunscroft.

523, seen here on Church Street, Sheffield, had also been ordered by an independent, but when they had been taken over by the PTE, the bus was delivered to them.

Oddities like these were difficult to keep spare parts for, and good prices were being offered for them on the open market. The new influx of minibuses enabled them to be withdrawn and sold.

It was known that certain people within the company were unimpressed with this particular venture, and were willing for it to fail. Elements of the Trade Union also wanted it to fail, although mainly because they saw it as a further erosion of staff wages and conditions. Indeed in some quarters of the Trade Union there was downright hostility to many of the ideas that Bob Montgomery was putting forward to turn around the company's fortunes. It took some time for them to come around to the new way of thinking, but slowly, the corner was turned, and some cynics were turned in to ardent defenders of the scheme.

Almost overnight, it had a positive effect on passenger numbers. Research carried out after the launch concluded that about 10% of ridership had previously used a car or other form of travel to get to work, but found the frequency and convenience of the service had made them look again at the bus. S&D quickly pulled off the service, and SUT reduced their frequency, but Yorkshire Terrier were harder to dislodge, and some customers just didn't like travelling by minibus.

When Bob Montgomery went to America to explain the Eager Beaver concept, the audience were aghast that you could get away with such a name, never mind having it printed in huge letters on the side of a bus. Bob was somewhat perplexed, until someone explained that the name had different connotations 'over the pond'.

This influx of minibuses had a knock on effect on other vehicles throughout the fleet. A start was made on getting rid of the last 'oddities', with early Dennis Dominators 521, 523 and 524 being withdrawn and the unique East Lancs Atlanteans 322 and 323 at Dunscroft. A start was also made on the early 1600 batch of Roe bodied Atlanteans, at Herries and Rotherham, by transferring surplus Dominators away. The Atlanteans were chosen over older Fleetlines for their sale value (although they wouldn't see out the end of the year), in addition a small number were earmarked for conversion to Driver Instruction Vehicles. In the meantime, these vehicles were stored at East Bank.

The trials and tribulations of Rotherham garage were never too far away. This enormous building had been designed for a different age. As fantastic as a facility it was, it was now, too big for the number of buses operating out of it. Despite mileage being placed in to it from the closure of East Bank, it was still woefully under used. The palatial office accommodation was largely empty, with the ability to go from one end of the office block to the other without seeing a soul. The canteen facility had never opened and apart from drivers taking buses out in a morning, and bringing them back at night, most staff used the facilities in the Town Centre.

Around one third of the engineering facilities weren't being used and the building was being heated by two enormous coal fired boilers, built in to the structure by the PTE, to support local business. Frankly, it was a white elephant, and its losses were costing the company serious amounts of money.

Politically it would have been unacceptable not to have an operating location in the town, but did it really need to be so big? Designed for 150 buses, with plenty of room for expansion, it was now holding less than 120, all under cover. There was lots of pressure from the non-executive members of the Board to keep the building and find alternative uses for parts of it, but what?

The Directorate were convinced action was required, and initially looked at other options for the site. Negotiations were reopened with NFC to take on the site. They were really keen, as it had ample parking and engineering facilities, enabling them to vacate a number of their locations. A site was identified at College Road that could easily accommodate about 80 SYT vehicles, with main engineering service being transferred to Greenland, with non 'town' services being reallocated to Greenland, Herries, Halfway and Doncaster.

Negotiations continued throughout the year, but came to naught. NFC eventually lost patience and backed away from the deal altogether. It was now up to the Directorate and local managers to try and establish a profitable operation for the garage, with several service changes implemented to trim frequencies and affect efficiencies, especially on the Whiston corridor.

Compass had been extremely successful in winning tendered work from West Riding, and had increased its fleet to 30 buses. It had purchased vehicles from outwith SYT, as well as others going on loan. It had been necessary to move to larger premises at Flanshaw Way in Wakefield, and further expansion was likely.

The Government had decided that the radio frequencies used by SYT, and other bus operators throughout the UK, were to re allocated, and that instead, a new 'Band III' was to be made available. The company had been fully committed to radio communication since its inception in corporation days, and developed plans to replace the entire radio system garage by garage. Initially, the new service 52 unit was equipped with a variant with an open 'hot mike' system, but for main fleet, a complicated system had to be developed that could pinpoint vehicle locations, as well as allowing different style of calls to be routed to individual garages. Doncaster was chosen as the initial location for trials, and was successfully rolled out across the company, but it was a £1 million investment the company could have used elsewhere.

Above

Compass was coming on leaps and bounds and was expanding rapidly.

Buses were now being acquired from outwith SYT, and this Leyland National had originally been with Burnley and Pendle.

Seen on the top park at Greenland garage, the buses still came through the company for preparation and painting.

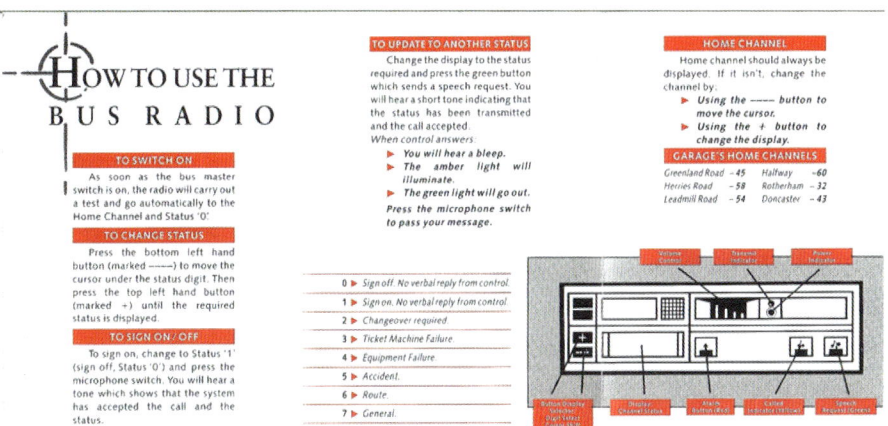

Above

Leyland Atlantean 1728, pictured at Doncaster garage, was painted in one of the three trial liveries, for what would eventually become, 'Sheffield Mainline'.

Although rejected, it's easy to see that the initial idea was to restructure the fleet livery into a common theme, based on diagonal 'wedges' of colour.

It never ventured into service in this garb, although it did make it to Meadowhall head office for viewing, before rejection.

Plans were now being made for the next 'unit' style of operation, this time based on double deck buses. Services 81 to 84 and 86 in Sheffield were known by staff as 'The Track'. Essentially unchanged since tram days, these popular services operated from Ecclesall and Bents Green in the west, through the city centre to Middlewood, Roscoe Bank and Stannington in the north, with odd extensions to Ringinglow, Ewden Valley and Dungworth. Operated from Herries garage, they were good strong, profitable services. Competition was provided by S&D on the Stannington end and SUT over the Middlewood to Bents Green service.

Using similar principles to the Eager Beaver operation, this time, existing staff were used to man the service, on a separate keyboard (rota). Engineering would also be on conventional lines, not separated out (indeed the separate engineering idea for minibus units eventually withered on the vine, whereas the operational unit structure was strengthened).

Drivers were to be given customer service training and a slightly different uniform with a blazer being preferred to the conventional body warmer.

Unit 81, as it was known, was to be managed by Tony Gilmour, a popular company Inspector. Initially, 20 vehicles were to be used on the service, and the search was on for a new brand name. The first effort was an overall midnight blue, to which was to be added silver stripes, with a fleetname of 'Sheffield Steeline'. Despite being painted on one vehicle, it was rejected. Next, two buses were painted in a similar style to the Eager Beavers, one in cream, red and blue and the other in cream red and brown. Again neither was acceptable nor was the suggested fleetname of 'Sheffield Citybus'.

A young designer called Ray Stenning was contacted for a livery proposal, and in the sheaf of designs he created was a new fleetname. Sheffield Mainline was born, married to a new, eye catching red and yellow livery. The buses chosen were eight to ten year old, Alexander bodied, Leyland Atlanteans. They had been well maintained, and with their dual door bodies, would easily scoop up the crowds on these busy services, serving large housing estates and the huge student population on Ecclesall Road. They were given an extra heavy clean, with some buses receiving moquette seats upstairs, in attempt to deter vandalism.

Traditionally, service changes in Sheffield were carried out on a Sunday (the pay week being Sunday to Saturday; Rotherham and Doncaster being Monday to Sunday), so the new service pattern started on 28 May, but the new livery, and associated launch, didn't occur until Tuesday 30 May – the Monday being a public holiday.

The new image was bright and strong, suddenly making the normal SYT livery seem dull in comparison. The local 'Star' newspaper carried several pages of complaints about the new image, but it was unlike anything seen before. The service pattern gave a 7.5 minute interval between Holme Lane junction in Hillsborough and Hunters Bar, with lower frequencies on the outer ends, where the service pattern split. On reflection, this was too low, and in the September service change package, this was increased to every 5 minutes, but did encompass the new strategy of taking the best services, making the most profitable use of the resource and then marketing it to the max. In its first few weeks a promotion was run that offered prizes and free travel to customers.

The main competition on the route reacted in two different ways. S&D, the only competitor that SYT really respected, acted professionally, and made changes to its tendered and commercial journeys to dovetail in to the new service pattern. SUT on the other hand, had bought a number of second hand Atlanteans from Lothian, and had been using these on the route. They were 17 years old, and although they had been well maintained in Edinburgh, the same could not be said about their treatment in Sheffield. They were not fitted with power steering, and were notoriously slow. They inserted additional, unregistered journeys and had started blocking bus stops and stands to prevent SYT buses from serving them.

Above

Getting dressed and ready for the new competitive battle, in the weeks leading up to the relaunch of 'The Track', feverish preparations were underway at Herries garage, home to the new Unit 81.

Here we see a phalanx of Leyland Atlanteans, having been painted, being fitted out with vinyls and being given heavy cleans, to get them ready for launch day.

Herries, built in 1952, was modelled to some degree on Stockwell bus garage in London. A fiercely independent place, drivers were known by other Sheffield garages as the 'Hillsborough Bus Company'. The garage was yards away from Sheffield Wednesday's ground.

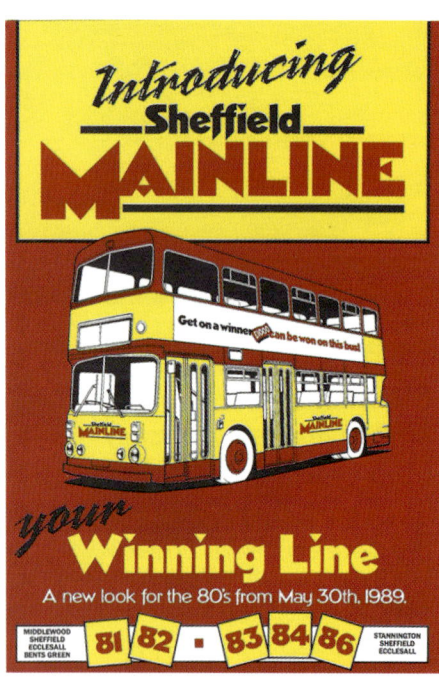

Above

Leyland Atlantean 1706 is pictured turning into Cumberland Street, Sheffield, early on the first day of Sheffield Mainline operation.

The new livery certainly caught the eye, although yellow is not an easy colour to paint, the variant here being called 'Canary'.

Profitability on the routes became very good, and the aforementioned frequency problems were soon corrected, as it was notable that some journeys were having to leave people behind, because they were full. The previously mentioned, extended journeys to Ringinglow, Ewden Valley and Dungworth were separated out in May, but were incorporated in to the main service from September, with an increase in buses to operate it.

The competitive scene was not stagnant in other areas. In Doncaster, a new entrant to the market, Wilfreda Beehive, a well-known operator of high class coaches and holidays, had assembled a fleet of former Bristol Omnibus, dual doored, Leyland Nationals and a variety of former WMPTE and GMPTE double deck buses. They started competition with SYT and Yorkshire Traction on a number of corridors, initially going for the Skellow, Scawthorpe and Woodlands corridors.

Yorkshire Terrier, having now established its base in the former Central Works, consolidated its operations, by moving on to the Loxley and Wisewood corridor in competition with SYT services 13 and 14 and starting new express services to Beighton and Killamarsh via the Mosborough Parkway. This was a pre cursor to them buying new premises on Rother Valley Way in the south east of Sheffield, when they were required to vacate the works for a retail development.

The well-respected independent A&C Wigmore had sold out and was now being transformed in to a new company known as Northern Bus, still based in Dinnington. They would go on to collect an amazing fleet of Bristol RE and VR type buses, and enter both the commercial and tendered market in all spheres of the company's operation.

Andrews had branched out from its tendered and occasional journeys on service 24 to Rotherham by launching a new service in Rotherham to Dovedale Road, exactly mirroring SYT service 114, and eventually going on to match SYT's service 121 to Sunnyside.

Clockwise from top left

SUT's Engineering Director, Bill Devlin, had done a deal with his opposite number at Lothian to acquire these Atlanteans from a Barnsley breaker. With no power steering, they were heavy lumps to drive.

Wigmores had sold out, becoming Northern Bus in the process, although it kept hold of its premier route to Dinnington.

Wilfreda and Andrews had moved to other areas of the company's patch to compete, finding niece markets to serve, whilst Richardson's was still the only public transport option to Manchester Airport.

Sheafline had acquired additional resources, with this Atlantean coming from East Yorkshire.

Above

The purchase of Richardson Travel's bus network, required the purchase of a small amount of secondhand stock, to enhance the fleet.

In both cases, the initial owners had been London Country. The Leopards were left white, and had 'Airport Link' vinyls fitted.

The two Leyland Nationals were of the short variety, and they were prepared and painted at Greenland.

Leopard 95 is seen on the forecourt of Greenland garage, while National 3, is seen in Crystal Peaks Bus Station.

Richardson Travel had been content to manage its small portfolio of tendered and commercial services, having added a service from Sheffield to Greasbrough in Rotherham, via Attercliffe. Its main bread and butter was the route to Manchester Airport, although it had created a niche on the Dearne Valley network to Sheffield and Doncaster, mainly in competition with Yorkshire Traction.

National Express, newly privatised and hungry to expand, had decided to target the Sheffield to Manchester Airport corridor, which at that time had no direct rail link. Richardson's had doubled the frequency to hourly for the summer season, anxious not to be outdone, but with limited facilities and finance, would find it difficult to defend its position.

In this scenario, SYT decided to purchase Richardson's' bus services, taking them on from the end of June, although SYT had been assisting with drivers, buses, management expertise and cash beforehand. The owner, Roger Richardson, would continue his coach hire business, before eventually moving to Sussex. In the main, existing vehicles from within SYT were prepared to take over the incoming services. Two, short length, Leyland Nationals were purchased (3 & 4) for service 258 to Thorpe Hesley and four former London Country Leyland Leopards (92 to 95) were bought from dealer stock, kept in the white livery they were delivered in, and pressed in to service with 'Richardson's Airport Link' vinyls, for the Manchester run.

Most of the services were operated out of Greenland, the exception being service X40 to Mexborough, which went to Rotherham, and the Sheffield to Doncaster night services, which were added to the existing Nightline keyboard at Leadmill.

Unconnected fleet arrivals arrived in the same month, these being two brand new Dennis Javelin coaches (78 and 79) with Duple bodies. The company had plenty of experience with bodywork from this manufacturer, but quality issues on those delivered in 1980 and 1981, had meant most had been withdrawn and sold. These were a completely new design and also introduced a brand new livery of grey, yellow, white and red. In addition, a small Premier fleetname was added to the Coachline image (the totally unconnected Premier coach unit was based in Doncaster).

The end of June heralded another minor fares increase, but this only affected two 'off peak' fare bands, and was the lowest increase since the company started operating. Also, on the last day of the month, Wilf Kemp, Engineering and Personnel Director, retired. He wasn't directly replaced, as Bernard Keane had been promoted to Associate Director of Engineering when Alan Jones had exited the business. The other duties were shared with Bill Bland and Chris Dyal, who were promoted as Engineering Executives.

Above and Below

Investment in Coachline saw the purchase of two Dennis Javelin coaches, with Duple bodywork. They also launched a new livery, to replace the scheme used since 1985. 78 is seen at Meadowhall, about a year after delivery.

Could you get away with an advert like this for Savercards today (below)? In less stringent times, this would be seen as mildly amusing, nowadays, somebody would be offended, and bus companies generally shy away from such advertising.

From 27 August, changes were made to the Savercard scheme. The 'Shoppacard' off peak ticket was scrapped and a new 'Saver 7' was launched to help attract new patronage, who perhaps couldn't afford the monthly ticket in one go. Initial take up of the new ticket was high, but it was only available in the 'go anywhere' network version. It would be several years before customers could buy these tickets on bus, and for now, you would have to go to a Travel Shop, or a Post Office to get one.

The summer of 1989 was a hot, sultry affair. Like all good things, it had to come to an end, but a glorious Indian summer was beckoning for the revitalised SYT. The Eager Beaver and Mainline concept had proven to be a winning combination for the future direction of the business. This strategy was to be rolled out across the network, but it was time to hit back at some competitive battles that had developed throughout the year.

Above

Dodge S56, 187, pictured in Sheffield Interchange, was delivered in 1987 in Little Nipper livery.

By September 1989, it was reallocated to Herries, repainted in Eager Beaver livery, and was set for a busy few months on services 13/14 to Wisewood and Loxley.

The redeveloped interchange was completed in 1990, but saw less than twenty years of full use, before this lower section was sold off for redevelopment.

Passengers had long eschewed using the facility, preferring to use buses that took them to the shopping areas of the city centre, some distance from the shiny new facility.

Yorkshire Terrier had made inroads in to the Wisewood and Loxley market, which had only been partially repelled by minor changes to the existing service pattern from SYT. The decision was taken to convert these services to Eager Beaver operation, launching a new unit at Herries.

Previously, these services had operated on a combined 15 minute frequency between the city centre and Hallowmoor Road Top, at Wisewood, before the 13 continued to Malin Bridge, and the 14 continued in a loop to Loxley. The new service pattern was to be every six minutes to Hallowmoor Road Top, with the 13 terminating at Hallowmoor Road Bottom, and the 14 continuing direct to Loxley, terminating in a loop on the hitherto, unserved, 'The Chase'. This would abandon the Loxley New Road corridor to the tendered 61 service , but would be a faster, direct link to this popular estate on the west of the city. The PTE decided, in their wisdom, that one bus per hour on service 13 should continue to Malin Bridge off peak, and that was built in to the service pattern.

For the vehicles to operate this service, the resources had to come from in house. Work had been ongoing during the summer to convert the Dennis Dominos in to minibuses, by removing the central section of eight seats, and replacing it with a standing 'pen', meaning they could then be driven by minibus drivers.

Work had also been undertaken on their troublesome Maxwell gearboxes, converting them to semi-automatic, using parts from Leyland Atlanteans. These buses were initially going to be painted in Eager Beaver livery and transferred to Herries, but, that idea never materialised, and nine surplus S56s from the first and second batches were collected from around the company and prepared instead.

The second Eager Beaver route from Greenland replaced services M26 and M27. The old 92 route number returned, on a service between the city centre and Fishponds, on the eastern edge of the Woodthorpe estate. This had been an area locked in a competitive battle with S&D and Yorkshire Terrier on their services 91 and 25 respectively, and a new ten minute frequency timetable was devised to tackle this head on. Again, the proposal to use the Dominos was investigated, and rejected, and a further small batch of S56s from 1988, were repainted and added to the fleet at Greenland, operated as part of Unit 52.

The other major service in the area was the long established 93, operating from Woodhouse, via Stradbroke, Manor Park and the city centre, before heading east through Brightside and Wincobank to Firth Park, although that northern section had only been taken over from service 4 as recently as June 1987. It was decided that it would benefit from conversion to Mainline operation, and the frequency was increased to every 10 minutes, as it would also be one of the first buses serving the Meadowhall shopping centre, under construction, on land formerly occupied by Hadfield's steelworks.

A batch of five year old Dennis Dominators was drawn from examples at Greenland, Halfway and Rotherham and subjected to a heavy interior clean and repaint in to the bright Sheffield Mainline livery, mainly at the paint shop at Greenland, but some were done by Plaxton at South Anston.

In each case the same formula was used for staff recruitment, this being external applicants for Eager Beavers, and existing staff for Mainline operation. The idea would be that eventually the new drivers on Eager Beavers would flow through to double deck driving, and this was the new entry system for initial applicants in Sheffield. Initial Unit Managers were Colin Wheeler for service 13 and 14 and Geoff Davison for service 93, both popular members of the Inspectorate. The drivers on service 92 reported to Mike Robertson. All these changes, together with other minor changes across the network took effect on 3 September.

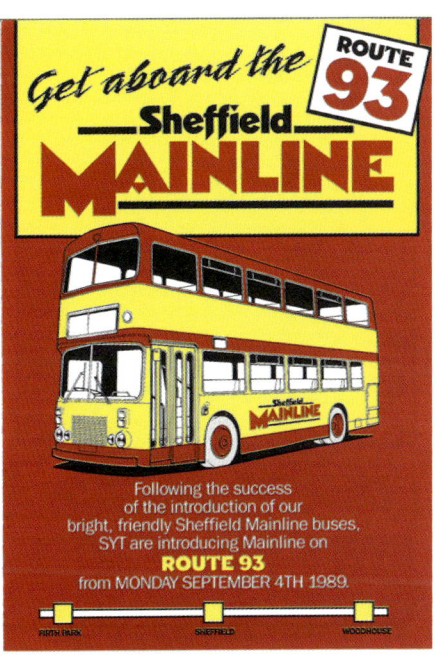

Top

Dennis Dominator 2446 is seen in Sheffield Interchange, freshly painted in the Sheffield Mainline livery, for the very busy service 93.

Above

The new Sheffield Mainline livery suited the lines of the Alexander 'R' type body well. Simple, and easy to maintain, it quickly grew in popularity.

Sheafline had one last throw of the dice, taking on board four, former London Country, Leyland Tigers, despite them being wholly unsuitable for the duties they were to perform.

This example is seen, apparently out of service, in Fitzalan Square, Sheffield. Sadly for them, time had run out.

This change saw to the end of further 1600 series Atlanteans at Herries and Rotherham and Greenland's entire fleet of Alexander bodied Fleetlines in the 1500 series was withdrawn. In most cases, they were sent to store at East Bank, but a few Fleetlines were kept as a 'warm' reserve at Herries. The 1600 series Atlanteans were finding willing buyers all over the country and Drawlane owned Midland Fox were interested in as many Fleetlines as they could get their hands on for operation in Leicester.

The ATL group (which included SUT) had been purchased by National Express in August, mainly for access to its coach operation on the west of the Pennines. They weren't interested in the bus operation, and were making noises about selling that part of the business.

Sheafline, who had now expanded slightly by winning tenders to operate the 260 and 261 Westfield Circulars and the 8 and 9 Inner Circle, had purchased an additional four, former London Country, Duple bodied, Leyland Tigers, which they continued to operate in dealer stock white. They had, however, ran in to significant difficulties in maintaining their fleet. The facilities at the old Tinsley tram sheds could be best described as primitive, with only basic pit and lift equipment available. They had already been warned by the Traffic Commissioner about their standards, and had reached out to the newly formed Drawlane group for assistance.

Drawlane had been formed out of a property company called Endless Holdings, based in Salisbury. They had purchased a number of former NBC owned bus companies, one of which being North Western, based in Liverpool. North Western had been formed from the splitting up of Ribble Motor Services in September 1986, and as part of that process, they had inherited a large quantity of Park Royal bodied Leyland Atlanteans. North Western offered mechanical services to Sheafline in the form of a number of these Atlanteans, and had cemented that relationship by painting a small number in Sheafline livery.

The Traffic Commissioner finally lost patience with Sheafline, who had no professional officers to call on for administration, and revoked their operator's licence to at the end of August, suspended for 12 weeks, in order for them to try and find a buyer. Drawlane would seem to be that suitor.

At the same time, Groves, the small independent operator based in Darnall, had also run in to problems maintaining its small fleet, and had attracted attention for its unreliability. It also was to have its operator's licence revoked

At the end of September, SYT, through a holding company called Hallamshire Bus, which had been created in January 1989 with independent management, purchased SUT from National Express through another company called Sheffield United Transport Limited. As part of the deal, SYT would withdraw from the Manchester Airport market.

Again, via Hallamshire Bus, Sheafline was purchased from its owners, who were retained as drivers, from under the noses of Drawlane by another new shelf company called KT530 Limited. Drawlane immediately took all its property away, although they continued to make noises about returning to the area. This threat was taken seriously by SYT's management, so much so, that members of the operational and commercial teams were sent on clandestine missions to review operations on Merseyside, Surrey, Leicester and Manchester where Drawlane had a significant presence.

Groves was the next operator hoovered up by Hallamshire Bus. Its operation being transferred to the new KT530 (trading as Sheafline) company.

Finally, in what had been a frantic period of consolidation, West Riding and SYT agreed a swap of operations, with S&D being bought by Hallamshire Bus, being renamed as the Sheffield & District Traction Company, with West Riding purchasing the operations of Compass Bus. The new S&D were to operate from the SUT premises on Charlotte Road, with the Handsworth garage closing, being retained by West Riding. Hallamshire Bus was then 'purchased' from its management by SYT.

This entire combine would take some sorting out, and a new manager to the business, Martin Lewis, former Commercial Manager of Ribble, came on board as General Manager. Initially each was to be operated as an autonomous business, but some urgent action had to be taken to restore some sense of reliability. The engineering issues at Sheafline were addressed by purchasing a large quantity of Mk1 Leyland Nationals from West Riding. They had been well maintained and were painted in either overall cream or in their previous owners' red, or green and cream livery.

Above

Apart from the Leyland National, none of the acquired businesses buses entered the new Hallamshire Bus fleet.

Above

West Riding, as part of the Compass Bus/Hallamshire Bus deal, decided that it didn't need certain parts of the fleet, and two coaches, and a rebodied Leopard, came south.

Bova 71, seen on Granville Road in Sheffield, was repainted into the new Coachline livery and was retained.

The somewhat offbeat, Irizar bodied Volvo 72, seen on the Norfolk Park estate, was only briefly placed on fleet strength, and was rapidly sold out of the business.

SYT had hoped that West Riding would include the virtually new Leyland Lynxs in the purchase deal, but they were spirited away quite quickly, after a short period on loan, back to West Yorkshire. They also removed the last ECW and Park Royal bodied Atlanteans, leaving just the Leyland National fleet. To replace that stock, a further batch of secondhand buses, also Leyland Nationals, arrived from Yorkshire Traction.

A few buses came in the other direction, West Riding not wanting to be left with marques it no longer operated. In the main this consisted of a rebodied, Plaxton, Leyland Leopard (69), a Bova coach (71) and a Irizar bodied Volvo (72), new in 1980, which didn't see any service with the company, although the Bova, new in 1984, was repainted in the new Coachline livery.

As the year came to a close, two new liveries appeared on the rag, tag, inherited fleet. In a similar style, the new SUT livery consisted of red and grey with white tapelines. Sheafline's was white with a red roof, blue skirt and white tapelines. Only two vehicles ever carried the SUT variant, but the Sheafline version was rolled out quite rapidly.

In October, a radical reorganisation of the Operation and Commercial wings of the company was undertaken to streamline how the new SYT was being run. Sadly, these events also coordinated with redundancies, but wherever possible, volunteers were taken first, some on an enhanced scheme involving pension rights.

Bob Montgomery had inherited the structure put in place at deregulation. In the previous twelve months, the engineering operation had been split away from operations, and it was now time to reform the way the garages operated. The old practice of individual garages planning and scheduling their services was swept away in to a new district structure. On top of that, a central services function was developed to assist this new structure, within the rest of the company.

Assisting Bob in his endeavors, Ian Davies was retained as Associate Director, having an overview, but mainly being concerned with Sheffield. Bob Rowe looked after Doncaster and Peter Edwards was promoted to be Area Manager for Rotherham. Central services consisted of John Parkin in charge of Personnel and Recruitment, Mike Newton in charge of Training, Graham Hogg in charge of the commercial and marketing function, Steve Arnold in charge of public relations and Brian Keith who was to be the company's eyes and ears on the new Supertram project, that had recently started construction.

Under the area managers, a new planning function was put in place, with the slightly mis named Marketing Managers, going on to plan new networks and find new business. Gary Nolan looked after Sheffield, Richard Simons looked after Rotherham and John Swann looked after Doncaster. They would have a team of experienced schedules staff from around the garages under them, led by Bill Allen and Mike Nuttall.

To support this team, Ian Blackburn was placed in a new role, using developing computer software, to head up project Bus Driver, which tried to match real time data analysis with a functional, simplified timetable.

Individual Garage Managers were replaced with Operations Managers who would support and look after the Unit Managers in the future. Dave Henderson, Graham Willis, Andy Mycock, John Asquith, Bert Middleton, Malcolm Woodward and Don Philpotts took up these roles. Further changes were afoot, with a big emphasis on cleaning, a much maligned and forgotten about activity, now under the charge of Colin Fowlston, who would develop more effective ways of removing graffiti and making bus travel more luxurious

Wilfreda Beehive had started to make inroads in to the SYT network by registering, essentially identical services, to Edlington and Rossington.

One of the first acts of the new structure was to investigate the best way of getting rid of this new predator, but to start with, extra buses were drafted on to the routes and new variants 453 and 454 were registered around Rossington to relieve the fight, as well as remove the tendered Little Nipper services in the area.

The Sheffield Mainline concept increased its services in November when Shiregreen services 47 and 48 were extended across the city centre to Herdings, replacing parts of service 43 and all of service 28. Effectively two figure of eight services, over the core part of the route, the frequency was every 7/8 minutes. A number of Mk1 MCW Metrobuses were repainted for this route, and it was added to the keyboard of Unit 93, with Geoff Davison expanding his role as manager for this as well.

Clockwise Above

The new liveries for SUT and Sheafline were based on the same template, sweeping away all previous images.

The SUT variant, however, was only applied to two buses, but the Sheafline version spread rapidly.

The other refugee from Compass Bus was Leopard 69, which found a new home at Leadmill, although it didn't normally get as far north as Leeds, where it's shown.

The MCW Metrobuses for the 47/48 were drawn from existing stock at Greenland. They weren't the best vehicles, but they were only a stopgap, and most be withdrawn by the following year. 1895 is waiting time on Flat Street, on these very busy services.

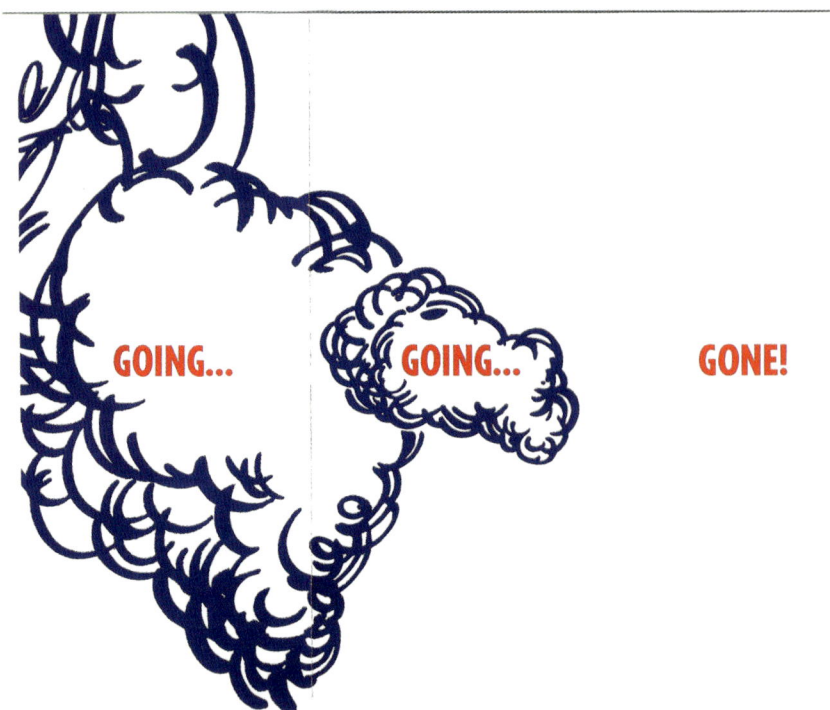

Fitted with lifts in the rear portion of the vehicle, they were based at Greenland, but weren't owned by the company. They were driven by a special pool of drivers.

It had been a momentous year for the company. The corner had been turned, so much so, that the year ended April 1989, had shown the company making a profit of just over £2.75 million. The dark days were over for now, the buzz words were expansion and quality, despite the fact the Government was still thinking about splitting the company up, although they accepted that SYT was making moves to privatise through an ESOP. Great strides had been made in sorting out the newly acquired companies, but 1990 would be the year these plans would come to fruition.

ON NOVEMBER 1ST ALL SYT BUSES WILL BE SMOKE FREE

 At SYT we try very hard to give all our customers the best possible service. That doesn't just mean making sure the buses run when and where you want them. It also means making every trip with SYT as pleasant as possible.

That's why we keep our new Eager Beaver and Mainline buses especially clean. And why we've now decided to make all our buses smoke-free zones.

Of course, we made sure that you wanted our buses to be smoke-free first. We asked passengers their opinion and we found out the reaction to smoke-free buses in other parts of the country. The result was a big thumbs-up for no smoking on SYT buses.

No smoking will mean fresher air on board all our buses. They'll be cleaner and they'll smell sweeter too. In fact it will guarantee a healthier, more pleasant environment for passengers and crews alike. And that has to be good news for every one.

YOU ONLY GET THESE GREAT SERVICES FROM SYT

On the first day of November, smoking was banned on all SYT buses. Unbelievable as it now seems, smoking was allowed on the upper deck of double deck buses, and towards the rear of single deck vehicles. There was the usual outrage in the press, but what some people hadn't noticed was that every minibus was non smoking, and that major route 52, had been converted to non smoking overnight in March, without even a whimper of complaint. Initially a soft approach was taken, but laterally, fines were to be enforced for non-compliance.

As the year ended some minor service changes took place to reintegrate some aspects of tendered operation, that were now with the new SUT/Sheafline operation, back in to SYT, with the S&D tendered work in Rotherham moving back. Tendered routes operated by SUT in Barnsley were sold on to Yorkshire Traction.

The company had also won a package of Tertiary College services for disabled customers from the PTE, and as part of the deal, nine Carlyle bodied Freight Rover Sherpa minibuses had arrived in a special red and black livery with a yellow stripe.

Clockwise from Left

At deregulation, most of the driver training fleet consisted of ex Sheffield Daimler Fleetlines from 1973. Most were repainted overall white. By 1989, they were in need of replacement.

The Roe bodied Atlanteans in the 1600 series, had proved to be readily adaptable for driver tuition duties, having semi automatic gearboxes. M114 is seen at Tinsley Tram Sheds and taking a breather outside The Dome leisure centre in Doncaster.

Chapter 5
1990

This Page

1990 was a year of innovation and new ideas.

Pictured at the rear of Rotherham garage, on the internal perimeter road, MCW Metrobus 1894 is on the newly constructed guided busway test track, being inspected by the garage engineering management.

Passing by is Dennis Dominator 2440, newly repainted into a test livery for Rotherham Mainline, has been released from the paint shop, and was barely dry.

At the very end of 1989, Tony West, a former detective with South Yorkshire Police, joined the company as Security Manager. Whilst the incidence of graffiti and vandalism had tailed off, there were still flare ups, especially around school services and in the evening when groups of youths would use the bus as a replacement for the youth club.

As part of a professional approach, the company would now treat each incident as the police would, giving it a unique reference number, and following it up with detailed witness statements and record keeping. This would also include better liaison with local authorities, as well as the police forces that the company served. Joining Tony on his mission were Terry Walls and Dave Owen who transferred over from the Inspectorate, as they had previous police and military training.

The company was now in the position of being confident to place orders for new buses. During the summer of 1989, a small number of manufacturers had demonstrated new chassis for the last decade of the century. Volvo provided a B10M from Burnley & Pendle, with an Alexander body; Optare contributed a Delta with a DAF Chassis; Leyland showed off its revised Lynx integral and Renault, a new entrant to the UK market, brought along one of its 'PR' make of integral chassis/body.

In the event, the Volvo made the best impression, and the company ordered 50 with bodies by Alexander, the PS type, with a restyled front end, first supplied to SBS in Singapore. In addition, the company ordered a further 50 Renault S56 MkIIIs, with a revised Reeve Burgess body, for further expansion of the Eager Beaver concept. These were due for delivery in May.

Hot on the heels of the restructuring of Operations, Engineering also broke itself down in to functional units, more in keeping with the way the business was now operating, compared to how it was on deregulation day.

Although not a full member of the Board, Bernard Keane was effectively in charge as Associate Director. In addition to Colin Fowlston, looking after cleaning, the actual day to day issue of putting enough buses on the road in a safe condition was down to the two Engineering Executive's, Bill Bland and Chris Dyal. Bill looked after Sheffield and Central Engineering with Roger Sims, Keith Peacock, Malcolm Tomlinson and Dave Hearson taking day to day charge. Under Chris, Phil Fowler, John Clayton and Dave Biggin looked after Doncaster, Rotherham and Halfway respectively.

In a similar set up to Operations, a central services function looked after company wide matters. Ray Giblin looked after supplies and purchasing, Bob Wilson looked after technical services, Mel Baskerville looked after recruitment and Ken Mason looked after the management services (stats/safety) function. This section also looked after apprentice training through Steve Hicks.

The first major service change of the year was on 25 February and was the start of the integration process of SUT/Sheafline in to the business. The SYT 'family' was to consist of a number of brands, each performing a specific role in the service provision.

Above and Below

Renault tried to enter the UK bus market in the late 1980's, with little success. SYT trialled this PR series single deck on service 51.

The bus that won the 'big bus' order for Volvo, came from the Burnley & Pendle fleet.

Although displayed with the more angular front, the company had picked the more stylish 'S' front that had been supplied to Singapore.

Burnley 66, is seen in the town's Bus Station.

Above and Below

The majority of the allocation for service 51's conversion to 'Mainline', was made up from the unique batch of 10, Northern Counties bodied Dominators.

2315 is seen on the first morning at Lodge Moor terminus.

For the 97, a batch of Mk2 MCW Metrobuses was repainted, but one Mk1 was also treated to the yellow and red paintbrush.

1887 is turning into Commercial Street on its way to service 97's original terminus at Nether Edge. Within a year, it would be going to Totley and Totley Brook instead.

The quality, high frequency, brand was Mainline, running at least every 10 minutes. Eager Beavers was to the same standard, but with minibuses. SYT's core red and cream buses were to provide services that didn't quite make the frequency grade, but were still profitable. Fastline was to be SYT's core limited stop network within and beyond the county. Little Nipper was for low frequency, commercial and tendered services, using minibuses. Sheafline was going to be for former 'core' SYT services, that made little, if any, profit and provided an internal competitor, to the main brands on limited corridors (a so called spoiler, reducing the opportunities for competitors to get a foot in the door), whilst bringing lower costs. Finally, SUT was going to be used for low cost tendered, conventional services.

The first part of this plan, was to move some mileage between the two companies. Services 1, 23, 32, 34, 35, 39, 44, 91, 94 and 98 were all transferred to Sheafline. Most of these services had been operated by SYT buses from three garages, or S&D and whilst technically profitable, they had a greater chance of being more so, using the new Sheafline pay scales, now operating from Charlotte Road.

In return, a significant chunk of what had been 'competing' SUT mileage was removed from sections of SYT services. This had the effect of reducing the number of buses at Greenland and Rotherham, but plans were in hand to restore the allocation at these garages and drastically cutting the SUT fleet, removing elderly Atlanteans and Nationals.

At the same time, service 51 at Greenland was converted to Sheffield Mainline operation, doing so with the entire batch of Northern Counties bodied Dominators (2311 to 2320) and Alexander bodied 2290/2291, with Phil Travis looking after the drivers on this route. Leadmill was also added to the Mainline 'party' with the conversion of service 97 between Nether Edge and Hillsborough/Parson Cross, with a batch of Mk2 MCW Metrobuses and one Mk1 (1887) at the same time. The new Unit manager appointed there was Alan Bullas. Extra buses had to be drafted on to the 81 group at Herries to fill the holes left by removing the SUT and S&D journeys on the corridor, with Dominator 2234 becoming the first at Herries in the bright red and yellow livery, although some SUT journeys continued on service 86 out to Dungworth.

Savercards were now valid for use on SUT/Sheafline services, showing how the purchase was beneficial to the wider public, as well as making it easier to transfer mileage between the two companies.

As part of the changes, the somewhat unloved, Marshall bodied Leyland Atlanteans (from the batch 1807 to 1835) were transferred from Rotherham to Doncaster and Dunscroft, with some also seeing service at Leadmill, starting the process of replacing the final East Lancs bodied Atlanteans, and completing the task of withdrawing the company's last Fleetlines, from there. Leyland National 28 decided it was time for a dip, into the uncompleted Ponds Forge Swimming Pool, whilst operating a journey on service X38 to Penistone. The unfortunate bus was withdrawn, and the remains taken to Herries for spares. Dodge 106 was stolen from Doncaster garage and was found, burnt out, down a side street in Attercliffe, Sheffield. This wouldn't be the first, or last time, a bus had been stolen from the company's premises.

There was a cloud on the horizon as the Government had instructed the Monopolies and Mergers Commission (MMC) to look in to the acquisition by SYT of the four former operators now being reorganised in to SUT/ Sheafline combine. As this was going to take some considerable time to investigate, eating up valuable management time and resources, the company was directed not to make any material difference to the structure of the new company, in case the MMC should direct SYT to dispose of the business. The instruction, issued on 23 March, would not hamper the day to day workings of the group, but would prevent it from making large scale changes to the setup of the company, and must ensure it is financially independent from the main SYT fleet. This would also have ramifications for the ongoing ESOP.

The Government classed the area the company operated in to be one of a 'significant' part of the UK. The MMC took the view that parts of the surrounding counties, served by SYT, would be lumped together to show one huge tract of land. From the east coast to Manchester and from Leeds to Worksop and the Derbyshire Dales, despite SYT having only a limited amount of mileage in areas out with South Yorkshire.

Above

National 28 did not win its diving competition, and was scrapped.

The MMC came on a fact finding trip, to see how the market was performing, and the scale of other competition. SYT had even sold a redundant Fleetline to Andrews, who had it prominently displayed at their new premises in Attercliffe, which was soon to be raised to the ground for construction work. SYT was also at great pains to show that they did maintenance for outside companies, including competitors.

Above and Right

The Lyceum Theatre in Sheffield was to reopen with a multi-million pound refurbishment. SYT, made a sizeable contribution, for which they received some 'debenture' seats for staff use, as well as painting Dominator 2172, based at Greenland, in an overall advert livery, that was eye catching, but would also drum up support for the fundraising efforts. Other adverts on buses in 1990 were Herries Dominators 2114 and 2144 both advertising Milka chocolate, and Dominators 2170, 2173 and 2174 advertising Trophy Bitter

Tuesday 1 May dawned bright, sunny and very warm. The first Volvo B10Ms had been prepared for a launch at the, yet to be completed, Meadowhall Shopping Centre. Marques, tents, food and drink had been provided for a spectacular 'drive through' moment to the assembled guests, which included industry figures, the trade press, as well as members of staff and unions.

These buses came with a completely different internal design. The famous 'split step' arrangement, a long held feature of bus design in the area was gone, replaced with three shallow steps. Light grey Formica was used extensively and a new seat moquette was introduced in two shades of grey with red, blue and yellow stripes. While initially good to look at, the yellow quickly discoloured, and needed frequent attention to keep it in good order.

The initial batch of 38 were going to go to Herries, for the upcoming service change in north Sheffield, but due to space constraints in the garage, the buses were allocated to Greenland, and took up duties on services 47/8, 51 and 93. This released the Mk1 Metrobuses, to be temporarily allocated to Herries.

Overleaf and Below

To celebrate the biggest fleet investment the company had made so far, a launch was held for the new Volvos at, the still incomplete, Meadowhall Centre.

Peter Sephton is seen starting proceedings, as a brand new B10M 'bursts' through the packaging to be welcomed by a crowd of shareholders, manufacturers, press, television crews and staff.

The new buses were sleek and noticeable in the bright yellow and red livery. Driver training started immediately, and they would enter service over the summer of 1990.

601 was taken to Ladybower Reservoir in the Peak District for a photo shoot.

The new Beaver body was larger and more refined compared to previous efforts, and was also fitted with the new interior. 303 is seen prior to being vinyled at Greenland.

The new Renault S56s had also started to arrive, with a revised version of the Beaver bodywork, and with the new interior moquette. Initially, they were allocated to Herries and Greenland for the north Sheffield scheme.

The first 'bus driver' led network design project, was implemented on 27 May, and would again involve some quite complicated mileage swaps, and have a snowball effect on vehicle allocations. The principle of bulking up core routes was maintained, and three further routes went over to Mainline operation, these being the very busy, cross city services, 53, 75/6. In addition, further Eager Beaver operation was introduced on service 33 between the city centre and Herries Garage, the 89 between the city centre and Ecclesfield and the M45 and M46 being renumbered as 45/6 with a revised frequency. With the exception of the 45/6, which was operated from Greenland, the other routes were operated from Herries.

Service 79/779 was cut in frequency and was no longer a circular service and was joined by a new service 90, operating through Hillsborough to Parson Cross. Changes were made to other services, most notably the 17, which now only operated to Fox Hill and the 42 which now operated from Grenoside to Totley Brook. Sheafline's service, was restricted to tendered journeys on service 91/8, which operated in the evenings and Sundays and new services 472 and 474 from Chapeltown to the city centre. Services 31 and X8 were also transferred to them. All other competing SUT/Sheafline services, such as the 49, were withdrawn.

In order to operate these services, a cascade of vehicles took place. Firstly, the aforementioned transfer of Metrobuses from Greenland to Herries was only a temporary measure, until more Dennis Dominators could be painted.

The Metrobuses had been suffering from severe corrosion issues, and although only eight years old, it was in the company's interest to keep older Atlanteans, instead of spending huge amounts of money rebuilding these buses. Once enough buses were painted, these Metrobuses were placed on reserve at Dunscroft or Rotherham, awaiting a buyer.

The entire batch of Northern Counties Dominators was also transferred to Herries. This, together with the influx of minibuses, led to the withdrawal of all semi-automatic Atlanteans in Sheffield, including the unique 1675 to 1680 batch, fitted with Alexander bodywork. This also enabled some earlier Voith gearbox examples to migrate to Doncaster, enabling further inroads to be made in to their older stock. The first Dodge S56s were also placed in to storage at Dunscroft, together with the expensive to operate Dennis Dominos.

It would be fair to say, that not all the changes made in north Sheffield had been well received, although the level and quality of service had markedly improved, whilst eliminating costs. Drivers at Herries briefly considered industrial action about changes to their keyboards, but this was eventually settled. By July, further minor changes were put in place that restored service 17, but also matched it with a new service 18, becoming a huge north/east Sheffield circular service, killing off service 90 at the same time. New Unit managers had been appointed for this change, these being the very well respected Terry Conley for the 53, 75/6 at Herries and Steve Rogers who was now looking after the 45/6, 92 and remaining Little Nipper vehicles at Greenland.

East Bank, which had been the storage centre for withdrawn buses, and used to prepare buses for sale, was leased to an indoor karting experience called Trax. The garage was emptied during the spring, and the buses on site, were either sold or transferred to Dunscroft for storage.

The New Network for North Sheffield

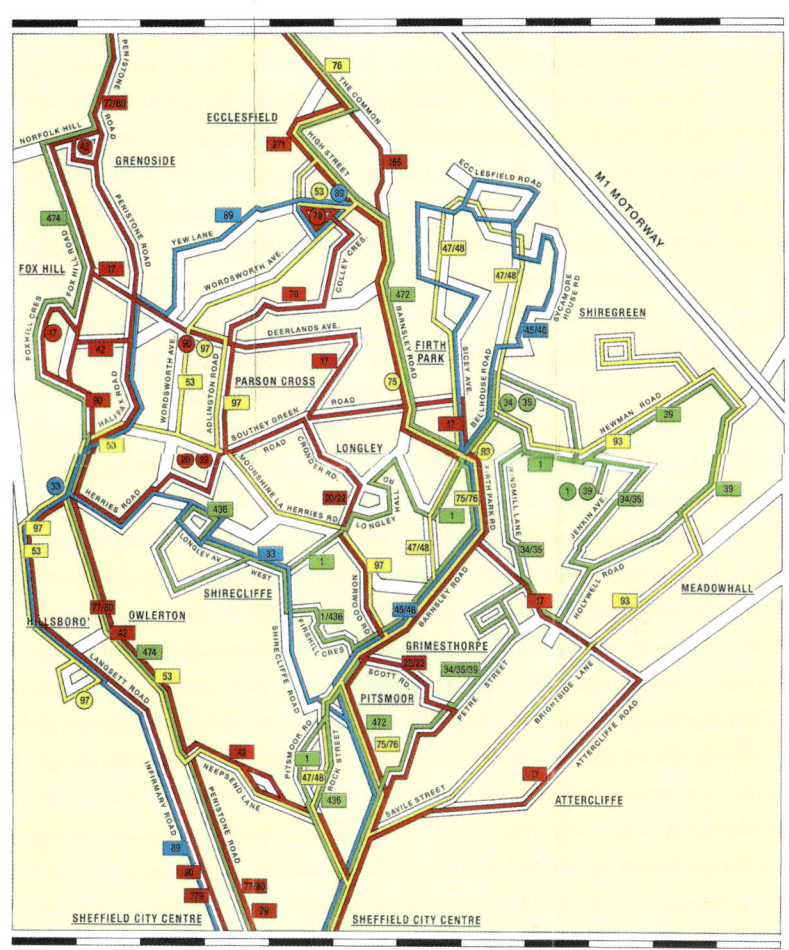

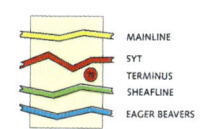

Wilfreda Beehive had been busy moving on to more sectors of the SYT network in Doncaster, and would eventually cover most of SYT's commercial network in the former borough boundary. Additional buses were used to protect SYT's revenue, but a thorough review of the area's services was under way.

Andrews had caused significant damage to service 114 to Dovedale Road, and part of the new minibus order was diverted to Rotherham to begin Eager Beaver operation in the town, augmented by existing stock. Service 114 was converted on 18 June, with buses operating every 10 minutes, which was a 25% increase on the previous service pattern.

Your new, faster, more frequent bus service is here.

Above

The streets of South Yorkshire were starting to become very bright, with yellow being the predominant colour.

The Eager Beaver brand had spread to Rotherham to thwart competition with Andrews and some older Dodge S56s were repainted to help out. 150 is seen outside Rotherham Bus Station.

325, seen in Church Street, Sheffield, is on the recently revitalised 33 to Shirecliffe and Herries Garage, being closely followed by MCW Metrobus Mk2 1933 on its way to the north of the city. 325 would move quite quickly to Rotherham to help out there.

Such was the desire to get buses painted, some external contractors were used, with varying results. 2249 and 2251 were spray painted by Northern Bus, but they got the upper deck proportions wrong. Corrective action saw this put right by the paint shop at Greenland.

The pair are seen at Greenland, and 2251 is also shown, posed at Dungworth.

A recession was now beginning to bite, as the boom years of the late 80's came to an end, and budget constraints at the PTE had led to cuts in reimbursement for concessionary journeys. A fares increase was brought in on 1 July, affecting all single tickets, at the same time as the PTE doubling the fare charged for concessionary travelers. Rising tensions in the Gulf, also led to a surcharge being imposed on fares in October, initially temporary, it was never removed.

Halfway garage had been losing money for some time. Despite its location in south east Sheffield, it was right on the border with Derbyshire, and had been heavily dependent on schools and colliery contracts to pay its way. The closure of so many collieries in the past six years, had hit revenue hard, and it was about to lose all but 8 school contracts. It had strong commercial routes, but, these could all have been operated from Greenland and Rotherham. The elephant in the room was the cost of Rotherham, but that was a battle for another century.

Two options were put on the table, one less palatable than the other. The first option was a simple closure. This would have involved a number of redundancies, but most of the mileage would have been preserved. It was unlikely that the school contracts would have been economic anymore, and would have reverted back to the local authorities. The second involved partial closure of some of the engineering facilities, a reduction in administrative functions, negotiations on wage rates for contract services and the standardising on one vehicle type for the garage.

The second option was chosen. Firstly, all administration was to be undertaken by Greenland and Rotherham garages. The dedicated canteen was closed (leaving vending machines and 'mashing' facilities intact) and the new workshops on Old Lane were leased to a company called Stardes, who provided specialist transport facilities for rock groups, and had used the spare land at Halfway for parking their trailers.

The service pattern was revised, with a big push on the Fastline brand for services to this important corridor, now coming under attack from Yorkshire Terrier and Chesterfield Transport, on tenders. To operate the new network, a small fleet of Dodge S56s, that had been displaced from elsewhere, were gathered for tendered routes, but the initial idea, to place all the company's Mk2 Metrobuses here, fell foul of the design of the garage, which had a upward sweep on the exit, preventing these buses from safely exiting the garage, although they did visit from time to time. Dennis Dominators were retained, and for schools, a small batch of Atlanteans and Nationals were used, eventually gaining a yellow 'School Bus' panel under the windscreen. All other surplus vehicles were moved to Dunscroft for storage.

During August, the MMC indicated that SYT should dispose of SUT/Sheafline, as they claimed the purchase had been against the public's interest. SYT lodged an appeal, but this was going to be an ongoing battle for a number of years. Whilst local authorities and the PTE had welcomed the purchase, some other competitors saw it as anti-competitive and would like SYT broken up or, restricted from operating competing services and a ban on tender bids.

The first week in September brought about a massive change in retail focus to the region. The Meadowhall Shopping Centre, on land in Brightside, Sheffield, right beside junction 34 of the M1, opened on 4 September and SYT made a huge package of service changes from the previous day, to cope with revised travel patterns to one of Europe's largest indoor malls. It was claimed over 18 million people were just one hours drive away from the centre, and SYT wanted a share of that pie.

The most high profile of these changes was the Meadowhall Express. Operating as two routes, the 501 from the city centre and the 601 from Rotherham, each were to be operated by articulated vehicles.

Both batches had been painted in a quite pleasant, overall midnight blue livery, with a stylised dome motif (the centre's main advertising focused on its enormous dome). The rear portion of the buses, behind the 'bellows' was left blank, so that retailers in the centre could buy the space for their adverts. There were no takers for this, and they were remained blank. This service also replaced the City Clipper. Other services were diverted or extended to the new Interchange, which also had an area dedicated for the, under construction, Supertram as well as a four platform railway station.

Above

The Fastline Dominators were good people movers, and efforts were made to get as many as possible transferred to Halfway.

2474, seen entering Sheffield Central Bus Station, has had its seats modified to be in facing pairs, to disrupt vandalism that had been a problem on these buses, with their high backed cushions

The Leyland Atlantean fleet at Halfway was scaled back, and mainly relegated to schools work. 1771, 1773 and 1774 are seen in the garage yard, awaiting their scholarly loads.

Below

The Meadowhall Express livery was easy on the eye and replaced the previous City Clipper and Fastline liveries on the Leyland DAB artics.

In the weeks leading up to the new services, the buses were required to maintain the City Clipper and, unusually, Rotherham based 2011, is operating the service at Moorfoot, Sheffield.

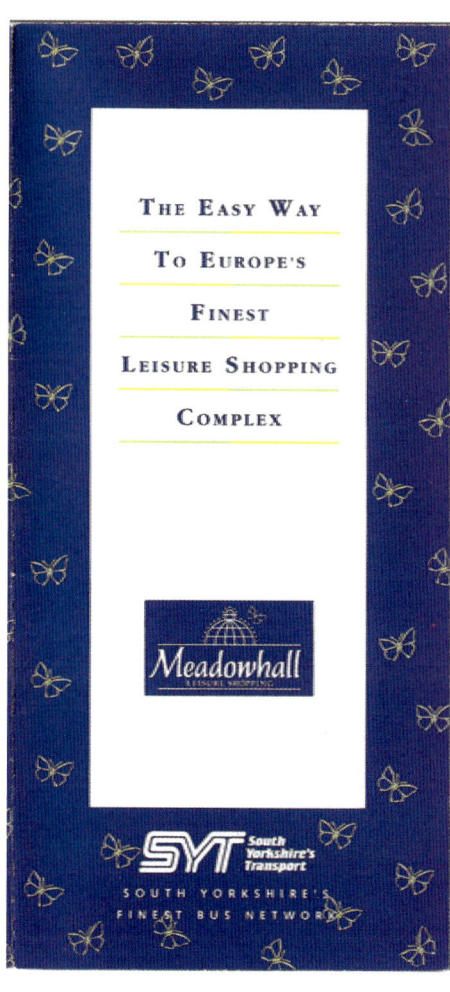

Rotherham garage extended its Eager Beaver fleet by converting existing service 130 from Brinsworth to the centre, every 10 minutes. Vehicles for this were sourced from the new batch of S56s allocated to Herries, being replaced there with earlier Dodge S56s from storage. On the same weekend, Greenland service 41, a very busy service between the city centre and Crystal Peaks was converted to Mainline operation using surplus Atlanteans from Herries, together with some further repainted examples, although this was only a stopgap measure.

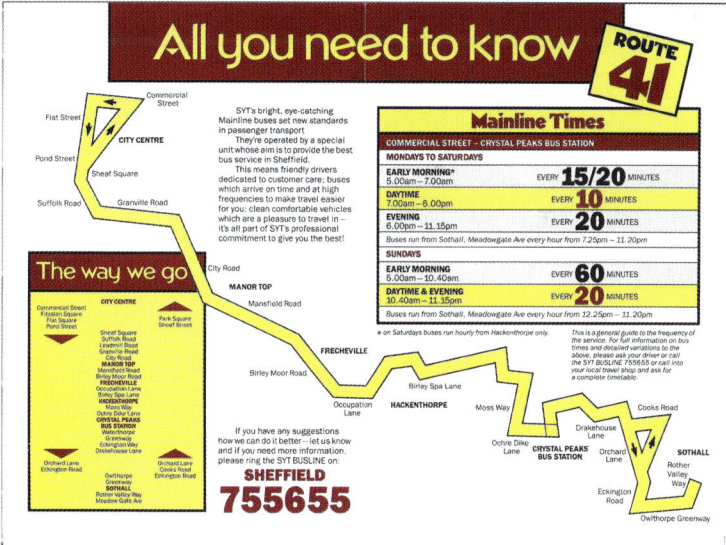

Above and Left

Existing minibuses were repainted, in addition to buses being transferred in for the conversion of service 130 to Eager Beaver operation. 174 is seen at Meadowhall Interchange.

The conversion of service 41 to Mainline operation required several Atlanteans to be resuscitated from storage and repainted. Cutting a fine sight is 1714 and 1717 inside Rotherham garage

Doncaster has always been an important place on the great highways of the UK. The Roman's called it Danum, and its shape hadn't changed much in the intervening years. Despite being bypassed by the A1M and M18, it was still a busy market town, with a high dependency of jobs in manufacturing and coal. An important railway town, with its enormous overhaul works, it was sat conveniently on the east coast mainline. Effectively shaped like an 'X', development had taken place to the north and east during the 1970s, but was constricted by mine workings and extensive peat moors.

Doncaster had also been an important border town between operators, and at one time, had an extensive selection of independent operators serving the surrounding towns and villages. Whilst the majority of these had been bought up by SYPTE in the 1970s, the final, traditional independent, Leon Motor services, operated a profitable service to the village of Finningley on the borders of Nottinghamshire. East Midland operated into the town from the south, Lincolnshire Road Car from the east and Yorkshire Traction, West Riding, South Yorkshire Road Transport and Yorkshire Rider from the north.

Due to its geography, congestion in Doncaster could get chronic, especially if the A1M or M18 were closed, and all that traffic would flood back on to the traditional roads. In addition, the world famous racecourse could gum up the town for hours on big meet days.

In PTE days, two very busy services had been joined together as a cross town service from Rossington in the east to Edlington in the west. One of the garage's most profitable services, it had suffered from unreliability, and with Wilfreda Beehive now competing on both legs, the opportunity was taken to restructure the service. In addition, the huge Cantley Estate, also on the Bawtry Road corridor, was included in to the service pattern with service 170.

Above

Doncaster Transport had adopted a striking new image in 1972, for this fiercely independent borough, which was sadly missed when the PTEs brown and cream paintbrush took over.

Leyland Royal Tiger 54 leaves the town's North Bus Station on a jointly operated service to Skellow,

The final 12 Volvo B10Ms entered service at Doncaster on 10 September, as the Mainline concept was brought to the town. Initially, these buses were to be based at Dunscroft, painted in a black, red, cameo version of the SYT livery, revolutionising the Thorne Road corridor out to the important, and profitable villages and estates in the north east of the county, but the incursion of Wilfreda Beehive, caused these plans to be changed. Three routes were involved, but the opportunity was taken to restructure the pattern.

With the 12 new Volvos, and repaints of some late model Dennis Dominators, the new network took shape as new services 55/6 on the Rossington side (Doncaster, under John Swann declared the UDI on route numbers from now on, refusing to comply with the former countywide pattern), with the 170 continuing to serve Cantley and services 455/6 serving Edlington. The revised pattern was based on the same, not less than ten minute frequency pattern, but overall the service replaced the existing 454 to 456 services, and was more reliable, as they no longer crossed the town centre.

The new image was somewhat surprising. Initially, all Mainline operations were going to use the yellow and red livery, with only the fleetname being changed. Jack Meredith, who had been SYT's Chairman, was repulsed by the thought of these coloured buses running through 'his' town, and refused to let the board paint them like this in Doncaster (he had also shown his displeasure by refusing to travel on one of the new Volvos in Sheffield, at the May launch, because of the paint scheme). Instead a compromise was reached in that the red skirt, roof and between deck bands remained, and yellow was restricted to two narrow bands, above the skirt and between decks. Instead, the main bulk of the livery was grey. Whilst looking fresh when newly painted, the grey wore badly, and never had the wow effect that the yellow gave.

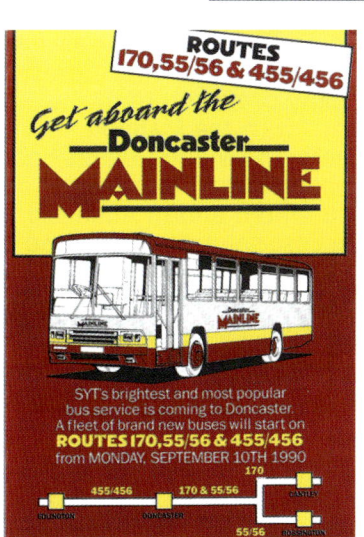

At the same time, surplus Dodge minibuses were swept up from around the fleet and placed on to a revised service pattern to Scawthorpe, with new Little Nipper services M53/5 replacing existing SYT service 154. All these changes killed off the remaining East Lancs bodied Atlanteans and pushing the final semi-automatic versions to Dunscroft. Ernie Slater was the Unit Manager for Mainline and Lenny McKie looked after the minibuses. The fight back was now on against Wilfreda.

Above

The Doncaster Mainline image looked fresh when newly painted, but the grey quickly dulled.

639 and 2453 are posed at the Lothian Road terminus of service 176, before the launch of the service.

The East Lancs bodied Atlanteans were beginning to look tired, and their withdrawal removed the individual look that Doncaster had retained.

1576 is pictured at Broomhouse Lane terminus.

Above Right

Guided buses are nothing new, but SYT worked with Yorkshire Rider, to share data and promote the alternative to councils and Government.

The test track built behind Rotherham garage wasn't huge, but incorporated a straight section, corner and stop point, to show level boarding.

1894 is shown on the track with Yorkshire Rider's Leeds heritage liveried MCW Metrobus, 7575, performing for invited guests and fellow operators.

Leeds did get guided buses, some years later.

September also brought about some exciting plans for how the company proposed to move forward with the Mainline brand in Sheffield. Guided buses had long been a feature of buses on the continent and in Australia. A low cost solution, it enabled buses to be fitted with small wheels, horizontal to the driving wheel, which could push up against pre-defined concrete tracks, but enabling flexibility in areas that hadn't got space for this infrastructure, by then being able to go on existing roads.

In order to test this principle, which was also being suggested by Yorkshire Rider, a swap of knowledge, resulted in a small piece of test track being built at the rear of Rotherham garage, which included a straight section, an incline and a curve, to show the capabilities of the technology. A vehicle was required to be fitted with guide wheels to show the concept and Metrobus 1894, which was in the storage line at Rotherham, was spruced up and fitted with the necessary equipment, ready to show to the press and public. Sheffield Mainline GB was ready to go.

The main plan was that Mainline would complement existing rail services and Supertram. The first corridor suggested for this treatment, was the long south Sheffield commute to Totley and Dore. SYT proposed that British Rail should slew its track south of the city, on the midland main line, to allow a guided bus track to be inserted on one side. The cost was estimated at £10 million, and that was the sticking point, who was going to pay? SYT were happy to provide the vehicles and services, but wanted British Rail and Sheffield City Council to provide the infrastructure. There was little appetite from either, although they welcomed the idea, and said they'd discuss it.

The last major change of the year occurred at Rotherham on 5 November. The Mainline concept was now introduced here using a number of late model Dennis Dominators on the very busy Maltby corridor (services 100/1/2) the 115 to East Herringthorpe and the cross town 137/8 between Thrybergh and Kimberworth Park and Richmond Park.

The opportunity was taken to extend the 137 via the very steep, and previously unserved West Hill to Blackburn and Meadowhall from Richmond Park, enabling service 118 to be withdrawn.

The new Mainline livery for Rotherham could be said to be the most pleasant, Trialed initially on bus 2440, it simply replaced the red of the Sheffield version with blue. However, at the Board's insistence, a red band was added to the skirt area, which made it look a little fussy.

These services were the bread and butter of the garage, and were very profitable. Increases in frequency were introduced, especially on the Maltby corridor, which went up to a 7/8 minute frequency, with the promise of bus priority measures, although this took another eight years to achieve, and a new owner, to introduce.

The Eager Beaver concept was also extended, with service 103 converted to high frequency operation and extended to the newish Morrison's supermarket in Bramley via the expanding Flanderwell estate. The difficult to serve Whiston and Broom Valley corridor also received a revised pattern of service with the 134 and 135 circulars being introduced, with an increased frequency. The desire to remove conventional bus operation from this area was thwarted, as the company retained the 125 to Rotherham Hospital, over worries that the minibuses, and conventional routes that ran south to Aston, Crystal Peaks and Dinnington, would be unable to cope.

This big bang approach had quite an effect on the fleet at Rotherham. Earlier Dominators were transferred out to Herries, releasing Atlanteans for storage or for fleet use in Doncaster and Dunscroft. Further S56s were transferred from Herries for the Beaver services, with older Dodges being painted up in compensation or for allocation to Rotherham. The new Unit Managers were Terry Quinn for Mainline and Dave Gregory for all minibus work at the garage.

The final Marshall bodied Atlanteans were also withdrawn from Rotherham, two going on to work for Sheafline, with the rest making their way to Dunscroft, which now had an extensive fleet of vehicles on site for storage. So many vehicles had been assembled, that moves were made to hire some out.

Bottom

With and without red stripe on 2429 and 2440 at the rear of Rotherham garage.

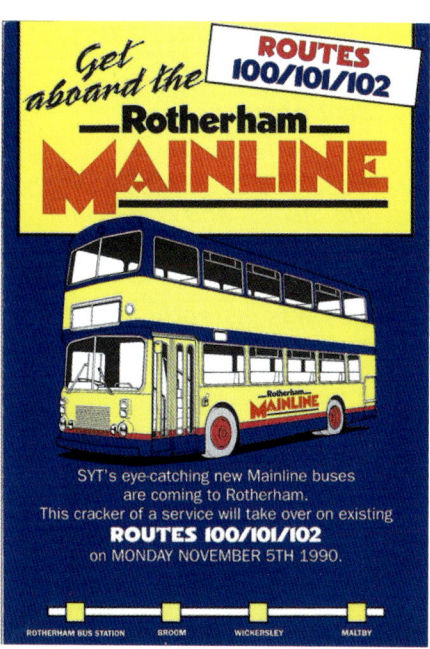

Right

The state of the Leyland Atlanteans that returned from London & Country was abysmal.

Seen here in Tinsley Tram Sheds, used for storing long term derelict vehicles, 1708 has been returned with heavy offside accident damage.

Invisible in the photograph, the staircase had been pushed in by several inches, and crates of mouldy bread had been left on board.

The bus was instantly withdrawn for scrap.

London & Country, one of the offshoots of the former London Country, and part of the Drawlane group, had won two routes in south London, the 78 and 188, and had ordered a fleet of Volvo D10Ms for their use. However, delays in getting the chassis bodied at East Lancs, meant they required buses to help out until all their fleet could be assembled. A batch of mainly Alexander, but some Roe bodied Atlanteans in SYT and Sheffield Mainline livery, were made available for hire, and they departed in November for a holiday in the capital. It would be fair to say that they weren't particularly well cared for whilst they were away, with the most spectacular example being bus 1708 which was in collision with a bread van. When it returned to Sheffield, the bus had to be instantly withdrawn, as the body had been damaged beyond repair, however, inside the bus, was still the contents of the bread van, slowly mouldering away.

Service 52 in Sheffield had been doing very well in battling the competition, but suffered from bunching, especially on days when the M1 was closed for repairs or accidents, when most of the east side of Sheffield would come to a standstill. A new way of regulating the service was required, and an option presented itself in the form of Datatrak.

Datatrak was a system developed by Securicor to track and monitor its high value cash delivery services throughout the UK, using VHF radio antenna. A beacon was fitted to each bus used on service 52, which was connected via the existing Band III radio. This gave real time location information, on each vehicle on the service. This could be viewed on a screen showing basic information as to where the bus was, back at a dedicated position in the 'Beaver Hut' at Greenland. Initially for a six month trial, whilst the system proved worthwhile, the cost of equipping the fleet was seen as prohibitive, coming on top of the adoption of Band III radios the year before.

As the year came to an end, a number of high profile members of management left the business. Bill Bland became the new Engineering Director for GM Buses. Martin Lewis left the new SUT/Sheafline combine, which had closed the Tinsley Tram sheds operating centre. He was replaced by Bob Rowe, who took on this responsibility in addition to being Doncaster Area Manager.

It had been another busy, yet profitable year for the company. The year ending April 1990 had the company making a profit of £1.35 million, whilst down on the previous year, it took in to account the purchase and associated restructuring costs of SUT/Sheafline.

Clockwise from top left

Sheafline received a pair of Marshall bodied Atlanteans for their fleet. Former 1817, pictured in Sheffield Interchange, is now Sheafline 2.

With Ponds Forge under construction, Leyland DAB 2010 does a trip on the 500, in the dying days of the City Clipper.

Beavers at rest at Crookes, Moorsyde Avenue terminus, with 222 first off the blocks for a short working to Ballifield.

1032 is one of Doncaster's elderly Nationals converted for Wheelchair services. Pictured in Hexthorpe. 2111 is seen in the delightful village of Bolsterstone, Olympian 100 in Bradfield and Renault S56, 322, is seen on Arundel Gate, Sheffield.

Chapter 6

1991

Right

New entrant Basichour, trading as Sheffield Omnibus, went after the lucrative Low Edges to High Green market. Initially launched with ex Preston Atlanteans, as they expanded, a rag tag fleet was assembled.

Bus 1128 is seen heading for City at Firth Park.

Glynn Pegg had tried two attempts as bus operation. The first, at deregulation, was on tendered services in Rotherham, using a hired in, Smith's, Ford Transit, seen here at Rotherham Bus Station.

That venture had been uneconomic, so eventually, an operation was commenced in Sheffield, attacking services to Dore, the busy interurban Sheffield to Doncaster corridor, and High Green.

With intensified competition, this also proved uneconomic, and the smart Leyland Nationals, outshopped in pseudo Rotherham Corporation colours, disappeared.

The year started with a new entrant to the market. Set up by two former Ribble managers, Basichour Limited, trading as Sheffield Omnibus introduced a competing operation over the route of service 76 between Ecclesfield and Low Edges, using a selection of time expired Leyland Atlanteans, that had last seen service with Preston Bus, and were operated in their colours of French blue and Ivory. They had obtained premises in a haulage yard at Green Lane in Ecclesfield.

SYT responded by reactivating some Leyland Atlanteans, operating duplicate journeys between Sheffield Lane Top and Woodseats, giving a five minute frequency over this section of the busily trafficked 75/76 route. The company also responded with a new promotion called 'Mainline Mania', which gave away cash and prizes in exchange for scratch off tickets that were distributed by drivers.

This response was also to tackle a small entrant in to the market, Glyn Pegg, trading as Rotherham and District.

Having previously tried to operate tendered services in Rotherham, he had now returned to the fray using Routemaster buses, previously deployed by GM Buses in Manchester and Leyland Nationals on routes to Dore and High Green. The Routemasters retained their red livery, whilst the Nationals were outshopped in blue and cream, reminiscent of the former Rotherham Corporation livery. The growing pressure of two operators on the corridor meant that that operation was uneconomic, and it closed in March.

The Rotherham Mainline concept had proved quite effective in stimulating travel demands in the town, and it was to be extended in January on the East Dene services (111/112). A few eyebrows were raised at the frequency enhancements however, as it was now 6 buses per hour on each route. Further Dennis Dominators were repainted for the service, this time coming from earlier batches, in a slightly revised pattern with black added to the blue skirt instead of red. This concept was also rolled out to Sheffield, where black was added on repaints.

Another bumper package of new buses was announced for delivery. A further 40 Volvo B10Ms were due, this time split between Rotherham and Sheffield and a further batch of 40 Renault S56s, the last for the company.

Also announced was the departure of Bob Montgomery, who had secured the Managing Director's job at Dublin Bus. A combative figure, he had polarised opinions within the company, but there is no doubt that without some of his foresight in to how a bus company should order its route network, SYT would have been a mess. This had an effect on the roll out of further Mainline and Eager Beaver schemes, whilst some expansion did take place, it was more muted and gradually petered out.

Whilst he was still in post, the next major package of service changes occurred in south Sheffield. Whilst not as major as the north scheme from the previous year, it mainly effected the Abbeydale and Chesterfield Road corridors, but did include an expansion of Mainline operation. Services 53, 75 and 76 were unchanged, but long standing service 97 was rerouted from Nether Edge to Totley and Totley Brook, taking over the southern leg of service 42 and all of service 24. Service 41 was extended through the city centre, replacing Sheafline service 436 to Batemoor, whilst the Nether Edge corridor was now served by service 22. Part of the Hemsworth service was given to Sheafline, whilst the section via Scarsdale Road was absorbed by service 42.

Sheafline also gained the Hutcliffe Wood and Norton corridor services, that use to be covered by SYT services 36 and 43, as the use of these had dropped markedly due to the service enhancements on services 47, 48 and 76. As part of the same package, but on the other side of the city, service 70 and 71 were also converted to Mainline operation, and this required some additional resources to be deployed.

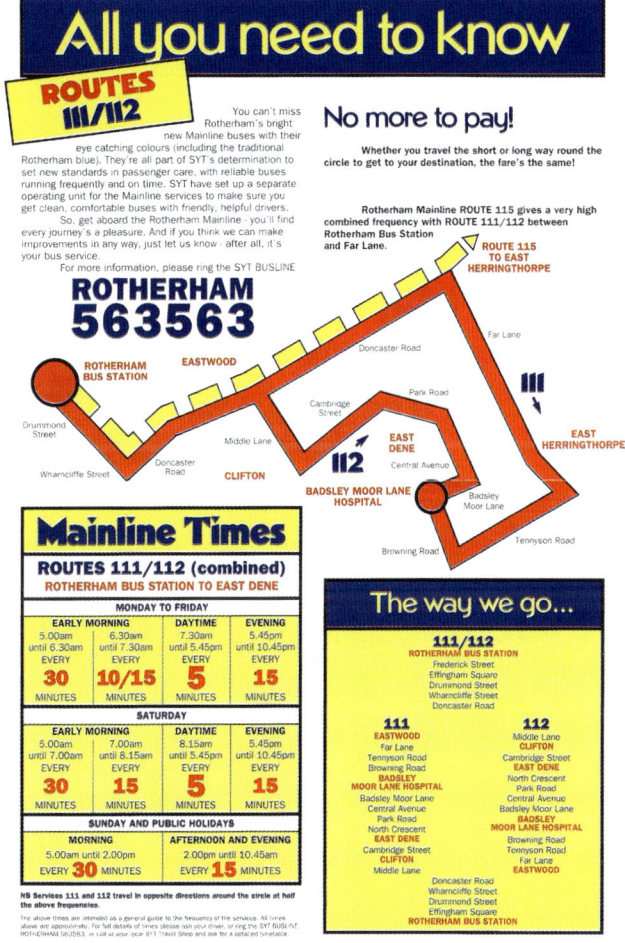

Top

Minor changes were made to the application of the Rotherham and Sheffield Mainline liveries, in anticipation of the receipt of the next batch of Volvo B10Ms, which included some black on the skirt.

2265 is seen at Rotherham Bus Station and 2415 is seen at the front of Greenland garage.

This particular practice was discontinued by 1992.

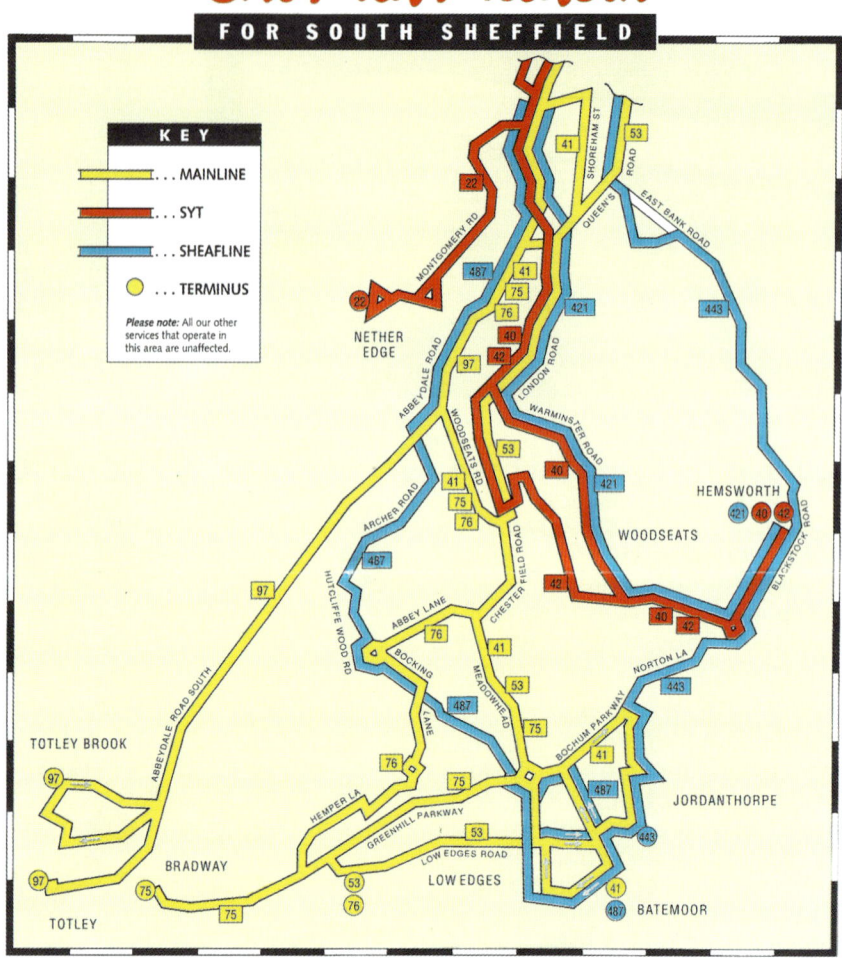

The New Network
FOR SOUTH SHEFFIELD

Below

Roe bodied Atlantean 1774 was back from its punishing ordeal in London, and had been repainted in Sheffield Mainline livery for use at Greenland.

This long term Halfway bus, had been made redundant by the 1990 service change at the garage, and is seen here in Haymarket performing a journey on the Prince of Wales Road Circular, via Darnall.

Many Leyland Atlanteans had to be repainted and put back in service at Greenland, including a couple of Roe bodied ones that had been in London (1767 and 1774), and additional Dennis and MCW buses had to go through the paintshops, which had been boosted by the building of additional capacity at Rotherham

The company had won its initial appeal against the decision to dispose of SUT/Sheafline, but the MMC appealed again. The Court of Appeal accepted that SYT did not operate in a 'significant' geographical area of the UK, and that they should be allowed to keep all the purchased entities. The Government disagreed.

With a recession now underway, the Government capped the amount of money that Local Authorities could spend on tendered services and concessionary fares. That led to SYPTE making cuts to services across the county. SYT being the largest operator of this mileage, would have to make deep cuts to services. SYT could not rely on its ploy of using Sheafline as a way of negating tender costs, as it had lost the evening tenders on Sheafline services 23, 32, 421, 434, 435 and 439 to East Midland, now owned by Stagecoach. Some difficult decisions would have to be taken as to what stayed and what went, but overall, the company was on track to remove over 2 million miles of service by the year end.

Minibus links were axed, which mainly affected Little Nipper services that were regarded as 'non-core', but it also affected lots of other routes. Some journeys were incorporated in to the timetable as commercial, with one of the biggest casualties, Sheffield's all night bus network, being saved in this way. SYT found a way to retain the majority of services on Friday and Saturday nights on a commercial basis, but the lengthy services to the Dearne Valley never returned.

Fares were also planned to increase, which would see changes made to the times that off peak fares were charged, removing this from evenings and Sundays. This got bogged down in political shenanigans, which wouldn't be fully resolved for years.

A small package of changes was implemented in Doncaster, to continue the fight with Wilfreda Beehive, who's fleet looked particularly shabby. The service to Woodlands was converted to minibus operations in one of the last large scale uses of the Little Nipper brand, with new services M77 and M78 replacing long established big bus services 177 and 178. Mainline operation was introduced on to services 175 and 176 to Intake and Lothian Road, again to battle with Wilfreda.

In the meantime a new Operations Director was appointed from the Go-Ahead group, Keith Moffatt. He had a slightly different view on how the bus operation should be managed. He took a dislike to the SYT brand and livery, describing it as 'orange and brown' and would prefer a simple red and white livery, similar to that of Go-Ahead Northern. Whilst he argued for a marketing led approach and quality service, he mused that need not be with brand new vehicles. His view was the company should make less changes to the network, and apart from a major package in Doncaster, service changes did die down under his watch.

Two second hand, three year old, Plaxton bodied, former Wallace Arnold coaches (1010 and 1011) arrived at the start of spring in the revised Coachline livery. Also joining the fleet were two former Sheafline Leyland Tigers (67 & 68), with the other pair going to Doncaster (62 & 63) for Premier Coaches work. Changes were made to how Coachline was managed, and Martin Tongue retired from the company to be replaced by Phil Travis from Greenland. In a previous life, he had been part of the management team at National Travel East. The Coachline unit was also 'sold' internally to SUT/Sheafline, and was moved to Charlotte Road garage from Leadmill, to reduce overhead cost.

Above and Below

There were certain similarities in colour use between the new Doncaster Mainline livery and the new Coachline identity.

Grey was very 'on vogue' in the early 90s, but had the tendency to loose its sheen quickly and look like undercoat.

Two secondhand Volvos came from Wallace Arnold, largely to expand coach operations and withdraw earlier Leopards from the fleet.

1011 is seen awaiting the return of its party of travellers. The black on the front dash was not an improvement.

Above

The Leyland Tigers received as part of the purchase of Sheafline, were distributed to Doncaster, for Premier Coaches duties, and to Coachline, again to remove unsatisfactory Leopards.

62 is seen at Hatfield Marina, whilst 67 is seen at the rear of Rotherham garage.

A big package of changes was instituted to the Thorne Road and Armthorpe corridors in Doncaster on 13 May. A revised pattern, simplifying services around Dunscroft, Stainforth, Thorne and Moorends, meant that only occasional journeys now served Lindholme and the link to Goole was now tendered by East Riding Council from Moorends. It did give an enhanced frequency on the main road though. Mainline operation was brought to Wheatley Hills by the conversion of service 179, which was also diverted to the Silver Jubilee Close terminus, replacing service 190. New Little Nipper services M71 and M72 replaced big buses in parts of Edenthorpe and Barnby Dun, but the most outstanding feature of the package was the introduction of Eager Beaver operation on services to Armthopre with new service 81 and 82 replacing big bus services 181 and Little Nipper service M81 to M83.

The new Armthorpe services used the first of the batch of new Renault S56s placed in operation, on a revised five minute frequency, battling against Wilfreda Beehive, who were becoming something of a competitive force.

The remainder of the batch was divided between Herries and Greenland, with those at the latter going on to service 52, including the 1000th Beaver body produced, which was handed over to the company in a ceremony at the Aston Hall Hotel in July. Three of the batch had a revised seating layout with longitudinal seating on the nearside to assist standing passengers.

Service 92 was withdrawn and replaced with an extended service 64 which now operated from Charnock to Woodhouse via the city centre using Eager Beaver minibuses. Some of these new S56s released older buses to go to Doncaster to help out with these frequency enhancements, as well as allowing the replacement of older buses on services to Hyde Park, Beckett Road and Hexthorpe. After a short stint on tendered services in Sheffield, the Iveco Fords found a home here as well. Changes to service 601 at Rotherham saw half the service diverted via South Street, renumbered as 602, and converted firstly to Little Nipper operation, and then to Eager Beavers.

The first batch of Dominators (2101 to 2110) were initially put on reserve following the Armthorpe changes, but most were quickly drafted to Leadmill to replace Mk1 Metrobuses that were showing signs of body fatigue. Some of these early Metrobuses were sold on for further service, but most found their way to various Barnsley scrapyards.

The next batch of Volvo B10Ms (651 to 690) started to arrive from Alexanders. Twelve were allocated to Rotherham, and they released Dominators from services 115 East Herringthorpe and 137/8 Thrybergh – Meadowhall/Kimberworth Park to upgrade the Kimberworth Park/Rockingham services (139 to 142) also from 13 May. The remainder of the batch were allocated to Greenland, making a start of withdrawing Atlanteans from Mainline work, most of which went to Dunscroft for storage.

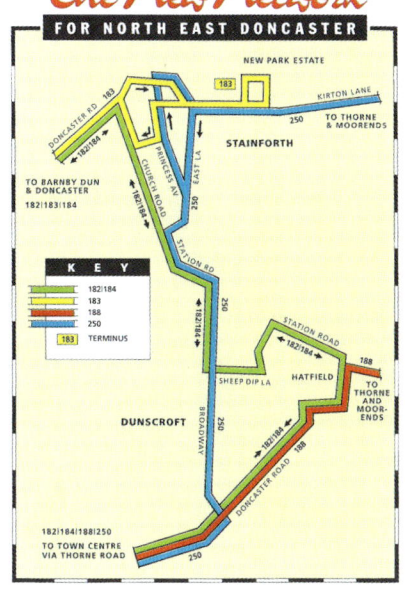
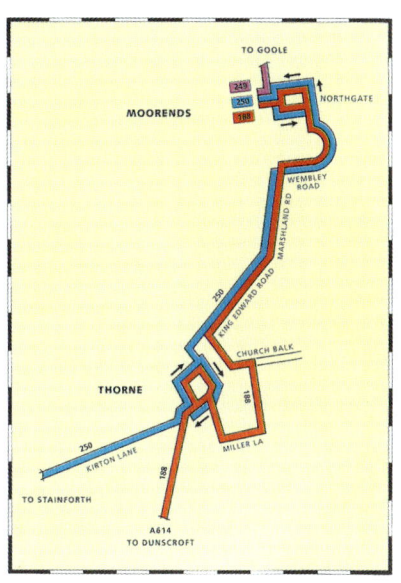

Above and Below

The second batch of B10Ms had a slightly revised cab window, and now incorporated black into the livery design.

653 is seen speeding along Frederick Street in Rotherham and 684 is seen at Crystal Peaks on the newly extended 41, cross city service to Batemoor.

381 had the honour of being the 1000th Reeve Burgess Beaver bodied bus, and was adorned with vinyls to mark the event, as seen in Sheffield city centre.

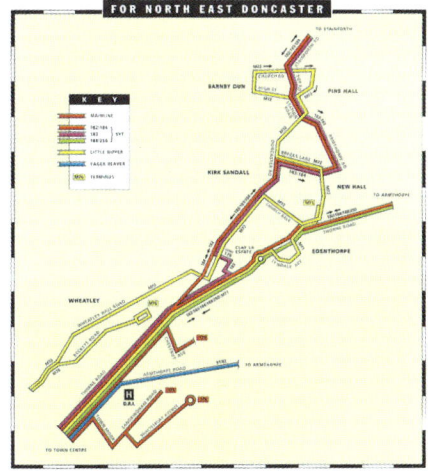

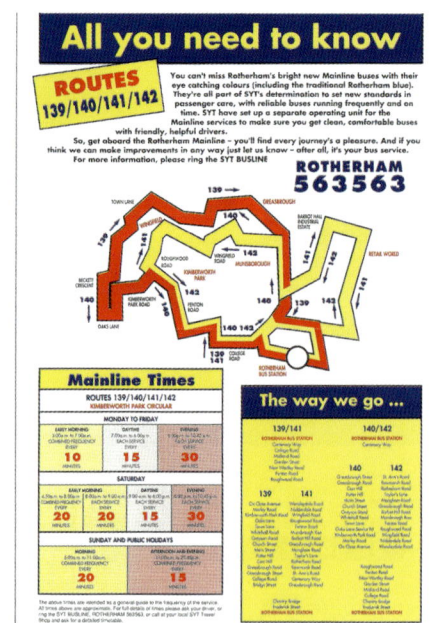

Above

Ex Sheffield Atlantean 287 had been converted to open top configuration by company apprentices in 1986.

Named 'Catherine Howard', the bus is seen here in 1986 taking visitors to the East Bank garage open day, held in August of that year.

This vehicle exists today, gloriously preserved, and has been given a new roof.

Sheffield had suffered quite badly from the early 1980s recession. With closures in the steel and engineering industry taking their toll on the economy and bus patronage. The government had created a new vehicle for development called the Sheffield Development Corporation (SDC). Its remit was to provide infrastructure and incentives to encourage businesses to relocate to the Lower Don Valley. In order to try and attract would be investors, the SDC sponsored an open top bus tour around the area, operated by SYT's open top Atlantean 287. Fares were charged, but of modest cost, and concessions were available. Whilst a novel idea, it was not perpetuated.

The city had also won the right to host the 1991 World Student Games, and during the summer, many thousands of athletes from across the world, came to compete in the biggest athletic event after the Commonwealth and Olympic games. SYT had hoped, after being so heavily involved in promoting the event, by sending the company's Showbus vehicle around Germany to promote the games two years earlier, that it would win the contract for contestants and officials travel. However, the contract was won by East Midland, much to the embarrassment of the company.

It wasn't all bad news. A new 'Games Saver' ticket was introduced. This ticket gave unlimited, one day travel, on all SYT buses in the city. Whilst not hugely successful, it did encourage the management to look again at selling day tickets on bus, but that would eventually come a couple of years later. To go with the promotion, a new route map was produced, showing the most frequent services.

The competition had been busy, with Sheffield Omnibus now covering parts of services 47, 51, 53 and 93 with their own versions. Andrews, who had managed to pick up virtually all the Sheffield schools tenders, for three years from September, were also busy running buses in between these journeys, and then causing mayhem in the city centre by parking buses all over the area so their drivers could get a meal relief.

Northern Bus, the new name for A&C Wigmore, also ventured in to the city, operating a Parson Cross circular service, using time expired Bristol VRs. SYT hit back, by taking some Leyland Nationals out of reserve, and registering a competing service, over their main 208 route from Sheffield to Dinnington via Thurcroft. Common sense eventually prevailed, and both parties went back to their respective corners.

Above

Andrews business model revolved around school tenders, infilling the remaining hours with commercial journeys on SYT's most profitable routes.

With no canteens to think about, during the afternoon dinner period, their buses caused chaos parking in bus stops around the city centre.

A trio of former West Midlands Fleetlines are parked on Arundel Gate, whilst their drivers find sustenance.

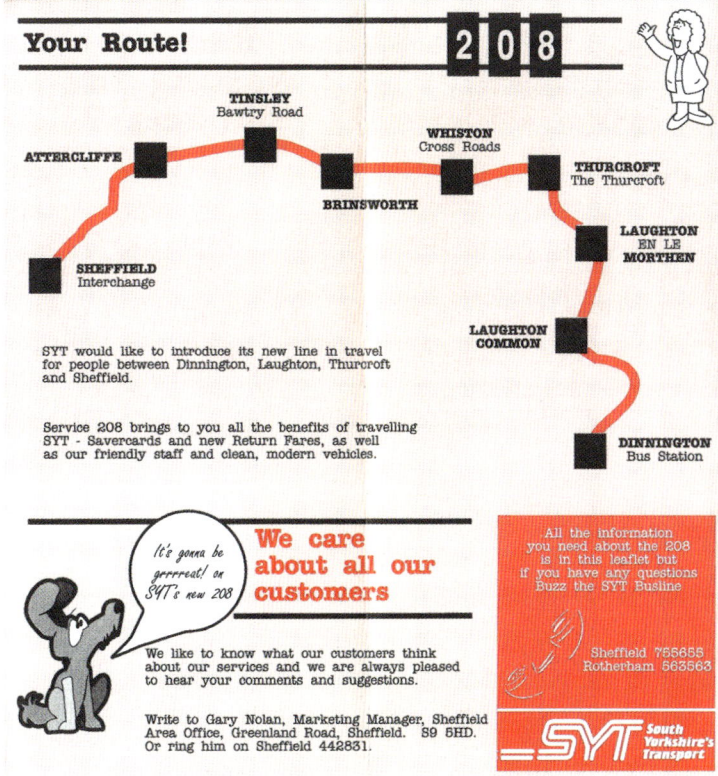

Above

The Mainline conversion of service 69 necessitated that the three Leyland DAB artics allocated to Rotherham, 2011 to 2013, needed to be repainted into the attractive blue and yellow livery.

2012, seen here, has also received silver wheels, which were a decidedly non standard colour for the fleet at this time.

The final Doncaster Mainline conversion started in July, converting the very busy 165 and 166 Bentley corridor, using more Dennis Dominators. From now on, Doncaster would use a combination of different techniques to try and rid the town of Wilfreda Beehive operation. Examples being using Eager Beavers on a new service 66 to Lothian Road, on top of the existing Mainline 176, although in this case, it would eventually replace it.

The harsh world of commercialism, and the ongoing recession, meant that further sacrifices had to be made to keep SYT on the road and profitable. A further round of economies, this time affected canteen provision with those at Rutland Way, Meadowhall, Doncaster and Dunscroft garages being reduced to vending machines only, following the pattern set at Halfway. Greenland canteen was refurbished and the foyer and office accommodation at the garage was also brought up to modern standards. The Castlegate canteen in Sheffield, was replaced by a smaller one on platform K in Sheffield Interchange.

Changes were also made to driver's uniform, with cream shirts being replaced by white and a new tie being distributed. White looked smarter, and was also cheaper. However, it would take over two years to get everyone in the same uniform, which also superseded the Eager Beaver uniform, as the allocation was based on a points system, which renewed in this timeframe.

The loss of schools contract work in Sheffield, coupled to changes to the way disabled persons travel was organised, meant a whole raft of vehicle changes in the autumn. Vast swathes of Leyland Atlanteans was now declared surplus, and were removed from the allocation at Herries. Those left in Sheffield were concentrated at Greenland and Halfway, with a further smattering at Doncaster and Dunscroft. The Sheffield Leyland National fleet, that had been adapted to carry wheelchairs, moved to Doncaster to replace their elderly Mark 1 examples. A large number of Dodge S56s were also surplus, and these went on hire to operators as diverse as London Buslines for tendered services in Slough and new entrant Wellcome in Newcastle.

A small package of service changes in Rotherham heralded the final Mainline conversion there, with service 69 to Sheffield being increased in frequency and converted to blue and yellow buses. The three dual doored Leyland DAB articulated buses were repainted in to Rotherham Mainline colours and were used alongside the Dominators, these having been displaced from their original use on Meadowhall Express duties. Further Dominators were also repainted for use on additional 137/8 journeys, in competition with Yorkshire Terrier, who had moved in to the town. The East Dene services 111/112 were converted to Eager Beaver operation on their existing frequencies. The final Mainline conversion in Sheffield was the important 60 to Crimicar Lane. Unusually for Leadmill, a number of Dennis Dominators, including 2101 and 2102, were allocated to the garage, and painted accordingly.

Thoughts had been given during the summer to disposing of the Leyland DAB fleet, which were distinctly non standard, and expensive to maintain. Bus 2001 was leased to Citybus/Ulsterbus in Belfast, and was repainted by them for the Tall Ships race, that was to take place in the province. Whilst they did buy articulated buses, they weren't interested in buying SYT's and when it returned to Sheffield, it was repainted in to Sheffield Mainline livery (which was also rolled out to the rest of the articulated fleet in Sheffield) before going on loan to London Buses subsidiary Selkent, to see if that style of operation would be successful in the capital. The bus also spent time on loan to Grampian Transport in Aberdeen.

The ongoing saga of the MMC investigation took yet another turn as SYT won yet another appeal. Although the Government would continue on to a further appeal, this process was sapping valuable management time, and money, when competitive battles were hotting up within the city.

Above

Transfers and repaints were the name of the game. National 23 went to Doncaster from Sheffield, 2166 was installed at Leadmill and 2260 is in its new colours for the busy 165/6 Bentley services in Doncaster.

Above and Below

The congestion, seen here in Church Street, Sheffield, was giving ammunition to local politicians that something had to be done. At peak times, parts of central Sheffield ground to a halt.

The Meadowhall Express brand lasted less than a year when painting commenced into the Sheffield Mainline livery.

There was a concern, from the new Operations Director, that the company had too many brands, and that cohesion was being lost.

2004 is seen on the top park at Greenland garage.

With so many buses now competing for road space, parts of Sheffield city centre resembled a bus park. High Street, a relatively short, bus only road leading from Castle Square to Church Street and West Street, was now one of the most congested in Britain. Sheffield City Council, although generally sympathetic to the company, could no longer let the situation get any worse, and were proposing a traffic regulation order, restricting the number of departures, from each of the congested stops.

Supertram construction would place additional pressures on road space within the area and SYT decided that the best course of action was to volunteer a solution, before any regulatory approach could be devised. SYT proposed a 'sector' approach, with various streets only being available to buses from certain sectors, with all services out of the city boundary being forced to use Sheffield Interchange. Whilst a noble effort, it relied on other operators also taking part, which was unlikely, but also, didn't take in to account the needs of passengers, who having got buses that took them exactly where they wanted, no longer wanted to be decanted at the, somewhat remote, Interchange.

The Supertram project, now in full construction mode, was concentrating the minds of the management as well. The route had been planned by the PTE, to provide maximum revenue for it, whilst operating on some of SYT's busiest corridors. That would have an effect on how SYT served these areas, but in the meantime, there was the reduction in revenue from construction to think about as well, as some streets/areas would be cut off for considerable periods of time whilst tracks were laid.

One thing SYT could never be accused of not having, was innovative ideas. The company now proposed an idea called the 'cozy stop'. Bus stops throughout the county were the responsibility of the PTE, but the quality varied enormously. Some stops had shelters, paid for by advertising, whilst others were relics from the former corporation days. Vandalism was also a problem at some, with glass shelters being replaced with Perspex, or in the worst case, aluminium sheeting.

Cozy stop was to combine a bus waiting area with facilities for topping up 'smart' travel cards, real time information and flat boarding facilities for the elderly and infirm (the thoughts of wheelchair bound passengers using normal service buses was a few years away yet). Some of these cozy stops would incorporate shops or small beverage machines to enable the journey to be more like the experience of travelling by train.

The company went to the expense of preparing and installing a prototype at the rear of Sheffield Arena, so that councilors and politicians could try out the concept. Bus 690 was fitted with an electronic destination blind to show how the 'bus of the future' could look modern and compliment light rail systems.

As with all these initiatives, well meaning, and well thought out as they were, there was little to no finance available. Guided buses, cozy stop, real time information were ideas that would eventually see the light of day, just not in Sheffield. SYT was ahead of its time in proposing these theories and ideas, and if it had still been owned by the PTE would have undoubtedly come to pass, but in the harsh commercial world of bus operation, there was no appetite from local authorities to progress these ideals.

Skills, the well known coach operator based in Nottingham, had purchased the former Reg Drabble coach business in Sheffield in 1990.

They had used the operating location on Petre Street, in Sheffield's east end to launch bids for a small amount of tendered operation in the area, including the once prestigious X32 service to Leeds. A vastly improved train service had made the X32 unprofitable and on Sunday it was operated by Skills on tender.

During the early part of 1991, the business had passed to a company called Beenak, which was part of Julian Peddle's Stevensons empire. Renamed as Don Valley Buses, it was operating a handful of minibus tenders, in a green, white and red livery. SYT made an offer for the company, which was accepted. Moves were made to replace some of the fleet with surplus Dodge S56s from the reserve fleet at Dunscroft.

Savercard had proved to be a very popular way of maintaining loyalty to SYT services throughout the county. One of the most popular was the seven day variety and efforts were made to make this readily available to purchase, from small shops and newsagents.

Clockwise from Top Left

690, seen here in Sheffield Interchange, had been fitted with electronic destination displays and cut outs, in the skirt panels, to facilitate guidewheels for demonstration of the cozy stop plans.

Beenak, or Don Valley Buses, was welcomed into the SYT fold.

A former Nottingham Dodge S56, very similar to SYT's own, is seen outside Greenland garage on a PTE tendered service to Dinnington.

The Mercedes semi coach was more use to the motorway than the estates of south east Sheffield, but is undertaking a Sunday tendered journey.

To standardise the newly acquired fleet, surplus S56s were repainted into a white, green and red livery. Former 153 is seen on the Manor Estate in Sheffield.

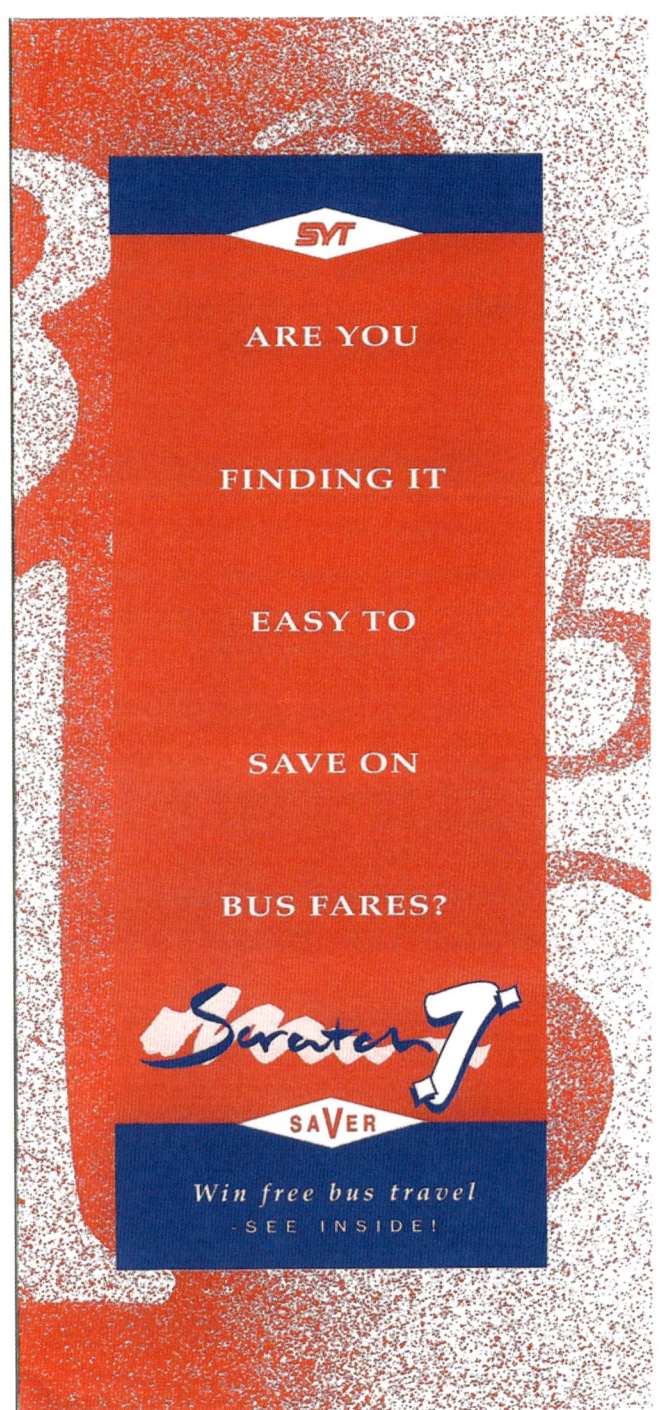

Generally, if a shop wanted to sell Savercard products, the shop would have to set themselves up as an agency, with a vast amount of paperwork to go with it. By converting the design of the ticket to be 'scratch off', it would be easier for smaller shops to sell, as they would simply account for the amount they sold on a simple form, in addition to earning a commission on every sale. The 'Scratch 7' was born and was rolled out from December, initially only in Sheffield.

Once the relevant seven consecutive days had been scratched off, revealing the dates underneath the silver panels, the user could fold over a simple, self-adhesive strip, making it both water proof and tamper free. It also had the advantage of being able to be sold as a 'book' of tickets, that employers could buy in bulk, and give to their employees as and when required. It also made the card 'anonymous' meaning that it could be passed to family and friends, when the initial purchaser didn't require it. It was an instant hit, and gave thoughts about rolling out the concept throughout the business.

George Watson had joined the board of Sheffield Omnibus, that was now busy setting itself up with additional premises in Chesterfield, as well as breaking in to the Nottingham market. Earlier in his career he'd been the General Manager at Clydeside Scottish in Paisley, and was a canny player on the deregulation field.

To his surprise, drivers at Sheffield Omnibus were accepting Savercard for travel, on payment of a 50p surcharge. SYT weren't overly concerned, as the revenue had already been taken by the company, regardless of whether the passenger used its service or not. The 50p charges also adversely affected the average fare of Sheffield Omnibus. Mr. Watson, somewhat perturbed at not seeing any revenue from SYT for this practice, presented himself at SYT's headquarters, demanding a share of the Savercard revenue. He was politely informed that the revenue from it was nothing to concern him, and that he might wish to discuss with his drivers where the money was going from the surcharge.

It had been another year of ups and downs for the company. The loss of Bob Montgomery was a body blow to the operational side of the business, coupled with tender losses and increased competition during the year, gave rise to the 'under siege' mentality to return.

Improved train services, paid for by SYPTE had also been eating in to the revenue stream, making some express services uneconomic. Passenger numbers dropped by 15% over the year, as the effects of the severe recession and competition, bit hard in to the bottom line. The company made a profit of £870,000 in the year ending April 1991, but with interest charges, and ongoing legal costs of fighting the MMC, a technical loss of £102,000 was recorded. 1992 was shaping up to be another grim period for the workforce.

Above and Below

On the prowl of paying customers.

The Volvo B10M fleet was now seen as one of the main selling points of the company.

The Mainline concept had been well received and garnered much public goodwill. All the company needed to do now, was convert goodwill into bums on seats.

Chapter 7

1992

Above

The sad remains of Dominator 2422 rest inside Rotherham garage, the morning after being stolen.

The damage is evident, and repair was not economical. The bus was used during the summer to repair other members of the fleet. The remains were cut up on site, becoming the first of the batch to be withdrawn.

January is a month with little to commend it. Invariably snow falls and bus patronage is lower, as the effects of Christmas catch up on weary shoppers. With a substantial recession ongoing, the outlook for the year ahead was less than positive.

However, for SYT, things got much worse, when on the 13 January, bus 2422 was stolen by two drunk teenagers from Rotherham bus station. As the bus entered the village of West Melton, near Wath, whilst negotiating a corner, the youths miscalculated the degree of steering required, ploughing the vehicle into a house. For both youths, their exit from the vehicle was unconventional, as they were thrown through the front windscreen, knocking themselves out.

The bus was taken back to Rotherham garage with severe accident damage, encompassing the entire front of the bus, as well as demolishing the first two bays on the nearside.

Whilst negotiations continued with Insurance companies, the bus sat, generally donating parts to other accident damaged buses, until the remains were finally cut up on site.

Together with other attempted vehicle thefts at Leadmill, the engineers started to fit 'secret' start switches, wired through the ignition, which would prevent anybody simply starting the vehicle, and driving it away. It took some time for drivers to get into the habit of pressing the secret start, with engineering being contacted many times to attend non starters, until Radio Controllers became wise to the problem. Instances of buses being stolen dropped dramatically after this action, although minibuses were easier to move, and this was a particular problem on race days in Doncaster, where normally an attempt would be made to take one vehicle away.

As it was a General Election year, SYT had to prepare budgets for the year ahead. Surprisingly, the company had to prepare two for the shareholders. The first was on the basis that Labour would win and the company would be retained in public hands. The second, should the Conservatives win, almost certainly meant that the company would be privatised. This somewhat barmy set of circumstances hampered the actions of the company throughout the start of the year. In addition, an appeal had been launched in to the latest MMC judgement, meaning that planning for the final integration of SUT/Sheafline, still couldn't continue, despite many competitors entering the market since the purchase.

Service changes were miniscule at the start of the year, and Ian Blackburn was moved from the 'Bus Driver' project to Sheffield area schedules. The project had delivered three area schemes, with some degree of success, but under Keith Moffatt, changes were to be kept to a minimum. In addition, Bob Rowe left his post as Doncaster Area manager to look after the company's plans to operate Supertram, as well as running SUT/Sheafline, with Peter Edwards taking control of Doncaster as well.

A new competing service 25 was registered in front of Yorkshire Terrier between Woodhouse and Moorfoot, worked by a batch of superannuated Leyland Nationals gathered up from around the fleet. These were in standard SYT livery, with a yellow front added, to make them stand out.

Sheffield Omnibus had grown to be an effective, if somewhat erratic, competitor, now extending operations on the Hillsborough/Wadsley Bridge/High Green corridor in competition with SYT services 42, 53, 77 and 80. They had also started operating later journeys than SYT, which had an effect on night service revenue, as they charged their normal fares. Yorkshire Terrier, on the other hand, had decided to exit the Rotherham market, to concentrate on their services in Sheffield and Killamarsh.

The long running saga over congestion in Sheffield city centre reached a crescendo in the spring, as the local authority sought action to implement a Traffic Regulation Order Condition, restricting bus movements within the heart of the city centre. A Public Inquiry was held, where SCC gave evidence of the severe congestion created by the number of bus movements through certain affected streets, these being Waingate, Haymarket, High Street and Church Street. The Deputy Traffic Commissioner supported the application, which restricted bus movements on the affected streets, by making a condition that services using these streets had to operate at least 1.5km beyond the Town Hall, or terminate in the Interchange or Flat Street, thereby encouraging more cross city services, rather than having services terminating in the city centre. Secondly, services which started outside of the Sheffield boundary, were not allowed to use the affected streets, and had to terminate in the Interchange or Flat Street. Finally, no new service registrations would be permitted.

SYT had raised an objection to some of the items listed and on appeal, it was determined that the Deputy Traffic Commissioner acted ultra vires, in that he had banned new bus registrations and did not specify any times when the TRC would apply.

Above

The competitive service 25 was launched with a hotch potch of tired looking Leyland Nationals, brought out of storage, or from use on competing service 208, when that was withdrawn.

1062, seen at Sheffield Markets, was in the latter category. They were all generally spruced up and given yellow fronts, but it was a world away from the ultra comfy image of the Mainline brand introduced just three years earlier and reflected the new Operations Director's philosophy.

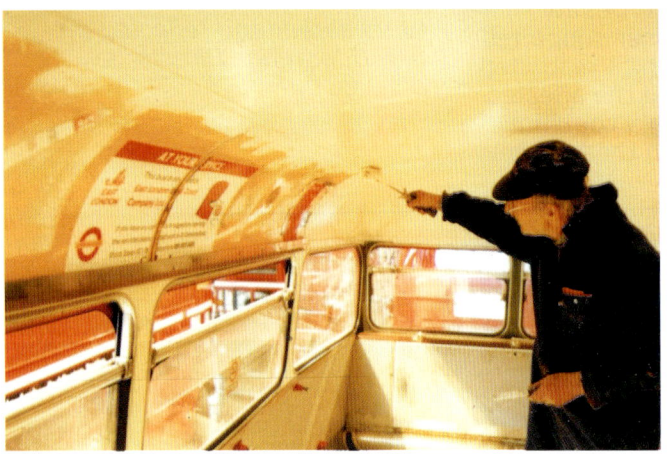

Above

The London Bus contract eventually gave birth to the Commercial Unit.

It's fair to say, when the buses arrived from London, they hadn't been properly maintained for years. The work to turn them from tired, unloved workhorses to the thoroughbreds that left the works was immense, and couldn't have been done without the skill and workmanship of the entire team.

This small spread of photos is a tribute to their work.

The appeal was allowed in part. The ban on new registrations was lifted, and the TRC was varied making it operational from 0700 to 1900 on Monday to Saturdays only.

The TRC came in to operation towards the end of the year and operators identified that Moorfoot became a suitable turning and terminal point, being just the right side of the 1.5km beyond the Town Hall

Wrapped up within the Council's argument was the idea that buses should be regulated and should be operated in a coordinated manner, regardless of operator. Whilst well meaning, it had little grasp of reality and the commercial pressures that bus companies now had to deal with, which in some case meant they were barely solvent. As part of the process, the Department for Transport gave £350,000 towards a feasibility study into guided bus proposals for south Sheffield, but this came to nothing.

With SYT having lost the chance of getting the fairly hefty Green Goddess contract, the company was now looking at other avenues for using some of its under utilised engineering assets.

At the end of 1991, London Buses had announced it was looking for suitable contractors to carry out a full refurbishment and modernisation, to its fleet of 500 AEC Routemasters. Unlike most other operators throughout the UK, London still had a small contingent of services, mainly through Westminster and the City, which required, conductor operation.

These buses, introduced in 1959, had, until 1986, received regular overhaul and body attention at London Transport's Aldenham works. With London bus tendering, and the breakup of London Transport into smaller chunks, the works had closed, and overhaul work had been undertaken at their garages or outside contractors.

Rotherham, had a surfeit of engineering space, and had the right grade and quality of workforce to take on such a role.

This was also a handy way of ensuring the garages survival, and finally put good use to its extensive facilities.

This was to be a huge contract, initially for 250 buses. The RMLs were to receive their biggest refurbishment since they had been to Aldenham. The refurbishment aimed to bring them up to date. The process included new interiors including re-laid floors and side walls, seats retrimmed, complete repaint, heating upgrade, Transmatic lighting, exterior panel changing where required, and new fibreglass front domes.

The repainting was contracted out to Graysons. In addition, the company also won a further contract to for a further 60 retrims that were being carried out by Leaside Buses. Overall, 34 jobs were created by the contract, with SYT hungry to add additional work.

Bodyshop Supervisor Allan Needham was charged with setting up the new 'London Bus Unit'. A trial bus was given to SYT and it took around three months to work out what would be required and the costs involved. The original contract had been split between several companies but with one of those, TBP falling behind, SYT gained an additional contract for 50 RMLs.

Below

Prior to the long drive south, once the buses were completed, and final checks were made, the workshop staff would normally call into a transport café at Canklow, to fill up on bacon sandwiches and fill up their flasks with coffee.

Such was the quality of the workmanship, many buses would make the journey up the M1 from the capital over the years.

Above

Repaints, during 1992 in Sheffield, had all been in the red and yellow variant, as seen on dual purpose MCW Metrobus 1957, seen in Dinnington Interchange.

The new Mainline image was launched on Dominator 2409, which also featured in the television adverts at that time.

Thankfully, the wheel trims seen adorning the vehicle, as it glides through the 'outside' bus wash at Herries, were not perpetuated.

Note the side advert, making use of the 'we've saved a seat for you' strapline.

May's General Election had been surprisingly won by the Conservative Party, and the outlook for SYT changed overnight. The next morning saw Yorkshire Terrier buses displaying 'Goodbye SYT' vinyls in their rear windows, sending a message to SYT drivers about the future of the company's ownership. The initial budget was based on control being retained by the local authority shareholders, but Government policy was now to force the remaining PTA companies (SYT and GM Buses) to be privatised.

The latest 'action' plan was devised, which changed the name of the company, as well as bringing in a bright new image and new marketing led initiatives to try and restore profitability to the company.

Kicking off on 15 June, the company was now to be known as Mainline. Well, that was the plan, but as the shareholders didn't like to let go, until the employees owned the company, it was to be known as SYT Mainline. If that sounds a little crackers, then it just showed how much resistance the company faced from its owners, whilst trying to provide an adequate and profitable bus service for the county. For clarity, it will be simply referred to as Mainline.

Mainline was to replace all other identities within the company. One brand, one service was now how the company wanted the passengers to see the business. The livery was based on the existing Mainline 'canary' yellow and 'post office' red, with thin bands of blue and silver, representing the previous district Mainline liveries.

The silver was quickly replaced, however with grey, as it couldn't be brush painted (Mainline didn't have spray painting facilities) and tarnished easily when going through the bus wash.

The first vehicle in the new livery was Herries based 2409. Throughout the early part of 1992, when buses required painting in Sheffield, they had been painted in Sheffield Mainline livery, regardless of if they operated on those services or not. This had led to all sorts of vehicles being outshopped, including Leyland Nationals and the MCW Metrobuses with Fastline specification.
Initially, Eager Beavers was to be kept as a brand, but after a few buses had been painted into Mainline livery, with a 'Beavers' logo on the front end, it was quickly dispensed with. Mainline had done well as a name in customer feedback that had taken place earlier in the year, with it being associated with quality.

Rotherham were quick off the mark, modifying the existing Rotherham livery with red and grey, but not in the correct proportions, and often retaining the local are identifier above the Mainline logo. Sheffield and Doncaster waited until full repaints to adapt their fleets.

Clockwise from top left

Once the new image was launched, the race was on to get the 900 odd strong fleet into the new livery. Early repaints concentrated on buses in SYT livery.

1902 is seen in Commercial Street, Sheffield. 2163 is seen in the rear yard at Herries.

2427, seen passing Sheffield's Sheaf Market, has been touched up by Rotherham garage, forgetting to paint the whole roof, getting the proportions wrong and leaving 'Rotherham' on the fleetname.

389 in an advert livery for Henlys at the rear of Greenland garage, has the 'Beavers' appendix to the fleetname. This was quickly removed.

26 and 2487 are seen in Doncaster. The silver quickly gave way to grey. 98 is on hire to Cygnet.

Above

The new B10Ms came in the new livery, with silver stripes.

691 is seen prior to entering service in Norfolk Park, whilst 714 has a healthy load, inbound from Cantley.

The red caterpillar moquette, which would become standard.

The image was launched using billboards and 30 second advertising spots on Yorkshire Television, the £600,000 cost of which, was questioned by the trade unions, on grounds of value for money, especially as people were being made redundant. The new tagline was 'we've saved a seat for you'. That was definitely true, as passenger numbers had dropped by 50% since April 1986, with the company now carrying some 120 million passengers per year. Not all of these had been gradual losses, with the biggest chunk coming when the cheap fares policy finished and at deregulation, but with heavy competition from other operators, as well as private motoring, and improving rail services, something drastic was needed to plug the holes and find a profitable future.

Whilst a start was made on repainting, initially, buses in the existing SYT livery, had fleetnames covered over with dark red and yellow vinyls. These didn't look great, but it would take at least three years to get the fleet looking completely the same. A new batch of 25 Volvo B10Ms (691 to 715) were also delivered in the new scheme. The first 12 went to Leadmill for service 97, eight went to Rotherham for the Maltby corridor and the final five went to Doncaster for operation on the Cantley corridor, fighting against Wilfreda Beehive. This initiated the movement of the East Lancs bodied Dominators to Doncaster and Dunscroft, where their large range fuel tanks were needed for the long runs to the north east. Surprisingly, towards the end of the year, Sheffield Omnibus placed in service three, almost identical B10Ms, which was a first for such an operator.

These new Volvo buses, 691 to 715, had a revised interior with a new moquette, referred to as the 'red caterpillar', matched to yellow hand poles and grey flooring and sidewalls. The new moquette felt warmer than the previous grey/striped pattern, and looked fresh.

Mainline was to be more than just a brand, it was meant to be a whole re evaluation of how the business operated.

At the same time, a further round of redundancies saw nearly 30 people leave the company, including nearly all the marketing department and Customer Services, with Travel Shops, and their associated staff, being transferred to the PTE. The new Mainline would now limit the amount of publicity it produced and a new agency called Oelrichs Communications would now take charge of the majority of the company's marketing collateral. It did seem a bit of a backward step to have a marketing led process for your business, with no marketing department and sales points, akin to Tesco asking the local council to advertise that it was selling beans.

Changes were made to the operational structure under Keith Moffatt, with Ian Davies being in charge of day to day operations, having direct responsibility over all the company's garages. Peter Edwards was now Deputy General Manager and Gary Nolan became Operations Executive, looking after the route planning for each area.

There was also to be a general 15% reduction in overheads, and work was to be started on removing over capacity within the company, by looking at facility closures. Meadowhall head office was to be closed, and the company was also looking at closing Halfway, Leadmill and partially closing Doncaster, and/or, closing Dunscroft. A general wage freeze was implemented and all staff over 50 years of age were offered early retirement/redundancy packages, with pension guarantees. In more general terms, the company was also looking at the possibility of moving all buses in Sheffield to one 'greenfield' site.

A start was made on looking for a replacement for the company's fare collection equipment, with Scanpoint, a Danish company, offering an alternative to Wayfarer, but also facilitating the use of 'smart' ticketing. A trial was scheduled to begin on service 60 and 97 in early 1993.

A new entrant to the market, South Riding, fronted by Andrew Gunning, formerly of SUT, appeared at the end of the summer, with a fleet of second hand Leyland Nationals, in a red and cream livery, (only adding a green stripe after Mainline proposed legal action, claiming they were passing themselves off as the old SYT) exactly three years after the sale of SUT to the company. The livery was actually a modification of Halton Transport's, as that's where the majority of the initial fleet came from.

Below

New entrant South Riding came along to upset the Mainline party.

Above

Open top Atlantean 287 was repainted in time for the 'Bus Only Day', and lead a cavalcade of vehicles on the day. It's pictured here at the Sandtoft Trolleybus Centre, prior to the event.

The confusion about the new brand is accentuated by having the SYT logo beside the Mainline one, on the upper windows. This fudge was forced on the company by the shareholders, until the company had been purchased by its employees.

When your shareholders meddle in your affairs to this degree, who needs enemies?

As a condition of the sale of SUT, and Mr. Gunning's departure, he was prevented from running buses in a competitive manner in the county for three years. In a somewhat bizarre move, Mainline decided to go to court, to prevent the new company using the same route numbers as it. The action was destined to fail, as the same argument was used against Yorkshire Terrier and Sheffield Omnibus. The question was asked by the Judge hearing the case, 'would you like to copyright the alphabet as well?'

A 'Bus Only' day was held in September and was well publicised on radio and television. The idea was to highlight how important bus travel was to the region and was also a good way of promoting the new Mainline image.

This wasn't helped by the Traffic Commissioners taking a very dim view of the actions of some operators, with regard to the proposed Traffic Regulation Condition, with Sheffield Omnibus registering an appeal with the Secretary of State for Transport.

The TRC came in to effect on 30 August, although further measures were to be introduced in October as well as spring 1993, mainly in connection with Supertram construction.

Changes were made to the Savercard system from the start of September.

The original Savercard areas were based on the pre 1974 boundaries, with everything beyond them requiring the purchase of the all encompassing 'super' version. This was now changed so that area cards matched their equivalent local authority areas. Three new 'Seven Day Saver' tickets were now launched, one for each district and a county wide version, and for the first time, could be bought on the bus from the driver.

Driver sales were encouraged by commission being paid to individual members, with take up being high from the off. However, following complaints about earning potential being limited by drivers who worked regular late or night shifts, and it being an administrative nightmare, eventually the commission payment 'pot' was rolled in to a higher hourly wage for all staff. The new 'Saver' wallets, were particularly useful for drivers, sadly not for their intended use, as many were used to secure squeaking panels and gum up holes that left draughts in the cab. The yellow wallets were easily foldable, and quickly overtook the sale of standard cards that required purchasing from travel Shops and agencies.

Also for sale were scratch off variants from newsagents and shops that were available for one day or longer. These weren't as popular as the on bus purchase, but still provided a vital role in assisting with pre sales for the company.

No further Renault S56s were to be ordered, but the company was still on the lookout for smaller, midibus size vehicles for routes with lower patronage, or for routes with high demand, but coupled with high frequency. Two entrants were made available to the company for trials.

The first was the Volvo B6. Based on an Austrian, Steyr, design, this short chassis coupled a small Volvo engine to a ZF gearbox. Bus 401 was bodied by Plaxton to their new 'Pointer' design. The Pointer was a square design, using equal spaced windows, with a more bulbous front end.

It had sold well, so far, on the Dennis Dart chassis, with Wilfreda Beehive purchasing some examples, but this was its first outing on a Volvo chassis.

The second demonstrator was a Dennis Dart with Northern Counties bodywork.

Bus 402 had received one of the trial batch of Paladin style bodies, with a large glass fibre, moulded front end structure. The body manufacturer was in some difficulty financially, and were not considered for further orders at this time.

Both buses were allocated to Greenland, regularly seeing service on route 52 as well as the 70, 71 and its recently introduced 711, which was a new cross city service competing with Yorkshire Terrier services 10 and 11, on the Darnall, Norfolk Park, city centre, Parson Cross corridor. Both had the new red, yellow, grey interior.

November was a momentous month for service 52. The once high profile Eager Beaver service had outgrown its minibus vehicles, and plans were made to exchange the minibuses for Volvo B10Ms from the main fleet at Greenland.

The new service pattern was for a five minute frequency over the entire route, and the buses were all given a 'touch up' paint job, to get them into the new Mainline livery, with route branding applied to their rear quarters.

Minibuses still operated on a Sunday for a short while, but in the main, the buses displaced from it went to other garages, especially Doncaster, to replace earlier vehicles; there no longer being a requirement to keep them on Eager Beaver routes. A number of Leyland Atlanteans, including the unloved Marshall variety, were gathered up from reserve, around the company, repainted and placed back in to the main fleet at Greenland to balance the numbers.

As the end of the year approached, the company could look back on a tremendous year of upheaval. There were encouraging signs on revenue and sales, especially the on bus 'Saver' range, that really seemed to have grabbed the public's imagination. For the year ended April 1992, the company made a profit of £284,000.

Clockwise from Top Left

The Volvo B6 was based on a Steyr truck chassis. 401 was given a Plaxton Pointer (assembled by Reeve Burgess) body for the trial, and it's seen at Moorfoot, Sheffield.

402 was the Northern Counties bodied Dennis Dart. Seen at Greenland garage, it didn't find favour, and was quickly sold out of the fleet.

The end of Eager Beavers on service 52 saw the first 25 Volvo B10Ms spruced up and livery modified for the increase in capacity. New style route branding was also fitted.

To plug the gap where the B10Ms came from, a huge number of Leyland Atlanteans were gathered from storage, repainted and put back in service. They also replaced Leyland Nationals as well.

With three different body styles represented, 1825, 1805 and 1756, seen on Greenland's top park, have bodywork by Marshall, Alexander and Roe.

Chapter 8

1993

Right

Generally, buses and trees don't mix. Bus 629, seen dumped beside the wash at Greenland, is going to need serious body rectification after this incident.

It would emerge in late spring, fully rebuilt and repainted in the new Mainline image.

The ownership of the company had to be settled in this year, as the newly elected Government had decreed that the final PTA companies should be sold. In the case of Mainline, that process was under way, but over the Pennines, GM Buses was to be split in to two companies for sale.

Moves were being made, but with the upcoming House of Lords appeal process in to the ownership of SUT/Sheafline still ongoing, it couldn't be finalised until that matter was out of the way. In the end, the Law Lords decided against the company, but as Mainline was being privatised anyway, the Department of Transport decided to let the company keep its acquisitions.

It could be argued that the whole MMC process was a farce. Politically motivated, the idea was based on a flawed charge that the purchase would affect a significant proportion of the UK bus market. The MMC had included Nottinghamshire, Derbyshire, Humberside (as was), West Yorkshire and Greater Manchester in its case, despite the fact the company actually only operated minimal amounts of mileage in these areas.

You could also argue that SYT's policy of buying up the competition was flawed as well, as it hadn't discouraged new firms from entering the market, but had actually encouraged it, as any competing company knew that it was handicapped in how it could respond. The matter was passed to the Office for Fair Trading to decide how Mainline should now deal with it.

Volvo B10M Bus 629 operating on service 51 came to grief in January, when it was in collision with a car at Lodge Moor. The car had misjudged the give way on Lodge Lane, and collided with the bus, pushing it into a tree. Substantial damage was caused to the nearside of the vehicle, which put it off the road until the spring.

The company still had to get itself in to better financial shape, and one of the first acts of the year was to close a significant chunk of Doncaster garage. The long battle with Wilfreda Beehive had knocked the stuffing out of the garage's revenue, and for now, showed no sign of abetment.

The engineering workshops, completed in 1984 were to be retained, as was the huge concrete apron in front of it, and a small portion of the existing garage which included fuel and wash facilities, but the office block and original garage was to be swept away for a Wickes superstore. A plan was put in place to execute this by the end of March.

For office staff, this meant a move to new premises in Duke Street, where an additional shop unit had been purchased. This also enabled a refurbishment of the canteen facilities. A home had to be found for the preserved ex Doncaster Leyland 188 and the Rossie Motors Daimler, which had been hiding around the building. Together with the PTEs trolleybus 2450, they all made their way to the museum at Sandtoft. A mileage swap would also be required, with Dunscroft gaining additional 'town' work.

The garage was always known, affectionately, as Leicester Avenue, as the frontage was on this road. With the new development, the chance was taken to rename the garage, Leger Way, as the entry/exit now faced on to it. For the purposes of this book, we'll continue to call it Doncaster.

The garage had made strides in getting the bus fleet in to the new fleet livery, with all sorts of unusual buses gaining the new Mainline colours. The former disabled persons Leyland Nationals could also be used for normal service work and looked fresh in the new livery.

Also closed during the year was the Meadowhall HQ building, with the directorate moving to a new location at Riverside Court on Newhall Road, Brightside, in Sheffield's east end. The existing canteen facilities in Rotherham were also closed, with staff moving to a former shop unit within the town.

Drivers' uniform was smartened up with a new Mainline tie and issue of blazers and grey trousers to all staff. The older cream shirts, brown trousers and body warmers were phased out by the end of the year.

Service changes throughout 1992 and the early part of 1993 were deliberately muted in an effort to restore stability to the service pattern. The forced changes in Sheffield city centre were increased under the third stage of the city centre traffic management order.

This made both Church Street and High Street one way northbound, with a whole raft of diversions being required to maintain a cross city access arrangement. The best example for this was service 95. A simple route, which since tram days had trundled between Walkley and Intake via West Street, Church Street, High Street and Commercial Street. In a southerly direction, between West Street and Commercial Street, the service now had to divert via Leopold Street, Pinstone Street, Furnival Gate and Arundel Gate, adding about a mile to its route, and having a consequent effect on its timetable. In a northerly direction, it was unchanged.

The PTE was also doing the company no favours by planning to introduce departure charges for the use of its bus stations and interchanges. At 40p per departure, this would cost Mainline over £500,000 per year. Further service changes would minimise this burden, especially in Sheffield, reducing the number of services operating from it.

The whole scheme looked and felt like a disaster, with little or no consideration for the passenger.

Clockwise from Top Left

The closure of half of Doncaster garage necessitated the movement of two preserved vehicles, that had been kept inside.

Doncaster Leyland 188, which had an old trolleybus body, and former Rossie Motors Daimler 220, were taken to the Sandtoft Trolleybus Museum, together with PTE owned trolleybus 2450.

The new Mainline tie appeared at the start of the year, available in standard, clip on or scarf, for ladies.

Above

After the TRC was implemented, scenes such as this were commonplace.

Buses jammed from one end of the central area to the other, fighting for the little remaining roadspace.

The one way gyratory in the Castlegate, Waingate and Haymarket area, could gum up for hours. Of course, it doesn't help, when buses load in the middle of a live traffic lane, as seen on Yorkshire Terrier National 41 on their service 123, which competed with Mainline's 95 between Walkley and Intake.

Also added into the mix was the upcoming construction works for Supertram, which would close one half of Church Street, High Street and Commercial Street (which if you take service 95, now involved a further diversion via Angel Street, Castle Street, Haymarket, Flat Street and Sheaf Street) as well as removing Castle Square (the hole in the road). On some days, early on in the scheme, buses could be log jammed from Moorfoot all the way to the Wicker (over a mile), and the Council had to tinker with the scheme to get it right.

In April, a small package of service changes was put in to place in Sheffield, which included the conversion of service 17 to minibus operation. This long standing route between Hillsborough and the city centre via Fox Hill, Parson Cross, Firth Park and Attercliffe, had suffered under the twin pressures of factory closures and house clearances in the east of the city and competition from Sheffield Omnibus service 18 which competed head on.

The service went to a 15 minute frequency, operating in the main between Hillsborough and Meadowhall, leaving the Attercliffe corridor to service 69 and 130, which had been revised to be a double deck route, again, in 1992. The tendered evening service continued to serve Attercliffe.

The Doncaster north east corridor was also restructured, again, to provide a more frequent service on the main Thorne Road corridor. A new X88 provided a limited stop service to compete with an improved train service, with five Volvo B10Ms being transferred to Dunscroft to operate it. There was also a revised pattern around Dunscroft village and Barnby Dun, with new minibus services 68 and 69 providing a better service around Edenthorpe, an area which had experienced some expansion in the past few years. This new pattern replaced former services M71 and M72. A special £5 weekly saver was introduced as a special introductory offer.

There was also a ticket promotion introduced on services 55 and 56 to Rossington, which was part of a company wide push on return fares and special route defined Saver tickets, which also encompassed service 93 in Sheffield and the Maltby corridor in Rotherham.

In each case, a special effort was made to get as many buses in the new Mainline livery operating on these services. The service 93 promotion, which also included an increased frequency, saw passenger numbers go up by about 5%. This was a valuable pointer for the direction of the company.

COMMITMENT TO CUSTOMER CARE

At Mainline our aim is to put you, our customers, first. With a fleet of 800 buses, Mainline is South Yorkshire's largest bus operator, providing travel to over 100 million passengers each year.
As all our 2,000 staff are committed to bring you a friendly, clean and, above all, reliable service - there's no wonder we're the region's favourite.

SAFE, CLEAN BUSES

Mainline have the region's top garage and maintenance staff, who are committed to keeping every single bus in top quality order for your safety and comfort. Our buses are cleaned inside and outside at least once every day.
We operate a no smoking policy for the comfort of all passengers.

FRIENDLY, HELPFUL STAFF

Our drivers have pledged to put you, our customer, first, and to make your journey as comfortable and hassle free as possible.

FREQUENT, RELIABLE SERVICE

Mainline's Service 55/56 buses run frequently every day of the week. We adhere to timetables wherever possible, although traffic congestion can sometimes make this difficult. Our endeavour is always to provide a service on which you can depend.

123

Clockwise from Top Left

Yorkshire Terrier, formed out of the closure of East Bank garage, had done well. They managed to purchase a small batch of seven, Plaxton bodied, Dennis Darts. Their 101 is seen entering Commercial Street, Sheffield.

The intensity of the fire that consumed 2269 can be gauged from these photographs.

Luckily, the driver managed to evacuate all the passengers, before the fire took hold, but it shows how an engine fire can rapidly spiral out of control.

Yorkshire Terrier introduced a small batch of Plaxton bodied Dennis Darts, in a revised livery, with Sheffield Omnibus introducing a batch of five new, Alexander bodied, Leyland Olympians, from dealer stock.

The Dennis Dominator had been a great servant of the company with over 300 in service. They had one small, but significant flaw, being the ability to catch fire. Since their introduction, a number of fires had occurred in the engine bay, mainly caused by fuel leaking from a ruptured pipe (these can occur at any time, and is not a deficiency in maintenance regimes), which then finds its way on to hot engine parts. Hidden within the body, were two 'chimney' arrangements, either side of the engine, which removed hot air from the engine bay, but also acted as an easy inlet for fresh air.

Most engine fires were extinguished fairly quickly causing little damage, but bus 2269, operating from Rotherham garage, managed to catch fire in this manner, and with an unfortunate wind direction, blowing it in to the body, destroying the vehicle. Such was the intensity of the heat, the back of the vehicle completely melted. There would be other fires, but this was the first that had such a devastating effect. When delivered these buses were fitted with an internal Halon gas extinguisher, but these were later banned and had to be removed or disabled, as they became an MOT failure.

The commercial unit was going from strength to strength, and had won additional contracts from London Buses, who were extremely happy with the work being undertaken. The company had now won a contract from Kentish Bus to refurbish 23 additional Routemaster's, for operation on tendered service 19 from their Battersea base, which included a new livery of maroon and cream. There was further good news for the unit as they also won a contract to fit new floors to London Buses' fleet of Leyland Titans and install wheelchair lifts in to a small fleet of Mercedes minibuses for their Selkent subsidiary.

A highly unusual request for a private hire came Mainline's way in May. To celebrate 50 years of the Dambusters raid, a special park and ride service was to be operated, with the focus being at Derwent Dam, culminating with a special fly past by the remaining Memorial Flight's Lancaster bomber. The only snag was, this was to occur on a weekday, when the fleet would be at peak capacity.

As this was such a prestigious contract, a special effort was made to get as many vehicles available as possible for the day. The engineers managed to restructure how they did their vehicle exams (VEXs) for the preceding week, freeing up spare buses for the service. To present the best image, only buses painted in the new Mainline livery were used from across the company. In addition, vehicles were hired in from Chesterfield Transport, Northern Bus, GM Buses, Stagecoach East Midland and Yorkshire Traction, with the combined fleet nearing the 100 mark.

All roads leading to and from the area were closed and an estimated 85,000 people were transported to and from the main event at Fairholmes in a constant procession of buses from surrounding fields along the Hope Valley and either side of Ladybower on the A57, that had been hastily turned in to park and ride facilities. The service operated from 0730 and was expected to continue until 1600 following the fly past.

The turnaround at Fairholmes is fairly restricted and it was envisaged that access would be limited to the Park 'n' Ride buses only. As with any large event, the problems can grow at the end when everyone wants to leave the site at the same time. It was thought that as visitors would have made their way down the entire length of the valley to gain the best viewing point, their departure would be staggered. What wasn't in the script was the use of the turning circle by coaches and private hire vehicles, which blocked the area for several hours.

Thankfully, the weather was very pleasant, and it was around 2100hrs when the last vehicles and visitors had dispersed. Despite this, it was much needed good publicity for the company, with nothing but praise from the organisers, as well as being an important revenue stream.

Above and Below

The Routemasters for Kentish Bus carried this stylish maroon and cream livery, although internally, they were the same specification as all other London Routemaster refurbishments.

The SYT logo wasn't removed from buildings until the ESOP was completed.

The new Mainline image was strong, although the use of three colours on skirt panels, kept the engineers on their toes.

New ticket machines were purchased for operation on services 60 and 97 at Leadmill. Based on the successful Wayfarer 3 platform, these were married to magnetic card readers, that could produce a whole range of new style tickets. In addition to the popular 7 Day Saver, two new products were offered. The first called 'Multi Ride' gave the ability for passengers to bulk purchase single tickets, deleting one every time the card entered the reader. The second product was called 'Travel Bank' which offered the ability to have an electronic purse, which could remove value every time the card was presented, allowing multi user flexibility. The initial trial was fitted to Volvo B10Ms and Mk2 Metrobuses, and replaced an earlier proposal for a system from Denmark.

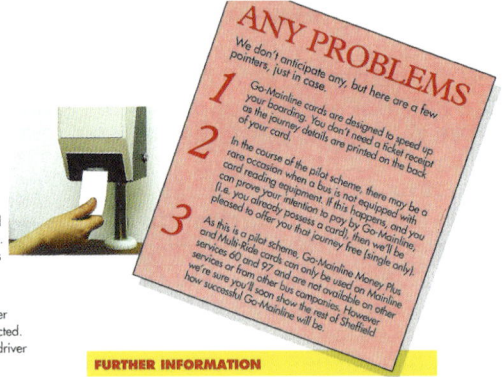

There were some initial teething problems with cards being accidentally damaged by customers (folded cards didn't read particularly well) as well as being 'eaten' by the machines themselves. Take up of the 7 Day Saver was good, but less so for the other products, but feedback about the machines from drivers was really encouraging.

The employees were now working towards purchasing the company in an ESOP. To further this aim, a new board had to be appointed to oversee the new company structure. The company was to be split in two, an operating company and a property/asset holding company. The first part was achieved by registering a new operating company called Mainline Group Limited, which was a wholly owned subsidiary of Mainline Partnership Limited, which was the vehicle used to purchase the company.

The new board consisted of:

Peter Sephton, Chairman and Managing Director

Ian Davies, Operations Director

Mike Pestereff, Finance Director

Bernard Keane, Engineering Director.

Top

The celebration livery on Dennis 2126 incorporated elements of the Mainline livery, and was designed by local school children within the city.

With its roof now intact, 2126 is seen rounding the doomed Castle Square, Hole in the Road, roundabout, at the bottom of High Street, Sheffield.

Sheffield celebrated the 100th birthday of its City status in 1993 and Mainline helped out by painting bus 2126, based at Herries, in a special livery to promote this and take part in the Lord Mayor's Parade. It didn't have a great start, however, as when it was lining up for the parade at Sheffield United's Bramall Lane ground, it managed to strike part of the overhang on the main stand, wedging elements of it in the roof. After several red faces, it took part in the parade, before repairs were undertaken at Herries.

Four Worker Directors were also appointed, representing the various employment grades throughout the business, these being Dave Edwards, Charlie Clarke, Trevor Simpson and Anthony Ward. Finally filling the lineup was ex NBC Chairman Robert Brook, who sat as a special adviser to the board.

There was an Employee Buyout Trust board as well which had Mike Nuttall, Stuart Laidlaw, Frank Gawthorpe, Mick Bullivant and Paul Green in place, ensuring the correct allocation of shares to employees.

One notable absentee from the new board was Keith Moffatt. He decided to leave the business, returning to the Go-Ahead Group. Ian Davies, who had taken his place, was well respected by both union, management and driving staff, and brought some long needed stability to the post.

The second company, SYPTA Properties Limited, used the old SYT company titles and now owned the residual property and assets not purchased by the new company. Bob Rowe was named the new Managing Director, and ownership remained with the former shareholders.

So what exactly were the employees buying? Unlike near neighbour Yorkshire Rider, the ESOP for Mainline had been structured in a way which, originally, gave the former shareholders a small degree of control. Sold to the employees was the right to operate the Mainline suite of services and its associated brand and fare products. The sale also included some buses that weren't bought on lease agreements (mainly elderly Leyland Nationals and Atlanteans).

What wasn't owned was the bricks and mortar that the company operated from. Instead, these went to the new SYPTA company, on the understanding that Mainline would then lease these to operate the service. This last part was not legally binding. The company would now be able to operate wherever it saw a commercial opportunity, and would no longer be restricted to its 1986 boundaries.

There were some hiccups along the way, meaning that the June deadline wasn't adhered too. These mainly concerned pension provision for existing staff, and their associated liabilities and the lease agreements for the bus fleet. As Mainline would affectively have few assets to call on, if it went bust, how would they get their money back? This especially concerned the Volvo fleet, which had been purchased using leases originating in Hong Kong, with the banks there being sceptical on the merits of employee ownership.

Each employee would receive around 100 shares for every year they had been employed by the company, which meant that some long serving staff received more than the directorate, although, so called, 'ghost' shares were issued to them.

The ESOP was finally completed on 15 November with each member of staff receiving an ownership handbook and badge, which was encouraged to be worn on uniforms.

The integration of SUT/Sheafline got under way in July, with the closure of Charlotte Road. Buses moved to Herries and Greenland, with Coachline reverting to Leadmill. Initially operating in their own livery, from September a swap of mileage meant the end of the separate image, with buses repainted into Mainline livery, eventually leading to the surrender of the separate Operators Licences.

Top

The new Mainline livery was being rolled out at the rate of five buses per week.

The East Lancs bodied batch from 1984, had settled in Doncaster, and were used extensively on the long range runs to the north east of the town, which benefitted from their long range fuel tanks.

2365 is seen, fresh from the paintshops on Duke Street, Doncaster, with Alexander bodied stable mate 2219, also freshly repainted, for company.

Clockwise from Top Left

Mainline's final absorption of SUT/Sheafline got underway during the year.

The fleet was renumbered into a common series with Mainline, and all sorts of exotic vehicles, some in better condition than others, were placed on fleet strength.

The two Neoplan buses, bought new by SUT, seen here with 803, were sent to Doncaster.

The National fleet came in various sizes and 863, seen in Moorfoot, Sheffield, was allocated to Herries for revised routes, which removed some minibus operation.

There were also two Greenway conversions. 805, seen in Waingate, was originally a Midland Red bus.

Noel Edmonds came to see the company to promote his 'Crinkley Bottom' attraction. He's seen, with trademark sweater, promoting the through ticket.

The opportunity was also taken to move the non standard Neoplans (802 and 803) to Doncaster. The continuing pattern of removing competing Sheafline services continued, with Sheafline taking less profitable work in return. This included the 287 group of services from Sheffield to Maltby from Rotherham and a restructure of the Shirecliffe and Hemsworth corridor in to a revised 33 and 34 service, replacing a mixture of mini and double deck buses.

Rotherham, had diverted most of its Sheffield to Rotherham services (69 and 130) to operate via Moorfoot in the city centre, but had also had to divert them via Angel Street and Corporation Street when returning home. Very few changes were made to local services, apart from minor alterations to services within Bramley, Sunnyside and the new Woodlaithes development, where patterns were increased.

Having got a taste for contract work, Doncaster got in on the act by operating a special service to a 'Noel's Garden Party', which was based on the popular BBC programme 'Noel's House Party'

As well as a special service from Doncaster town centre to the Racecourse, special express services were operated from Sheffield and Rotherham to the site. Although 35,000 visited the event, Mainline got less than 1000 people on the special shuttle services, but it was all good experience for future events.

The MCW Metrobus had only a small part in the Mainline fleet. There were just a handful of the Mk1 version still in service at Leadmill and 60 of the Mk2 variant, with 20 of these being to Fastline specification. They had suffered from an early age with body fatigue, mainly due to aluminium and steel coming in to close contact in the rear sub frames and a lack of adequate rust proofing.

Long faces were being pulled at the state of some of these vehicles and the need to either replace or fix the problems that they created. The first option was to refurbish the buses and replace the back ends of the vehicle which were, quite literally, falling apart.

Bus 1904, a standard Mk2 version, fitted with a Rolls Royce engine had suffered a rear end failure, and was admitted to works for rebuilding. In a complicated procedure, the interior was stripped of all fittings and the rear lower end of the bus was removed, after the engine, gearbox and associated other essentials had been disconnected. The rear end was then rebuilt with a bracing mechanism that gave a better support for the engine, as well as removing some of the stress points between the steel chassis structure. Once all associated welding had taken place, the bodywork was rebuilt, with a new rear window assembly that also added strength in to the structure.

The interior was refitted, but with a new PVC floor, which replaced the original treadmaster. The seats were upholstered in the new 'red caterpillar' design and hand poles were removed and powder coated in a yellow material. The refurbished bus, with adverts inside for Mainline engineering, re entered service, fully repainted, at Leadmill on service 56, which replaced minibus services M10 and M11. It was not unknown for drivers to start carrying a dust pan and brush around with them when driving this vehicle, to keep it in tip top shape.

Although a programme of rebuilding commenced on the Metrobus fleet, later rebuilds did not include the new floor or hand poles, with retrims being carried out in the former PTE moquette. The work never cured the problem, only stopping the rot, and some members of the fleet suffered premature withdrawal.

Fares hadn't been increased for some time, and two increases were implemented throughout the year. The first, in July, started to remove some of the anomalies of 'peak' and 'off peak' fares. The October increase was a direct consequence of the PTE imposing bus station departure charges. This met with some passenger resistance, but was unavoidable for the finances of the future of the company. To mitigate the effects of fare increases, a range of fare deals had been developed during the summer, initially on competitive corridors, but this was eventually rolled out across the territory.

Supertram construction work came to Hillsborough in September, leading to wide ranging diversions to services in this busy suburb and shopping centre. This had the effect of removing all buses from the heart of the area for over 12 months, and meant existing passengers had to walk some distance to the shops and other facilities. This not only had a serious effect on the company's cash flow and patronage, but also had a long term detrimental effect on the traders in Hillsborough. A special M14 service was operated between Hillsborough, Wisewood and Loxley, as the diversions meant there was no direct link on this corridor.

The first tram had arrived from Germany in August, and significant track laying had been undertaken at several sites across the city.

Below and Bottom

The rebuilding of MCW Metrobus 1904 was thorough and upto a very high standard.

The replacement rear end also included a revised rear window, which hid the massive steel reinforcement bars that had to be used to keep the body together.

The bus is seen in Leadmill garage and on Pond Street in Sheffield.

Service 501 in Sheffield was relaunched as 'Centre Link' with buses donning new vinyls to help promote this service to Meadowhall, with similar service 601 and 602 being promoted the same way, with window displays. The 501 was going to be a direct competitor to Supertram when it opened on the city centre to Meadowhall corridor. The term 'Savercard' was also dropped to be replaced by the less fussy 'Saver', which leant itself to easier promotion, and was quickly latched on to by the travelling public.

An open day was held at Rotherham in September. This was the first since the Greenland one in 1988. On an unusually sunny and warm Sunday, buses from throughout the company were assembled for the general public, of which 7,000 attended, to look at the garage facilities, as well as visiting buses from further afield.

Tours were given around the garage, and the ever popular 'bus wash ride' was operated. Trips were also given on the Guided Bus track. Rotherham also had a long standing arrangement with the French town of St. Quentin, Rotherham's twin in the country. They had sent bus 287 off there for a visit, to promote Rotherham and to stimulate visits from France.

Top

In its third livery in three years, Leyland DAB 2004, is seen in Sheffield Interchange, ready for a journey on the busy 501 to Meadowhall.

This route would suffer under Supertram competition, and fares offers were always in place.

The opportunity was taken towards the end of the year to float out three subsidiary companies from the Mainline brand. The first of these, Fleet Software had developed a computer package that monitored and organised fleet maintenance and workflow, proving the basis for a well managed engineering system. It could tell you when a bus required a VEX, when it required an MOT, when it needed painting and a whole range of other functions. So good was the software, it was specified by Stagecoach, Lothian and a whole host of other bus companies to manage their fleets.

The second was an insurance arm called Fleetrisk. Bus companies generally manage their own claims section, carrying their own risk, except for exceptional claims of loss or injury. Fleetrisk were now in a position to cater for other bus companies, as well as private users, and it was seen as a valuable revenue stream. Again, Stagecoach was quick to sign up and GM Buses also became a customer.

The final subsidiary was MGL Security. Since 1989 a security section had dealt with all manner of cases of vandalism, assault and willful damage to Mainline's buses and staff. This service was now available to outside interests, including local councils.

The severe competition in Doncaster had eased slightly and Wilfreda Beehive pulled off services 175 and 176. A minor timetable change was made to the service pattern here to restore profitability to the routes.

Halfway garage had long been looked at as a closure target. Heavy competition on its main routes from Yorkshire Terrier, Sheffield Omnibus and, to a lesser degree Stagecoach East Midland, had undermined any chance of profitability. A fightback had begun to restore patronage with a range of bargain return fares, but costs were still high.

The solution was to turn the garage in to a low cost operation. Drivers were offered a lump sum payment, in return for a lower hourly rate of pay. In addition, virtually all administration and engineering were moved to Greenland, with only minor work being undertaken in the remaining engineering pits. This course of action was put to a ballot, being accepted by a majority of the staff, but for those which refused to take the lower pay rate, they had to move to other garages. There was some bitterness towards this course of action, but the alternative was closure.

For the year ending April 1993, the company had made a small trading loss of £363,000, but with added restructuring costs, this ballooned to a loss of £4.2 million, most of which was left with the new SYPTA property company. The future now started to look brighter, the employees were in control of their own destiny (a process that had begun way back in 1988) and hopes of a profitable future were in everyone's thoughts.

Right

The Mainline livery could make any body style look good.

171 in Rotherham, 203 in Sheffield and 231 in Doncaster.

Chapter 9
1994

This Page

Commercial Street, Sheffield, and Rotherham based Dennis 2431, repainted in Mainline colours, is starting a circuit of the city centre loop on service 69.

Passing by is Metrobus 1938, with filler to the dome, awaiting its turn in the paintshop.

The Leyland National fleet that had been absorbed into Mainline the previous year was giving cause for concern. Problems with corrosion, and issues with black smoke being produced by the 501 engine, gave a poor image and tarnished the new Mainline livery. Thoughts were being given to replacement, and new vehicles and products were being developed by bus manufacturers across the UK and Europe. In the meantime, some Leyland Atlanteans were brought out of storage, repainted, and allocated to Greenland to remove some of the roughest members of the inherited fleet.

London had led the way at looking at all-inclusive transport, by introducing low floor buses into the capital. Chassis from Scania and Dennis had been developed that allowed low floor, step free access, throughout the majority of the vehicle. This had two advantages. The first was the ability to allow flat boarding for elderly customers, who found step entry vehicles awkward to negotiate. Secondly, it gave access to disabled passengers in wheelchairs, finally removing the stigma of travelling by public transport for this group. As an added benefit, it also enabled parents with children in buggies access, without the need to fold it up and place it in the luggage compartment.

Money for replacements was tight, especially in the formative months of the new company, but the need to look at new technologies, and think about replacing the National fleet, meant that Mainline would be looking for a partner to help out.

In order to assess the current market of low floor vehicles, a Go-Ahead group Dennis Lance was borrowed from their Coastline subsidiary. This vehicle was fitted with a bodywork by Wrights, built in Northern Ireland, which wasn't at that point, a mainstream body maker. Whilst not used in service (being based at Herries for the time it was with the company), it did give valuable insight in to new vehicle design and how the layout could be adapted to the company's needs.

A further Dennis Lance was also borrowed from Merseybus, fitted with Northern Counties bodywork. This was used on service 75/6 to give further technical knowledge to the management.

In the meantime, the National fleet started to be refurbished by the company, with body overhauls and repaints. In some cases, this included a full retrim in the new 'red caterpillar' moquette. A small number of Nationals were sent to Rotherham to replace minibuses on the 111/112 East Dene services. The local authority had placed speed cushions around the roads of the estate, and the Renault S56 minibuses, with their metal spring suspension, weren't coping well. As well as springs snapping in service, the comfort level of passengers was also affected, and it was found the Nationals were of just the right size to get around the estate, with the suspension easing discomfort levels.

The far reaching effects of the Sheffield TRC were still causing headaches for all bus operators.

Above, Left and Right

To replace part of the inherited Sheafline fleet, further Atlanteans were reconditioned, repainted and placed back on fleet strength.

The silver numbers, sported by 1701, were impractical, and not perputated.

The complex history of some of the buses sent to Rotherham to 'upgrade' the East Dene circular services, can best be described by bus 858.

Once SYPTE/SYT 1066, it was part of the Compass fleet and when that was absorbed, during the sale of that company to West Riding, it entered the SUT fleet, finally ending back in the Mainline stock.

Seen entering Rotherham Bus Station, these buses were a quick fix to remedy a problem, not of the company's making.

Above

East Bank garage, seen in the middle right hand side of the photo, was dormant and vacant by 1994. Across the road stood the similarly vacant Charlotte Road facility.

The new, employee owned, Mainline needed assets to help it grow and successfully negotiated to purchase the East Bank site and reopen it as Olive Grove, forcing the closure of Leadmill and Herries in September.

The huge Norfolk Park estate to the top left of this shot, would be obliterated by the turn of the century and redeveloped.

With Supertram construction now in full swing, including the removal of Castle Square, it didn't help when a Sheffield Omnibus Atlantean managed to drive over a flexible bollard, in the roadworks, snap an airline, effectively locking on the brakes, right on the junction of High Street, Castle Square and Fitzalan Square, quickly bringing the city centre to a halt. The ramifications went on for hours, and South Yorkshire Police requested that Mainline removed the offending vehicle.

Sheffield City Council were so enraged that they wanted to introduce, in association with SYPTE, a quota system of buses being able to enter the city centre. A sage observer may note that at no time did anybody mention restricting private vehicle use within the central area. Mainline had produced a number of proposals to reopen some streets to buses and increase stops, especially in Castlegate. It would take some time to see these ideas come to fruition.

Not to be outdone, Doncaster had approved a pedestrianisation scheme for the St. Sepulchre Gate and High Street areas, outside the Frenchgate shopping centre (still referred to by its previous Arndale name by older inhabitants) and Rotherham proposed a similar scheme for outside the bus station, at the same time the PTE was proposing a refurbishment of the facilities.

The new Mainline owned no property. This was in part a plan by the PTA to have some control over the new company. In earlier bus company sales, mainly former NBC fleets, some owners became overnight millionaires, as they sold on property and land for prices which actually paid off all the loans that had been taken on to purchase the company in the first place. The best example of this was Stagecoach, who had bought Hampshire Bus in Southampton, who then promptly sold on the garage and bus station in the city centre, the proceeds of which, covered the purchase price of the company. The PTA didn't want to see that in South Yorkshire.

Mainline had been locked into leases for all the operating locations current at the buyout. The length of lease varied, depending on how important it was seen to the company, and what development potential the PTA saw on the site. In an honest, an upfront discussion with the employees, the company laid out its options.

Mainline desperately needed finance to buy new buses. The Sheafline amalgamation, with so many elderly Nationals, had pushed up the average age profile to an unacceptable level. The PTE was also making noises about a maximum age for vehicles used on tendered services. Banks and finance houses required collateral in order to lend money against, and here was the crux, with no real assets to speak of, nobody wanted to take the risk on loaning the company any money. Mainline needed assets.

The company operated out of eight locations. Rutland Way in Sheffield was easy to close and move into some vacant space at Rotherham. That left seven operational bases. Leadmill, Halfway and Dunscroft were the smallest facilities, and each had been threatened with closure in the past. Halfway, however, where the staff had only recently taken a package of measures to save the garage was discounted, as it was seen as being relatively cheap to operate and was in a prime location on the Sheffield/Derbyshire border.

Leadmill was only on a lease until the end of 1994, so there was no doubt that it would close. It was in a prime development area, close by the rail and bus stations, however, it contained a lot of key facilities for the wider area, including clothing stores, lost property, ticket machine repair and cash counting. Dunscroft had the advantage of being on a relatively large site, with development potential, as such, the company had only been able to secure a five year lease.

Greenland was on a long lease and had developed into a huge garage, which now had several administrative functions and the main works facility in Sheffield. Herries was a modern garage, but suffered from being built at a time when buses were shorter, and it was a struggle to fit longer vehicles in the workshop and park correctly in the bays, using the herringbone system of parking. It did however, have a large external parking area, large staff car park and there was the possibility of expansion on to neighbouring land, which was at the time, a derelict factory. Also on a long lease, if it was to remain in the company, it would need a large sum of money spent on it in order to exist in to the next century.

Rotherham, as mentioned in earlier chapters, was the garage nobody wanted. Expensive to maintain, lots of uses had now been found for its vast, empty space, so much so, that only half the original garage was now used for its intended purpose. The commercial unit was now in a strong position, and was winning sizeable contracts. A long lease had been taken on and whilst a number of options had been looked at under SYT, it now had a future within the company.

Doncaster had already been downsized. The redevelopment by Wickes of the main garage had left a smaller building, leaner and better able to compete with the likes of Wilfreda Beehive, who had also taken further deliveries of new, Plaxton bodied, Dennis Darts. As part of the redevelopment of the garage, a new bus wash had been installed that could turn vehicles around faster, and give a better finish.

The 'new' workshop, had only been completed in 1984, had been financed by the PTE in such a way, that it would be almost impossible to extricate it from certain covenants to make it a viable site for development. The possibility of moving Dunscroft to the garage was to be explored again, the basis being the efficiency of the service that could be provided, but the current allocation now numbered 125 vehicles, so it would definitely be a squeeze.

That left two properties that were now owned by the PTA, both former bus garages, but both, currently unused. These were East Bank and Charlotte Road in Sheffield.

Above

Herries double deck allocation was 100% Dominator by 1994. The back yard is seen full of sleeping motors, in this Sunday morning shot.

With all the will in the world, the facilities at Leadmill could be best described as basic, in the 1930's built extension. However, the engineering staff there regularly turned out a smartly prepared fleet and undertook many heavy duty engineering jobs.

Trax, who had initially moved in to East Bank in 1989, hadn't been able to keep up a viable business, and returned the property to the company. Charlotte Road had only recently been vacated, but required a lot of money spending on it to bring it up to modern standards. Could new Mainline buy one, or both of these properties, allowing for the closure of one or more current garages, releasing them for development, and making it possible for Mainline to gain an asset that it could use to improve the fleet profile?

In the event East Bank was to be purchased and reopened, renamed as Olive Grove, with the subsequent closure of Leadmill and Herries.

It was going to be a tight fit. East Bank had been built with a capacity of 150 buses, but in later years had accommodated 200. Substantial work had been done in the past to secure its foundations and shore up the bus park at the rear of the garage, which had been sinking in the late 1970s. After Trax had moved out, the building had been left vacant, and would require modernising and repair, having suffered from vandalism. It was about to be transformed in to a garage with an allocation of nearer 250. The plans were put in place to get everything up and running for September.

The company had now partnered with Volvo to try out a new low floor concept bus called the B10L. Bodied by Saffle, but with substantial involvement by Alexander, bus 403 was initially going to be on trial for twelve months. The body was unlike anything seen before, and with one eye towards the London market, came with dual doors. 40, individually shaped seats were mounted on pedestals, fixed to the walls, allowing easier access for cleaning and maintenance. The new bus was allocated to Greenland, operating on service 52. Whilst no orders were placed for this type of bus, the chassis played a part in the development of the very successful B10BLE chassis, but the body style only sold in very small numbers to Citybus/Ulsterbus and Merseybus.

The competition was still fierce on the streets. In Sheffield, Yorkshire Terrier had consolidated its position in to a small number of cross city services, as well as express services to Beighton and Killamarsh. They had now moved in to new premises at Rother Valley Way in Sothall, and as well as buying some new Dennis Darts, they had also purchased some former British Airways Scanias, which they had been busy converting to service buses.

Sheffield Omnibus had now branched out on to the Stocksbridge corridor, and additional resources were now being used to fight them on that network of services. South Riding had been busy registering routes to Crystal Peaks and Stannington.

Below

No job was too small for the tightly packed Leadmill. Seen here, two MCW's, 1953 and 1927, are undergoing a rear end rebuild and an engine change.

The Saffle/Alexander bodied B10L was allocated to Greenland for service 52, but in this photo, it's been given a day out to Doncaster.

For the Crystal Peaks service, Mainline had fought back, initially with minibuses on service M46 from Greenland, operating via previously unserved roads in Birley, and then using double deck buses on services 145 and 146 from Leadmill. Additional journeys to Stannington were also operated from Hillsborough, by Mainline, just in front of South Riding, with some success, as they had got bogged down in tram construction delays.

In Doncaster, the war with Wilfreda Beehive showed no sign of slowing down. They had now registered on top of service X78, bringing them in to Rotherham and Sheffield, but moves were afoot to force them back from the fray. Wilfreda Beehive had also moved on to the Barnby Dun corridor, and additional buses were operated from Dunscroft to flush them out.

The commercial unit had won a number of new contracts, the first being further work strengthening floors on London Buses' Titan and Metrobus fleets. Haulage contractors had also come to the company to have vehicles painted and rebuilt.

The newly split GM Buses North, had inherited a large fleet of MCW Metrobuses and having no money for new vehicles, looked to Mainline to refurbish their fleet. An initial Metrobus was brought across the Pennines for assessment, and found to be in a worse condition than those examples, native to South Yorkshire. A complete strip down and rebuild followed, which proved to be particularly impressive to the new GM Buses North board, that further work was obtained.

Work was also obtained from West Midlands Travel, Hyndburn, East Yorkshire and major collision damage repairs for London Buses' South London subsidiary.

Not all the work was external. Doncaster based, East Lancs Dominator 2353 was badly damaged in an arson attack, whilst in service. The bus was taken to Rotherham where it received a new roof, floor and repaint, looking as good as new.

Clockwise from Top Left

The Sheffield Omnibus fleet had had small amounts of fleet investment, including five Leyland Olympians, including 1602, seen at Moorfoot, Sheffield, and three Volvo B10Ms, including 237, seen in their Ecclesfield garage.

Yorkshire Terrier had picked up a batch of former British Airways, East Lancs bodied, Scanias. Those windscreens would cause headaches, and several homemade solutions would be required. 92 is seen in Crystal Peaks.

South Riding were more of an irritation than a serious threat, but Mainline battled them on various corridors, including the Crystal Peaks via Birley route.

One of their Nationals is seen departing Sheffield Interchange.

Clockwise from Top Left

2358 was outshopped in this smart livery, seen at Sandtoft, for Doncaster's 800th Birthday.

2353 was less fortunate. Being the victim of an arson attack. Seen in Doncaster garage, before entry to the works at Rotherham for rebuilding.

GM Buses North, was a repeat customer for many years, and their Metrobus 5015, is seen being delivered back over the Pennines, after a full rebuild.

Also looking good was similarly bodied bus 2358 which had been outshopped in a special livery to celebrate Doncaster's 800th anniversary of being granted a charter.

Three Alexander bodied Dominators (2440/3/4) were bought off lease and sold to Capital Citybus, for use on London tendered service operation. This was seen as a one off move, as Capital were willing to pay quite a high price for them. A Volvo B10B, with Northern Counties body was also trialed on service 51, temporarily given fleet number 100.

Supertram started operation on 21 March between Commercial Street and Meadowhall. In an effort to be modern and different, the Supertram company had gone for a grey/light lilac livery, with matching seats. They had also gone for a complicated system of Australian made fare collection equipment, with at stop machines issuing a range of tickets. However, it proved quite easy for the criminally minded, to remove the contents of these. This added a further competitive battle to the streets, as despite the best intentions of the PTE, no coordination took place with any bus operator. The main two services affected by this incursion were service 69 and 501 operating on the Attercliffe and Meadowhall corridors to the city centre, although to a lesser degree, it affected patronage on services 25 and 93.

Service 501 was modified to now continue through the city centre to Batemoor, replacing service 41 on this corridor, with a new service 502 taking over former Sheafline service 436. This brought benefits of lowering costs as well as providing more competition to Sheffield Omnibus. The Centre Link branding, only applied the previous year was removed, and replaced by line diagrams. The entire fleet of Leyland DAB articulated vehicles were now based at Greenland for the revised service. The change, however, finally ended the former City Clipper link from the bus and rail stations to Moorfoot, although service 47 and 48 did the job just as well, just a short walk away.

Positive moves would be needed to repel Supertram, and older foes. A new, buy on bus day ticket, initially called 'Save & Go' (later renamed as the All Day Saver) premiered in May. Priced at £1.99, it gave an unlimited days' travel within South Yorkshire (a small surcharge had to be paid when travelling in to other counties). Initially drivers were paid a commission on sales, but the same problems that beset the system for 'Saver' tickets also bedeviled this product, and again the 'pot' was brought in to a wage agreement. A similar product, 'Student All Day Saver' was introduced in the autumn, priced at £1.50.

Price perception is an odd thing to work out. In this case, the psychological barrier of £2 has not been broken, it being seen as being cheaper, despite only being a penny less. It's a trick that was brought over from the supermarket industry, it did however give drivers nightmares trying to give the penny change, as so little copper coinage was tendered for fares. It was an instant hit and together with the sale of Seven Day Savers, on bus revenue was gradually going up.

In order to get some loyalty from concessionary passengers, a novel scheme was introduced that swapped bus tickets for TV Licence stamps.

Top

The new 501/502 cut right through Sheffield city centre and on to the southern suburbs.

Another set of vinyls for the artic fleet was required, this time showing the route in a diagrammatic form. 2009 is seen in Sheffield's High Street.

Specifically aimed at pensioners, who were a vital source of revenue, a set amount of tickets would see a set amount of stamps being issued. This scheme was also hugely successful, Mainline being inundated with applications (over 62,500), to such a degree, temporary administration staff had to be taken on to deal with the onslaught. This was good though, as it was taking vital revenue away from the competition. The promotion generated an additional 575,000 passengers over a six month period and would be repeated.

Coachline also introduced a service to Blackpool from all three urban centre's, via Manchester. A once daily round trip was introduced, but failed to get the required custom and was withdrawn at the end of the season.

Having taken the bold step to purchase the Company, the Board was keen to actively seek expansion, and was looking beyond South Yorkshire, to see where new opportunities may exist. In early 1994 a number of diverse locations were visited where networks, timetables and passenger loadings were monitored and the opportunities for complementary or competing operations assessed. Luton and south Leicester being two such areas studied.

In Suffolk intelligence had been gathered on one of the remaining council owned bus companies, that was worthy of further exploration. Ipswich Borough Transport (IBT) was, at the time, a traditional municipal bus operator, that had not really been challenged by competition, and was still being managed and operated in much the same way as it had been prior to de-regulation.

With high operating costs, driven primarily by platform staff pay rates being amongst the highest in the country, and a strong and dominant trade union, it was considered IBT would be unlikely to be able to respond quickly to a competitor. It also had a good network of local routes operating out of Tower Ramparts bus station, which it had exclusive use of.

Eastern Counties, the other operator in the area, operated rural and inter urban services from the Cattle Market bus station, located at the opposite end of the Town's shopping centre, so it seemed that the two operators had a tacit agreement not to step on each other's toes. Having analysed other operations across the country, there were very few other areas that featured the same opportunities, and therefore, it provided a good starter for the newly owned Mainline Partnership to expand.

Peter Edwards was charged with determining how this new venture should be set up, and during the spring of 1994, work commenced on pulling the pieces together. 10 Volvo B6s, with Plaxton Pointer bodywork, had been ordered for the new operation and, therefore, the proposed network had a restriction on its peak vehicle requirement, although it was planned to have a Dodge minibus as a spare.

An open-air site was found on the Ransomes Industrial Estate at Nacton, just off the A14, east of Ipswich. Ransomes had been a big producer of agricultural machinery (and former subsidiary of Sheffield based Newton Chambers) and the huge site they left had been split up into a number of separate units, including the local Volvo Truck & Bus dealer, who had agreed to maintain the buses under contract maintenance. The plot of land had a Portakabin, and cleaning and fuelling facilities had been secured. An Operator's Licence was applied for under the name of Don Valley Buses Limited T/A Mainline Ipswich

Having studied the IBT network, and with a steer from their excellently produced timetable booklet and maps, it was decided that rather than directly mirror their routes, it would be better to operate four frequent services along the inner sections of the busiest corridors.

Members of Mainline management spent time riding around on a couple of IBT services and drinking coffee in BHS overlooking the bus station monitoring loadings, followed by a couple of days driving around, planning the routes until the cover was blown.

The aim was to use the 10 buses on these services with a round trip time of 30 or 40 minutes delivering a 10 minute frequency where possible. Simple and efficient scheduling was proposed where buses and drivers would be paired for the day, and each was timetabled to drop back at lunchtime, to enable drivers to take a meal break.

Eventually, in October of 1994, with a plan formulated, the envelope containing the registrations was posted through the letterbox of the Traffic Commissioner's Office in Cambridge in the middle of the night. Parts of the timetable for the 10 minute services were registered at frequent intervals which was queried by the Traffic Commissioner because they had never encountered that concept before!

Above

The Ipswich fleet was of high quality, but expensive to operate. With an operator of the right experience, they were a sitting duck.

Ipswich Optare Vectra 169 is seen in Tower Ramparts Bus Station in the town, with Mainline's Ian Davies studying the loadings.

What would have been Mainline Ipswich's bus 411 is seen at the rear of staff car park at Rotherham garage, for a once over by the company's directorate.

Above

Glistening in the Yorkshire sunlight, 412 is seen being specially posed for photographs at the rear of Rotherham garage.

The logo was a modified Mainline vinyl, with a chunk missing from the bottom line, and Ipswich inserted.

Simple and classy.

In determining a manager for the new operation, Lyle Duncan, a driver at Dunscroft, who had previously managed Thistle Coaches, had the experience, and as his sister lived in the Ipswich area, it was easy for him to stay down there in the short term. Mainline's Human Resources department provided a Manager to help in the interviewing and recruitment of drivers, but rumours abounded - probably started by the 9/10 Branch Trade Union, that most of the applicants were failed former employees of either Eastern Counties or IBT which was to be expected, however with a depot, services registered and staff in place, the operation was good to go once the buses arrived.

The first of the buses arrived for inspection at Rotherham garage, painted in standard Mainline livery, but with Ipswich prominent in the underline of the Mainline logo. Fleet numbers 411-20 had been allocated and registrations M411-20 TET had been booked.

Meanwhile, Grampian Regional Transport had acquired Eastern Counties in July 1994 and the new owners were non too pleased about the introduction of further services in the Town. With two weeks to go before the Mainline operation was due to start, Moir Lockhead, Chief Executive of the GRT Group, contacted Peter Sephton, and made an offer to buy, the yet to commence, Mainline Ipswich operation.

A sum was agreed and Mainline literally walked away, but because the services had been registered the only way that to escape the obligation to run them without giving another 42 days' notice was to surrender the Operator's Licence, which was done as soon as possible. Whilst no other formal commitments had been made to staff and contractors, this was achieved with minimal cost.

Although Eastern Counties decided to not proceed with the network identified by Mainline, they registered a new cross town route that operated, and continues to operate, via Tower Ramparts, so that particular taboo was broken. The Town services became jointly operated with IBT until 2000. The vehicles were acquired, and the remaining deliveries went direct to Eastern Counties who rescinded the booked registrations and re-registered them as M584-593 ANG. Only two buses actually made it to Rotherham for certification (411 & 412), and the rest of the fleet was delivered straight to Eastern Counties.

As a postscript to the Ipswich project, the busy workload of the Operations Director meant he spent a lot of time away from his office attending meetings. To assist in spreading his workload and conscious that he had little time during the day to read trade journals, newspaper cuttings and general documents, his secretary created a folder for him to take said items home to read at his leisure. The folder had a clearly written label on the front stating 'Reading'. The folder was topped up during the day and left on the corner of the meeting table which adjoined his desk in an obvious position that he would remember to pick it up on leaving the office homeward bound.

A week or two after the Ipswich sale had been put to bed, the Chairman and Secretary of the 9/10 Branch of the TGWU, reported for a meeting and in their usual style made a point of being jovial as they entered the office and sitting at the meeting table. The said folder caught the eye of the TGWU Secretary who looked up and said. Oh, now that we've done Ipswich, is that where we are going next, Reading? It is believed that in defending their network from the Mainline proposals and the new Eastern Counties service had cost IBT around £4m.

Ownership matters were also taking centre stage back on home turf. Stagecoach, who owned East Midland, made it quite clear they would like to own the Mainline bus business. As part of the sale of the company, no takeovers could be allowed for five years, and claw back arrangements were in place after that date. However, a share swap, or equity stake, was allowed, and this was the route Mainline decided to go for.

The deal was that Mainline would swap 20% of the equity of the holding company, Mainline Partnership Limited, in exchange for 500,000 shares in Stagecoach, a move which would benefit Mainline to the tune of £900,000. Additionally, Brian Souter would sit on the Mainline board and a director from Mainline would sit on the board of Stagecoach South and North West.

The employees, now being the ultimate owners of Mainline, had to approve the deal, but some misgivings were voiced about the way East Midland had been managed since being acquired, with garage closures and redundancies. East Midland had, however, over reached itself in the new competitive market by bidding for tendered work as far away as London and Manchester, and whilst profitable, required some surgery to make it a fit and active company, which Stagecoach had done. The Mainline employees overwhelmingly backed the deal.

Brian Souter was keen to showcase the East Midland operation to the board, and in August, Ian Davies, Gary Nolan and Trevor Simpson visited the Head Office in Chesterfield, to meet the Senior Management Team, to understand the operational procedures followed by Stagecoach owned companies. They found that all processes had been simplified down to the basics, and that each Manager received, or produced, a weekly report, of one page, providing the results of their section. Similarly, the structure was slim, and the Head Office staff consisted of seven members, looking after 276 buses.

Whilst the Mainline employees welcomed the new shareholder, the MMC had other ideas, seemingly not content to allow the bus services of South Yorkshire to settle, and decided to investigate the share swap, having decided that they saw the deal as anti-competitive. Conclusions were not reached by the years' end, but it was yet another diversion on the main focus of the company, and its profitability.

Competitive activity in Rotherham, which had been quiet of late, allowing the garage to consolidate its operation, had begun between Sheffield Omnibus and Yorkshire Traction, over the latter's busy routes to Rawmarsh and from Sheffield to Barnsley, a market that Mainline had vacated some time previously.

Above

Stagecoach was no stranger to Mainline. Apart from some tender losses, in both directions, their was a cordial atmosphere between the two operators.

Leyland Tigers, such as 428, could regularly be seen operating into all areas of the companies territory. Stagecoach had promised an injection of 200 new buses, but would the authorities allow it?

Above

When Herries closed, dual purpose seated Dominator 2488 was reallocated to Rotherham, as Olive Grove had no buses with Gardner engines, and with one eye on reducing spares requirements, the engineering management wanted to keep it that way.

The bus is seen exiting Rotherham Bus Station.

Omnibus had also expanded a service from High Green to Barnsley, and in response, Yorkshire Traction had started additional journeys on their 165/265 service between the Sheffield and Barnsley. This impacted Mainline, as this was on part of the busy 75/76 corridor between Chapeltown and the city centre. Globe had also entered the Rotherham market, also competing on the Rawmarsh area.

All was not well at Sheffield Omnibus. A high profile incident, involving one of their MCW bodied Leyland Atlanteans mounting a grass bank, and toppling over, in the Wincobank area of Sheffield, raised the interest of the Traffic Commissioner. Their garage in Chesterfield was in the North Western Traffic area, and a vehicle inspection took place which concluded that vehicles were not being maintained to the correct standard and that measures would be needed to avoid removal of their operating licence.

Olive Grove opened for business on 4 September, and in the proceeding weeks, a new management team had been assembled to begin the process of welding two garages (Leadmill and Herries) into one. Bert Middleton was brought in as the new Garage Manger, assisted by Tony Gilmour, Terry Conley, Bob Adlington and Alan Bullas as Unit Manager's. Engineering was in the hands of Alan Hull.

Drivers had to get used to new routes and new colleagues. As part of the shuffle, some routes were exchanged with high frequency service 95 going to Greenland, at the same time gaining extensions to Base Green and Dyke Vale Road, replacing service 63 and 127. Services 145 and 146 also moved to Greenland, despite going past the front door of Olive Grove. There was no room at the inn however, and they were extended across the city, replacing services 25 and 64 to Woodhouse via Woodthorpe, an area which had been difficult to defend from Yorkshire Terrier.

Most Metrobuses were now based at Olive Grove, with Dominators going from Herries to compensate. The first day was a little fraught, as no water was available on site until later in the day, and it was certainly a squeeze getting all the buses in, with some now having to be stacked in the bays, in front of already herringbone parked buses.

There was, the seemingly never ending, cascade of staff out of the business, with some administration staff opting to take voluntary redundancy or retirement, with others becoming drivers. Coachline moved from Leadmill to Rotherham, clothing stores was closed and a new system of uniform ordering implemented and all cash counting was centralised at Rotherham. Lost property was now distributed to each garage.

Also strengthened at the same time was Don Valley Buses on Petre Street. This extremely low cost section of Mainline was now busy operating a number of evening tenders as well as trunk service 221 and 222 around the Aston estate in Swallownest, which undoubtedly, would have been lost under Mainline, or even Sheafline terms and conditions. Somewhat surprisingly, they continued to operate the tendered Sunday service to Leeds on service X32, using coach seated Mercedes minibuses for that. The Don Valley Buses licence was to come in very handy for competitive battles ahead (like the stalled Ipswich operation).

Go MAINLINE
the SMART way to travel in DONCASTER

BIG DISCOUNTS for paying in advance. No hunting for change, no waiting, no trouble - and great travel value!

PLUS INCREDIBLE INTRODUCTORY OFFERS
SEE INSIDE FOR DETAILS

CONCESSIONARY & SAVER PASSENGERS
2 more 'SMART' ideas from Mainline.
See inside for details.

IT'S SMART IT'S SIMPLE

We've invested in new technology to make your travel quicker and easier than ever before, and to offer you economical ways of paying your fare.

The new fare system makes use of what is known as 'smart' technology. The cards store information about fares, journeys, and usage. The equipment on the bus reads the information, deducts the right fare or journey, and prints out the details on the card. Passing your card through the machine is very easy - and if you don't know what to do, your Mainline driver will be pleased to help.

Whether you're a regular or occasional traveller, Go-Mainline cards make the bus the best way to go.

Here are some of the questions we've been asked about Go-Mainline - but if you have any other query, just call us, or ask your Mainline driver.

Q Do I need to buy my Go-Mainline card before I get on the bus?
A No. All cards are purchased from your driver and as soon as you are issued with your card, your first journey will have been acknowledged.

Q How can I be sure the machine has done what it's supposed to do?
A The card reader displays how much credit you have left and full details are printed on your card – just ask your driver.

Q What if the amount left on my Travel Bank card isn't enough to pay my fare?
A It is a simple process to add value to your card - just ask your driver.

Q What happens if my Travel Bank card gets damaged?
A Look after your card and take care not to fold or tear it. If it does get damaged tell your driver and your card will be replaced with a new one to the same value.

Q If the card reader on the bus is out of action, what do I do?
A Your card will be punched with a hole by the driver, and the minimum fare will be deducted next time you travel.

Q What happens if I lose my card?
A You must take responsibility for your card, it is valuable and should be treated like money.

Q What happens if there's no room left to print journey details on my card?
A No problem! Your driver will simply transfer your remaining credit to a new card.

For more information on Go-Mainline, call us on **Doncaster 762000**

MULTI-RIDE MEANS CASH-LESS, TROUBLE FREE TRAVEL FOR SENIOR CITIZENS

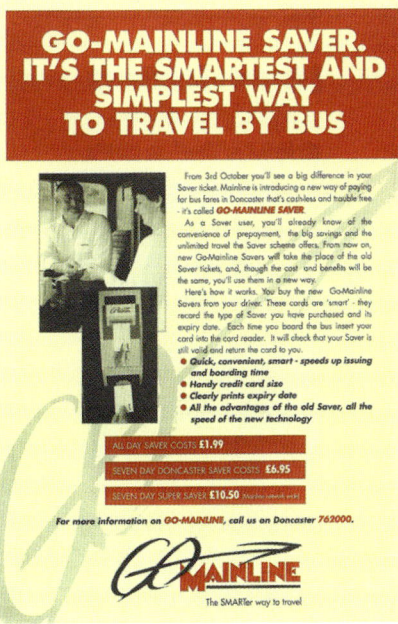

GO-MAINLINE SAVER. IT'S THE SMARTEST AND SIMPLEST WAY TO TRAVEL BY BUS

From 3rd October you'll see a big difference in your Saver ticket. Mainline is introducing a new way of paying for bus fares in Doncaster that's cashless and trouble free - it's called **GO-MAINLINE SAVER**.

As a Saver user, you'll already know of the convenience of prepayment, the big savings and the unlimited travel the Saver scheme offers. From now on, new Go-Mainline Savers will take the place of the old Saver tickets and, though the cost and benefits will be the same, you'll use them in a new way.

Here's how it works. You buy the new Go-Mainline Savers from your driver. These cards are 'smart' - they record the type of Saver you have purchased and its expiry date. Each time you board the bus insert your card into the card reader. It will check that your Saver is still valid and return the card to you.

- Quick, convenient, smart - speeds up issuing and boarding time
- Handy credit card size
- Clearly prints expiry date
- All the advantages of the old Saver, all the speed of the new technology

ALL DAY SAVER COSTS	£1.99
SEVEN DAY DONCASTER SAVER COSTS	£6.95
SEVEN DAY SUPER SAVER	£10.50

For more information on GO-MAINLINE, call us on Doncaster 762000.

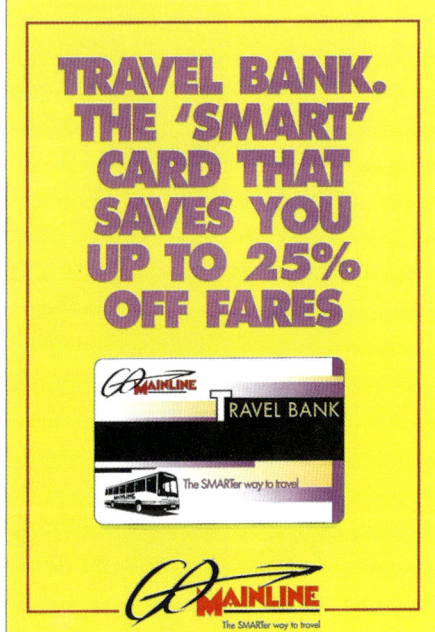

TRAVEL BANK. THE 'SMART' CARD THAT SAVES YOU UP TO 25% OFF FARES

Above

Another refugee from the closure of the two Sheffield garages was former Compass Leyland Leopard 69.

It wasn't often to be seen on high frequency city work, but somehow has escaped to the Tinker Lane terminus at Walkley, of service 95.

October saw the introduction of Wayfarer 3 ticket machines and magnetic card readers to Doncaster, following the successful trials on service 60 and 97 in Sheffield. Launched under the 'Go Mainline' banner, this was a fleet wide application, also including the buses and routes at Dunscroft. The same products that were available in Sheffield were also now available in Doncaster, with a slightly redesigned marketing package, which was mailed to all homes in the district, with a discount voucher for initial purchases.

The £300,000 investment also enabled more dedicated products to be offered on specific services. On the Rossington and Cantley corridor, a special 'Route Seven Day Saver' was introduced, priced at £4.50 for a week's travel. This was a full frontal assault on Wilfreda Beehive, who having invested in some newer vehicles, were now under assault from Yorkshire Traction as well. Doncaster had also won a package of routes (the 27 group) in north Nottinghamshire, serving rural villages between the town and Retford, mainly operated by minibuses.

Ticketing was also on the agenda in Sheffield. Competitors had always been able to offer cheaper fares, as their cost base was lower.

Sheffield Omnibus had been selling a 'Bus Card' on their vehicles for £3.95, for one week's travel, which was significantly cheaper than Mainline's, network wide, £7.50 variety.

A new variant was introduced called 'Red Saver' which gave a week's unlimited travel on services 53, 75, 76, 77 and 80 for just £3.50. Together with the introduction of service 72, which operated between Lowfield and High Green, via the city centre, it put Omnibus on the back foot. They couldn't really get any lower with their cost, although they had to match the £3.50 offer. In response, Mainline cut the price to £2.50, certain in the knowledge that the competition would respond likewise, but the 'war' was now on an equal footing, and Mainline had deeper pockets than Sheffield Omnibus.

The final end to off peak and peak fares was undertaken in two steps in October and December. In October, at the same time as the introduction of the new ticket machines, a single rate of fares had been introduced to Doncaster district, with little resistance. In December Sheffield and Rotherham followed suit, with a general increase included due to changes in fuel tax rebate outlined in the budget. The effect to the general traveller was muted, as most were now on some form of discount fare, either some type of saver, or using a return ticket. It did, however, raise the average fare, which the PTE used to measure the rate of concessionary reimbursement, which also increased the amount of revenue the company received.

The year ended with the Board ordering 25 new Volvo B10Ms and 30 Volvo B6s for delivery in 1995. This was a significant order for the fledgling company, but was required to meet growing emission targets, and rid the fleet of aging Leyland Nationals and early Dodge S56s, which were costing enormous sums to keep on the road. This blistering year of change had finished with a small profit of £306,000. Not a bad achievement.

YOUR NEW FARE GUIDE

WHY — Mainline are changing the fare structure in Doncaster in order to simplify the payment of fares. This is to assist the introduction of a new prepayment system, designed to reduce fare charges and speed boarding times.

WHEN — The new fares take effect from October 3rd.

WHAT
- The two-tier fare structure is being replaced by one all-day structure. All day and every day
- The new structure features a short hop fare of just 30p available on selected services
- No change to £1.00 or £1.50 maximum return fares charged on selected services
- Return fares still available on all routes

THE NEW ALL DAY FARE STRUCTURE FROM OCTOBER 3rd

Miles	Single	Return
Hop	30	60
1	40	70
2	55	90
3	65	110
4	75	130
5	85	145
6	90	155
7	95	165
8	105	180

THE OLD TWO-TIER SYSTEM APPLIES UNITIL OCTOBER 2nd

Miles	Standard Fare Times Single	Standard Fare Times Return	Discount Fare Times Single	Discount Fare Times Return
1	45	70	40	60
2	55	90	50	80
3	65	110	60	100
4	75	130	70	120
5	85	150	80	140
6	90	160	85	150
7	95	170	90	160
8	105	190	100	180

New from MAINLINE

RED SAVER SEVEN DAY

One week's unlimited travel on Mainline's Sheffield services 53, 75/76, 77/80

for only £3.50

If you're a regular traveller on services 53, 75/76 or 77/80, then this new ticket from Mainline could save you £££'s.

At less than half the price of a regular Sheffield 7-Day Saver, the new RED SAVER costs just £3.50 and lets you make as many journeys as you like on on Mainline's Sheffield services 53, 75/76, 77/80.

Mainline are pleased to offer this extra saving to those customers who travel regularly on these services but do not often use any of Mainline's other services throughout Sheffield.

the region's favourite

Chapter 10

1995

Above

The one that got away. Chesterfield was all poised to join the Mainline group, but was eventually purchased by Stagecoach. National 41 is seen in Eckington Bus Station.

One that joined the team. The well presented, if somewhat elderly Northern Bus fleet, was partially purchased by the group. In return, they were 'franchised' a number of Mainline services to operate. Two Bristol VRs are seen in Dinnington.

At the very end of 1994, Chesterfield Transport, and their employee shareholders, agreed to look in to the possible purchase, of their business, by Mainline. Chesterfield had taken the ESOP route some time earlier, but had run in to difficulties with an expansion policy which saw it running buses in Retford and the Peak District.

They had a huge operating garage at Stonegravels, which was now much bigger than their needs required. Some financial dealings had also been questionable, and a £2 million takeover by Mainline was on the cards.

Another purchase, that did go ahead, was for a stake in Northern Bus, the Dinnington based company that had been formed out of A&C Wigmore. They had been active in the tendered market, but for commercial work, despite an initial foray into the northern suburbs of Sheffield, they had largely stayed close to their Dinnington roots.

The purchase was structured in such a way, that initially Mainline only owned a slice of the business, with the ability to purchase the entire shareholding within a ten year period, or earlier, if a competing offer was made. As part of the deal, Northern Bus would take on some marginal Mainline routes, that although profitable, could be made more so, using a franchise style agreement. It also allowed Mainline to walk away from the deal, and retain the services, should the OFT or MMC decide the purchase was against the public interest. In this case, the ruling was favourable.

Northern Bus would take on a number of Dinnington orientated services from Sheffield, Rotherham and Doncaster, operating them with buses in their own livery, and charge their fare scales, but the ultimate responsibility for operating the service would still lie with Mainline. The 206/X3/X4/X5 from Sheffield to Dinnington and the 120/129 from Rotherham to Dinnington would pass to Northern Bus, to join their large network. In addition, later in the year, the once prestigious X32 to Leeds via Barnsley would also go to them. The improved, more frequent train service between the two cities, had taken a heavy toll on this once profitable service. Also joining Northern Bus, would be the 286 to Holmesfield, the N13 from Rotherham to Ulley and the X39 between Sheffield and Huddersfield.

Before transferring the X32 to Northern Bus, a feasibility study was undertaken into converting the three, Dennis Dorchester coaches (75 to 77) that had been operated from new by Coachline, for the service, subject to a full refurbishment. It was difficult to justify the expense, against the heavy competition on the route, and lack of profitability.

Rotherham Borough Council had been looking at investing in a high quality bus corridor in the town, to go hand in hand with the redevelopment of the barely adequate bus station. The PTE had already taken steps to completely rebuild the station and rename it as an 'Interchange'. The resulting building work had caused havoc to Rotherham services. The Council saw the future in a guided busway, similar in concept to that discussed for Sheffield and Leeds.

The Bawtry Road corridor seemed ideal to develop this strategy. A long, wide, dual carriageway that stretched from the town centre via Brecks, Bramley, Hellaby to Maltby and beyond. It had wide central reservations, and could easily accommodate a twin carriageway busway. Mainline committed to spend £5.5 million on new buses and associated infrastructure work, which would include better waiting shelters and improved frequencies. A bid was submitted to the Department of Transport for funds, but it would take another four years, a change of Government, and a change of ownership of Mainline, for the scheme to be implemented, but it wasn't a guided busway, but was a good package of bus priority measures.

The first of the year's intake of new buses started to arrive in January. Volvo had designed the B6 as their answer to the market leading Dennis Dart. Powered by a Volvo designed, 180 hp engine, coupled to a ZF gearbox, this was a new combination for the company. The bodywork was by Plaxton, built at their Scarborough factory, normally used for producing high quality coaches.

The first 16, of this batch of 40 were from stock, and had minor differences to the rest, although all had Mainline's, by now, standard grey, yellow and red themed interior. The batch of 40 was distributed to Rotherham, to operate on services 111,112, 601 and 602, Doncaster for the 81 and 82 to Armthorpe, Greenland for use on the 70, 71 and 711, and to Olive Grove for the 56 to Wybourn. In each case, it brought an appreciable increase in comfort and passenger perception to the routes involved.

For the Rotherham services, they replaced Leyland Nationals and Renault S56s, with the Nationals being transferred to other garages to replace non refurbished examples, and early Dodge S56s to be withdrawn and sold.

Above

The Plaxton bodied Dennis Dorchesters, delivered in 1985, were getting a bit long in the tooth for long distance coaching, and efforts were made to consider refurbishing them for the Sheffield to Leeds X32.

The route passed to Northern Bus, and the Dorchester's were used on less onerous tasks.

The first native B6s were a shot in the arm for Rotherham's fleet.

419, on Chantry Bridge, has already received a new panel, with grey substituting silver, and seems to be having issues with the destination blind. The blinds frequently twisted and split.

The Pointer was not one of Plaxtons best products.

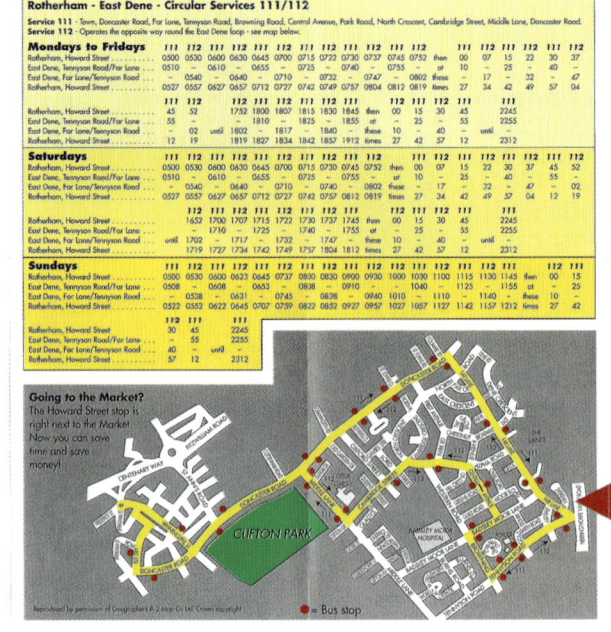
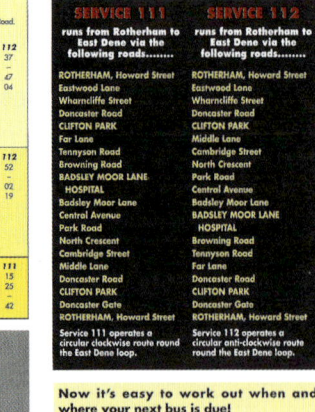

Below

Stagecoach were less than impressed with their early Volvo B6s, sending them back to the manufacturer and changing the order to B10Ms instead.

Sheffield Omnibus picked them up, cheap, and hurriedly placed them into service, as seen here at Meadowhall.

The Nationals, which had been introduced to the routes around East Dene to help mitigate the problems with speed bumps in the area, had also given the impression that the route had been downgraded, and had suffered a subsequent 15% reduction in passengers. A marketing effort, which included a fares promotion, coupled by road improvements by Rotherham Council, aimed to reverse this.

In Doncaster, they also replaced Renault S56s, which replaced the similar Northern Counties bodied variant, although they would shortly reappear, as well as providing more robust competition to Wilfreda Beehive.

In Sheffield, the 56 was a very short service that was performed on a tight, 30 minute cycle, operated every 10 minutes. Wybourn was about a mile from the city centre, but due to topography the estate was up a hill and a fair distance from main roads. It was also a very well used service, frequently carrying standing loads. For drivers, it was well known if you ever had any trouble on your bus in the area, a simple visit to the Windsor public house, have a quiet word with the landlord, and the problem would simply fade away. In later years, the buses would be taken off the 56 and allocated to a new 60A/60B service to Endcliffe Halls of Residence, being replaced by double deck buses.

It would be fair to say the Volvo B6 was not the best chassis Volvo ever built. Based on Steyr truck parts, it had a very limited turning circle and the ZF gearbox was initially problematical. There were also problems with suspension and brake snatch, but these were overcome under warranty. They could be slow, especially on the hilly terrain of Sheffield. Over time, the Plaxton body developed numerous faults, especially around the front dome and windscreen area, with cracking being a problem, causing glass movement and leaks. The driving cabs were also narrow and cramped, with Mainline's cash drawer design not helping those with wider legs. They did, however, see a full life with the company.

Not to be outdone, Sheffield Omnibus, in a desperate attempt to improve their image, had purchased the initial fleet of B6s that Stagecoach had acquired, but discarded quite early in their career, supplementing it with a small batch of new builds, with the same Alexander 'Dash' bodywork. That allowed them to dispose of the worst examples of their Atlantean fleet.

Outside interests were becoming big business for Mainline. The refurbishment unit had been busy winning contracts from all over the UK, and now that the Routemaster contract had come to an end, this was going to prove an excellent revenue stream for the company. Contracts had been signed with GM Buses North to start the process of refurbishing their Metrobus fleet, including new floors, rear ends and improvements to seats and ceilings. A harmonious relationship was also struck up with, Grampian owned, Eastern Counties (which lasted well into FirstGroup days) refurbishing 40 Bristol VRs to full DiPTAC standards, which included new floors, hand poles, reupholstery and repaints

London General sent an MCW Metrobus for full body refurbishment, including a new step entrance arrangement, as a trial to see if they wanted to order new buses, or go down this route. The bus, M808, was completely repaneled, new floor laid, rear end rebuilt with smaller back window, split step arrangement fitted to front and Transmatic lighting fitted (which was also fitted to all Mainline's B10Ms and later Renault S56s). The bus had to be brush painted, which was against London General's policy, but was to such a high finish, they couldn't tell the difference.

Above

London General M808, was completely rebuilt and reupholstered, and the quality workmanship shows through here.

In the end, the operator went for new buses, but returned to Mainline for high quality accident damage repairs, and other refurbishments, well into First ownership.

Above

The final London Routemasters rolled off the production line the previous year, but one or two additional vehicles were dealt with, occasionally giving the opportunity for a team photo.

Repainting contracts were signed with Grampian to repaint the fleets of Midland Bluebird and SMT, and to refurbish the entire fleet of Bristol VRs for Eastern Counties.

As well as being a valuable money earner, it helped ensure the survival of Rotherham garage, with its enormous overheads.

Work was also undertaken for Supertram, including at one stage, having parts of a tram on site for accident damage repairs. Retrimming of seats was also undertaken for them. This was in addition to security services being provided for them by MGL Security and replacement services, as and when required for track work etc.

Painting was also now being offered to outside companies, with the first to take up the facilities being SMT, from Edinburgh, who signed a contract for the repaint of their entire fleet, excluding those that required a metallic finish. So successful was this program, that Grampian, being SMT's ultimate owner, subsequently contracted the company to repaint buses belonging to Midland Bluebird and Lowland Scottish as well. Mainline now had paintshops in operation at Greenland, Rotherham, and Doncaster and to add additional capacity, a start was made at Olive Grove, repainting 79 buses in to Mainline livery during the year, the aim being to get as much of the fleet in to the yellow and red scheme as soon as possible.

The Mainline livery, despite being bright and fresh, was causing concern, especially around the rear ends of the Dennis Dominator fleet. The shelf/window arrangement above the engine was notorious for attracting dirt and being a real issue to keep clean, combined with the heat generated in the area. Initial attempts to keep the area clean, using hand operated lances, had the effect of removing the paintwork from the aluminium sheeting, and a different solution was required.

Three Dennis Dominators undergoing repaints at Greenland, were given a revised version of the fleet livery, to test practicality of application and if this aided cleanliness. Buses 2200, 2401 and 2441 were given various treatments, maximising the red section towards the rear, as well as the application of the blue and grey stripes. All three looked smart, but in the event, they proved no more adept at keeping the rear ends dust free, and were quickly modified to normal.

Above

The three trial liveries had one thing in common, more red around the rear bustle, to help prevent road dirt damage. All three were modified back to normal by the end of the summer.

2200 and 2441 are seen on the top park at Greenland whilst 2401 is seen in Sheffield Interchange, being attended to by the Wayfarer ticket machine repair van.

Above

Buses were washed, swept, or vacuumed, on return to the garage, on a daily basis, with heavier cleans taking place at periodic intervals.

427 and 612 get a good wash at Rotherham and Greenland garages.

Even vehicles destined not to be long in the fleet were treated to a repaint into Mainline livery.

Olive Grove based 1883 is seen in Chapeltown.

As part of the same 'striving for quality' approach, new methods of interior cleaning were also trialed at Olive Grove. A vacuum system was installed at each fuel pump, enabling staff to clean the vehicle using suction hoses, whilst it was being topped up with fuel and engine checks made.

This had the added effect of making the garage cleaner, as all waste paper and small dirt was trapped in the vacuum holder, whilst larger items, such as bottles/cans, went straight in the skip.

Buses went through the wash daily and each night they were checked for the operation of lights, heating and any sticky residues from chewing gum, was painstakingly removed by hand by a dedicated group of cleaning staff. Buses were also given a heavy clean weekly, which included washing the floor, windows and cab and cleaning of all seats. The days of buses being put in service with unpainted panels and seats painted over with gloss paint were over, and for the remaining time the company stayed independent, there was a real pride in fleet presentation.

Despite the MMC recommending that Stagecoach were allowed to keep their 20% holding in Mainline, coupled with a caveat that prevented Stagecoach from owning anymore of the company than that, the Government instructed that the share swap deal was against the public interest, and had to be undone. The justification for this, was that Stagecoach could potentially have a monopoly of services in the area, despite them only owning East Midland, which mainly operated in north Derbyshire and Nottinghamshire, reducing the competition in the tendered market.

The Directors considered going for a judicial review into the process, but having just fought a four year battle with the MMC over the SUT/Sheafline purchase, there was little appetite for that particular avenue. Stagecoach just considered it 'business', and entered into discussions to sell its share. If they had been allowed to keep their 20%, they had promised to inject 200 new buses into the company, but this wasn't to be.

As the year rolled on, there were a number of suitors interested in Stagecoach's 20%. Cowie, the operator of Grey Green in London (eventually subsumed into Arriva) were the frontrunners, but eventually, the stake was sold to FirstBus (as it was then called) for £1.75 million. The deal also included a substantial business loan to Mainline of £3.5 million, from FirstBus, for future investment in the company. Trevor Smallwood would replace Brian Souter on the board, with Peter Sephton gaining a seat on the FirstBus board in return. Again, the employees were asked to approve the deal, subject to approval from the MMC, which they did.

The Stagecoach decision was even more controversial when you consider that Yorkshire Traction purchased Sheffield Omnibus, Andrews, South Riding and Yorkshire Terrier in April, merging the companies into two groups, Andrews and Yorkshire Terrier. The purchase nearly equaled the number of buses being operated by Stagecoach in the neighboring East Midland area and gave rise to a second grouping in South Yorkshire.

Yorkshire Traction took little time in rationalising their purchases. They initially closed down the South Riding operation, merging it with Andrews on Attercliffe Common, but this location was required for a road widening scheme, and eventually the fleet was split to the Ecclesfield base of Sheffield Omnibus and Yorkshire Terrier's Holbrook garage. Sheffield Omnibuses base in Chesterfield was closed and together with the remnants of Andrews, was renamed Andrews Sheffield Omnibus (ASO), with a new fleet livery of light blue and cream. Around 80 vehicles were withdrawn from the combined fleet, mainly elderly Atlanteans and Fleetlines, being replaced with Leyland Nationals from Yorkshire Traction. There was also a slimming down of the network, and some areas reverted to being served purely by Mainline, removing their presence from Totley and Rotherham, for example.

To counter the continued competition on the Stocksbridge corridor, a new 'Green Saver' was introduced to services 57, 58 X66 and X67 between the city centre and Stocksbridge, giving seven days travel for just £4. An additional off peak service, the 21, was also placed into the service pattern, giving five buses per hour from Mainline. In the event, ASO pulled off the service, being unable to compete effectively, but in order to avert any OFT investigation, the 'Green Saver' continued for some time after, although the service pattern reduced with the end of service 21.

Further new buses arrived in May. The batch of 25 Volvo B10Ms were built to a revised specification, having a ZF gearbox and side mounted radiator. Internally, they were in the now usual grey, yellow and red theme. The first fourteen of the batch went to Olive Grove to operate high profile service 53 between Low Edges and Ecclesfield via the city centre. This route had competition from ASO, and additional journeys were operated by Halfway garage, between the peaks, to help out, using buses from the school fleet that would otherwise sit idle during the day. Further Volvos from the batch that had been bought initially for service 97 were also drafted on to the 53, as ASO were pulling off that route, double deckers were now required to cope with the patronage.

Above

Quality was the mantra from now on, coupled with fare deals and cleanliness.

The newly delivered Volvos were a considerable step forward on Leyland Nationals and Dodge minibuses they replaced.

B6 427 and B10M 717 are posed at Rotherham garage for a photo shoot, with their drivers looking smart in their simple white shirt and grey trousers/skirt uniform. A blazer, jumper and coat in maroon was added into the mix.

Above

The Frecheville corridor was refreshed with the new B10Ms, with route branding being used. 732 shows this off to good effect in Hackenthorpe.

The smart interiors were night and day to that being offered by Yorkshire Terrier, but price promotion was also required to win back customers.

The remaining 11 went to Greenland to improve the fleet on service 41 between the city centre and Crystal Peaks. These buses were fitted with route branding, similar to that fitted to buses on service 52 and a special promotion was undertaken to increase patronage by introducing a revised TV Licence stamp offer, specifically for the route. Heavy competition was provided by Yorkshire Terrier services 120 and 123. The TV Licence stamp promotion was again, phenomenally successful, and was rolled out fleet wide, again, from the late summer.

Surveys undertaken by Sheffield Hallam University into customer impressions of bus operators in South Yorkshire gave Mainline top marks, way above other companies, coming across as clean, dependable and trustworthy. The real issues were seen as being congestion and unreliability; issues that were out with Mainline's hands.

Mainline had always had a big presence in the Peak District National Park. One third of the city of Sheffield is within the park, and through a combination of historical operations, Mainline were the main service providers to Bakewell and Castleton from the city. From 1993, with support from the Peak Park Planning Board, a number of additional services had been added to the network, mainly on Sunday and public holidays, and by 1995 Mainline now reached places as far flung as Holmfirth, Glossop and Hayfield. It was good business, with buses regularly running full out to the most popular destinations such as Strines, where it was possible to travel out, have a long relaxing walk, grab a meal at the Strines Inn, and catch the bus home. It was also good for the driving staff, as they could stretch their legs by operating outwith the packed city streets.

Mainline was, however, looking further than that for its next venture, somewhere that a 'Seven Day Saver' couldn't get you. Adelaide in Australia was looking at franchising its bus network, and were looking for operators with commercial knowledge to take on the services and operate them in a professional manner. Two managers, Peter Edwards and Chris Dyal were sent to Australia to set up a local operating company, secure deals on parts fuel and cleaning services, and set up legal entities to bid and operate the services (Mainline Australia Pty.).

The initial contract was going to be for 30 months, with a five year extension if successful. Mainline assessed the routes and placed a bid for about 80 buses worth of work, out of a fleet of 800, in the outer north area.

The company was also hoping to secure the contract for Adelaide's guided bus network, the largest outside of Europe. Mainline management tried to engage with the workforce about an ESOP style arrangement, but to no avail, as the union thought they would lose their bargaining powers. In the event, the company didn't win, but it had been a useful exercise and numerous, essential, contacts had been made, that would help the company grow. The new Adelaide contractors rapidly dispensed with over 400 staff positions.

Right

Mainline drivers were some of the best and MCW 1956, seen in Bradwell, demonstrates the tight nature of some of the routes in the Peak District.

Adelaide's buses were in a familiar livery, and of the same manufacturer as Mainline's preferred supplier, Volvo.

One of their B10M artics, is seen in their garage.

Above

Low floor buses were in their infancy when Mainline borrowed this Wrights bodied, Volvo B6.

This bus proved the concept worked, and would eventually join the fleet, after demonstration in London, as fleet number 400.

Seen in its original silver livery in Sheffield Interchange and at Olive Grove garage.

Fares were increased, again, in May, generally affecting standard single fares. As in previous increases, no changes were made to Saver or special offer tickets or returns. An additional increase, due to changes in fuel tax, was implemented in December. There was little passenger resistance, and the additional revenue offset the costs of purchasing new vehicles and implementing a pay award, which now introduced 'Profit Related Pay' to all staff. That certainly focused the mind on getting higher patronage levels on Mainline services, which would show increased passengers and revenue by the year end.

Low floor buses were again in the news with the Government passing legislation on disabled persons' rights, called the Disability Discrimination Act. This would enshrine, in law, the right for inclusion on public transport of all groups of passenger, regardless of any disability or impairment. Mainline had already tried out low floor buses at Herries, but was now willing to make a substantial investment in accessible vehicles.

Wrightbus, based in Northern Ireland, had developed a smart little body on the Volvo B6 chassis, suitably modified and called the B6LE. Mainline borrowed the prototype for a trial (eventually adding it to the fleet, as bus 400, a few years later).

Shown to interested groups, and local Members of Parliament, an initial batch of 9 (441 to 449) were ordered to operate a revised timetable on services 13 and 14 from Sheffield city centre to Wisewood and Loxley, replacing Renault S56s.

The summer of 1995 was unusually warm and sunny, and with Yorkshire Traction having consolidated its operations, a 'show of strength' was required to remind them that this was a competitive environment, especially as they now viewed Sheffield as being quite nice operating terrain for them. In Rotherham, the northern part of the borough had traditionally been served firstly by Mexborough and Swinton and then Yorkshire Traction, although Mainline continued to operate a few journeys on services 298 and 299 to Mexborough and Conisbrough and had the 140 and 142 going past the door of the Parkgate retail complex.

A huge housing estate in Rawmarsh was their money-spinner, and to help persuade them not to encroach any further into Sheffield, Mainline registered two competing services into the estate. Services 108 and 109 were direct copies of Yorkshire Traction services, but were going to be operated by the, 'now redundant' Renault S56s, with Northern Counties bodywork, moving from Doncaster to Rotherham.

These minibuses had proved to be somewhat disliked by crews, even though they had better driving positions and a separate cab door.

They had been nicknamed 'scuds' on account of their shape (a reference to a weapon used in the first Gulf War) and now these 'scuds' were being targeted, as a weapon, at one of Yorkshire Traction's most profitable services. All the buses involved were repainted and fitted with a fixed destination blind which simply read 'Rawmarsh Circle'. Special fare offers were attached to the route and the usual 'Saver' range was available.

The initial take up was good, with additional journeys having to be added into the timetable, and additional minibuses resourced, to cope with demand. For their part, Yorkshire Traction briefly started operating a service to Maltby, and launched a competitive attack on the evening student market on service 52 in Sheffield, but with little success, they had pulled off by the autumn.

A major package of service changes was planned at all garages for the first weekend in September. The opening of Supertram, and consolidation of operations by Yorkshire Traction in Sheffield had sharpened minds to the commercial future of many services.

The main changes were in Sheffield. Services 13 and 14 went over to 'big bus operation', but as the new Volvo B6LEs weren't all ready, additional Plaxton bodied B6s were drafted on to the route, as well as some refurbished Leyland Nationals until all new buses arrived. A revised frequency of 7/8 minutes was offered, but with a greater level of comfort.

The minibuses displaced by this change went onto revised services 85 and 86 which replaced the Middlewood end of services 81 and 82 and double deck buses on the south end of the route. Services 81 and 82 were diverted to Stannington to replace service 86, providing with services 83 and 84 a five minute headway between Hunters Bar, the city centre and Roscoe Bank/ Hall Park Head. ASO retreated to operating between Ecclesall and the city centre on this corridor. This was all a direct consequence of Supertram, now finally operating to its maximum size.

Also in Sheffield, increased services were operated on the 47, 48, 53, 70, 71, 75, 76, 77, 78, 80, 97 and 711 on weekdays, to compete more effectively with ASO and Yorkshire Terrier. Service 41 was extended to Halfway, increased in frequency to every six minutes, with part of the service being operated by Halfway garage, with a small batch of older B0M's being allocated there to operate it. These buses were repainted and rebranded prior to allocation. There was a frequency decrease on service X55, as this had been hit by competition from Supertram, and passenger surveys had indicated that they preferred the higher frequency 41 instead, as this looped around the Moor and markets shopping areas. The 41 was also extended to Eckington in the evenings and Sunday.

Above

Supertram was now operating at its maximum length, and further changes were required to the network to compete. The trams initially wore this grey/lilac livery.

Some effect had been felt in the lower parts of the Mosborough estates, and Mainline's 41 was increased in frequency, but with a reduction in journeys on service X55.

Part of the operation, and some B10Ms were transferred to Halfway in compensation, such as 664, which is seen entering the bus station at Crystal Peaks, heading for the new terminus.

THE NEW RANGE OF MAINLINE SAVERS... MORE WAYS TO SAVE

When you're travelling frequently by bus, riding on a Mainline Saver is simply the best way to make your money go further. There's a complete range of Savers to fit in with your travelling needs.

Mainline Savers
- Save money and time
- Travel as many times as you like within your chosen area
- Choose a Mainline Saver for a day, a week or a month.
- Lend your card to family or friends

TRAVELLING ALL DAY?

Mainline's All Day Saver gives you unlimited travel for one whole day throughout Mainline's entire network in South Yorkshire. Mainline All Day Saver is available from your driver as a paper ticket* or from Transport Executive Travel Centres in Scratch card format.

| ALL DAY SAVER ADULT | £1.99 |
| ALL DAY SAVER STUDENT | £1.50 (WITH NUS CARD OR 16-18 PASS) |

*If you live in Doncaster or travel on services 60 and 97 in Sheffield, you'll be issued with a credit card sized 'smart' card that you simply enter in to a card reader on the bus each time you travel.

THE NEW RANGE OF MAINLINE SAVERS ARE NOW AVAILABLE. MAKE SURE YOU'RE RIDING ON ONE

TRAVELLING ALL WEEK?

Mainline's Seven Day Saver gives you unlimited travel for seven consecutive days within your chosen area. Mainline Seven Day Savers are transferable so that you can lend them to family or friends.

SHEFFIELD SEVEN DAY SAVER £8.30

Available from your driver for immediate use and allows unlimited travel throughout Sheffield.

DONCASTER AND ROTHERHAM SEVEN DAY SAVER £7.30

Available from your driver for immediate use and allows unlimited travel throughout Doncaster and Rotherham.

SUPER SEVEN DAY SAVER £10.95

Available from your driver for immediate use or for advance purchase from Transport Executive Travel Centres, main Post Offices and other selected outlets in scratch card format.

FOR MORE INFORMATION CALL MAINLINE ON 0114 256 7000

On all of these services, a renewed push was made on fare deals and returns and on the 'Red Saver' routes, patronage improved markedly.

Don Valley Buses vacated the cramped, rat infested, premises on Petre Street, for the much cleaner environs of Halfway. Further changes to working conditions there, improved the chances of winning further tenders in Derbyshire, and the schools unit continued to thrive, although their fleet was repainted into standard Mainline livery.

A change was made to the 'Saver' ticket product. These were now simplified into three products based on Sheffield, Rotherham and Doncaster combined and network wide. The seven day version continued to be sold on bus, and other special variants also remained. For longer periods, such as monthly's, these were now sold by agents in calendar months, via a scratch off card.

Easier to promote, and with less administration, they were instantly popular, although there was a noticeable drift towards on bus sales as the years went by.

Student travel had become big business for the entire company with money flooding in from abroad to the area's Universities and Colleges. Special fare deals and packages were introduced for them, and sales staff now regularly attended fairs to sell tickets and give advice.

Doncaster was busy changing services to cope with the new route pattern brought on by the closure of St. Sepulchre Gate and parts of the High Street, as a direct consequence of a traffic management scheme. Buses were diverted to surrounding streets and more use made of the North and South bus stations. Mainline purchased two, secondhand, Ford Transit minibuses, painted in overall yellow, to operate a free service called 'The Doncaster Connection'.

This was in a similar vein to the old Inner Circle service, but in order for it to survive, after the initial free period, sponsorship would be required from local traders and businesses to keep it going. This was not forthcoming, and the service was subsequently withdrawn.

Doncaster had also been busy in the private hire market, and had struck up a contract with a company called Demauris Associates, who provided private hire facilities to all manner of retail and leisure companies. To operate this contract, a second hand Volvo B10M (1000) was acquired from Shearings. In addition, the two Doncaster based, ex Sheafline, Leyland Tigers, 67 and 68, which had laterally been operating in standard Mainline livery, were brought in as back up. All three were painted in a revised Coachline livery, with a new fleetname, in style with the rest of the group.

Charlotte Road garage in Sheffield, now owned by SYPTA Properties, was placed on the sales market, but in the meantime, was going to be used as a base for a trial 'Park & Ride' service for the south side of the city. Mainline won the contract, and a small batch of 1988 Renault S56s was given a light refurbishment to operate the service. Part of the contract requirements, were that the buses were painted in a blue and grey livery, although some also appeared in partial advertising livery for local radio station Hallam FM.

Another contract win, was the retention of the disabled travel network in both Doncaster and Sheffield (Rotherham's network had always been won by small coach companies in the town). The new, five year, contract required the final replacement of Doncaster's converted Leyland National fleet, as well as the Carlyle bodied Sherpas operated in Sheffield. A contract was placed with Mercedes for a small batch of '709' chassis, bodied by Plaxton (111 to 122), to their revised Beaver body. Unusually, they were to have manual gearboxes, meaning that only a small selection of staff could drive them.

Above and Left

The inaugural journey on the 'Doncaster Connection' leaves North Bus Station in the town. Secondhand Ford Transit 105, does the honours.

The revised Coachline livery was smart, incorporating all the company's house colours.

Tiger 63 is seen in the yard at Doncaster garage and Volvo 1000 is seen on the top park at Greenland.

Clockwise from top left

The ever changing face of the Mainline Group.

116 and 113 are seen in Doncaster, bought new for disabled persons travel.

The Dominator still formed the huge bulk of the fleet. 2320 is seen loading in Sheffield's Church Street.

The Volvo B6 was now a familiar sight in the region. 447 is seen at Sheffield Interchange, whilst loan, Alexander Dash bodied 103, is seen in Doncaster on Park and Ride duties.

The launch of the low floor B6s brought a lot of interest from national politicians. Here is Neil Kinnock, discussing the merits of the new buses with Operations Director, Ian Davies.

These new buses would be allocated to Doncaster and Greenland, although one of the Sherpas (9) was repainted into Mainline livery as a spare, with the rest being returned to the PTE. They arrived with 12 seats, in a dual purpose configuration, which was very comfortable, and secure points for four wheelchairs.

All the Wright bodied B6LEs had arrived by the year end and were bedecked in a subtly changed livery, in which a new sub brand had been added, called 'easi access'. They had a slightly darker interior, enlivened with the usual red moquette and yellow hand poles. The launch was attended by local M.P.s David Blunkett, Helen Jackson and by former Labour leader, Neil Kinnock and a full colour leaflet was distributed to households along the route.

The year ended with an announcement that a further 40 Volvo B10Ms were going to be ordered for 1996 delivery and that for the year ended April 1995, the company had achieved a profit of £1.6 million. Steady progress was being made.

Right

Rear end advertising was used to great effect. The PTE Charlotte Road Park and Ride was resourced from existing stock.

Chapter 11
1996

This Page
1996 started snowy and cold, but Mainline kept the show on the road. 1910 makes a slippery start on West Street, Sheffield.

The year started with a contract win, and a contract loss. The win was contract to operate the town services in Goole. Whilst Goole had been served by Mainline for years with service 249 and X88, the town network had regularly changed hands, with East Yorkshire and West Riding having operated it in the past.

To operate the contract, Mainline ordered a further pair of Volvo B6LEs with bodywork by Wrights, as the contract stipulated low floor, accessible, vehicles. This pair of vehicles (450 and 451) weren't ready for the start of the service, so, a couple of standard B6s had to suffice until their arrival. They came in a non standard livery of red and yellow with large 'Goole Town' vinyls, in addition to standard Mainline fleetnames. A separate group of drivers were dedicated to these services.

The contract loss was of the 'Park & Ride' service to and from Charlotte Road. SYPTA had sold the premises to a local builder, who had plans to redevelop the site. Notice to quit had been given, but no date had been set. There were no plans from the PTE about a replacement facility. As and when the closure took place, Mainline would absorb the Renault S56s used on the service, back into the main fleet, simply painting the front ends back into fleet livery.

There were signs that passenger revenue and numbers were now on the rise, after a near ten year cycle of decline. Mainline set the target of 100 million journeys for 1996, and the year would be marked with service consolidation and further fares and marketing initiatives to beat the competition and woo car users back to the bus.

Student travel had become big business, and the number of foreign students in the area had ballooned. That, however, gave rise to a small problem; the language barrier. Whilst many spoke good English, it was difficult in a thick Yorkshire accent, to make the difference between the varied forms of 'Saver' tickets, understood.

Vinyl stickers started to be placed beside the entrance door which gave information in four of the most popular European languages, about fares information. This would also be useful to visitors arriving in Sheffield in the summer, for the Euro 96 football tournament, as several matches were to take place at Hillsborough.

To assist with negotiating the network, and for the first time in many years, a map and frequency guide had been produced for Sheffield and a joint one for Rotherham and Doncaster too. In full colour, with detailed maps, these were especially handy for visitors to the Euro 96 festivities, although the one for Rotherham/Doncaster wouldn't arrive until the autumn.

The new traffic management scheme in Doncaster was causing nightmares in the town. Duke Street, a once, mainly bus only thoroughfare, was now swamped with general traffic trying to negotiate a complex gyratory system. Traders were also up in arms, as shoppers were finding it easier to go elsewhere, than be sat in delays caused by the scheme. Timing changes were made to most services to cope with the problem, but further work would have to be undertaken.

The majority of the fleet was now in Mainline colours, with the last bus, Atlantean 1702, being painted in the spring.

Top

The livery for the Goole Town services was less flamboyant than the current Mainline style, harking back to the original Sheffield scheme.

One of the two Wright bodied B6s, is seen undertaking crew familiarisation work in Doncaster, prior to being launched.

Top

1702 was the final bus to be painted into Mainline livery, seen here on the top park at Greenland. By a quirk of being on reserve, and serving as a school bus, the bus hadn't seen a paintbrush since 1988.

Having tackled the main fleet, a start could be made on training buses. As manual gearboxes still existed in the fleet, an elderly Leyland Leopard was purchased and painted into Mainline colours. M106 is seen at Greenland.

For the double deck trainers, a predominantly red livery was designed. A start was made to renumber the 'M' fleet into the 9000 series, and 9112 is seen at Doncaster garage.

Second repaints commenced and Olive Grove used its capacity to repaint 2223, seen here in the garage's back yard. The Mainline livery enlivened even the dullest day.

A start was now made on repainting the training fleet into a new version of the standard colour scheme, which would replace the previous livery from 1989. This used more red, on the double deck version, and because there was still a requirement for manual licence holders, an elderly Leyland Leopard, with Alexander 'Y' type body, had been purchased and painted too.

Coachline had been set up by SYPTE in 1985 to compete in the high value, corporate, coach market. It seemed to be a standard plank of competitive thinking, prior to deregulation, to have some high end coaches, minibuses and dual purpose double deck buses. SYT/Mainline had inherited all three, and the coach business was the most difficult to crack.

The initial fleet of new coaches were three Dennis Dorchester that had been ordered by Leicester City Transport, but had been swapped, prior to delivery with three East Lancs bodied Dennis Dominators.

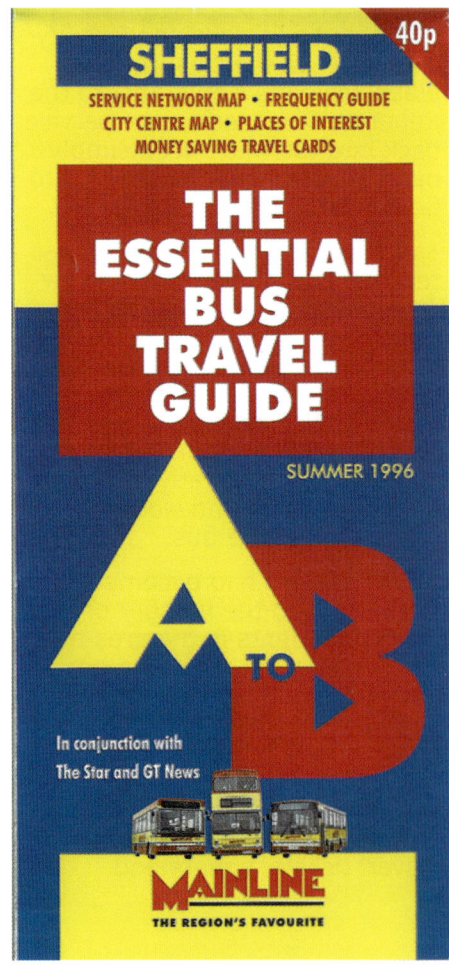

They were fitted with a Gardner turbocharged engine and three speed Voith automatic gearboxes. They were backed up with good quality dual purpose vehicles from the main fleet, as required.

This wasn't, however, the PTEs first foray into coaching. Doncaster had always had a thriving coach operation, mainly based on the operations of various independents that had been acquired over the years, but Doncaster Transport had a very exotic Ford, bodied by Caetano, on its books in 1973. The district had always kept a small fleet available, and for a while they were painted in a special tan and white livery, although just prior to Coachline being formed, a chrome yellow band had been added.

Sheffield, through the former Joint Omnibus Committee, had always had coaches, and ran local excursion programmes right through to the 1970s, but had been less focused on private hire, preferring to leave that to Sheffield United Tours and later to National Travel East.

Rotherham had shied away from coach activities, but with the purchase of Dearneways in 1981, a large coach fleet had been absorbed, and they too started a limited private hire operation, using when required, existing dual purpose coaches.

The new Coachline, had a livery of white with red, brown and yellow stripes, in a style very popular with the Plaxton Paramount body style then employed on the new Dorchester coaches. This was adapted for existing vehicles, although some dual purpose vehicles wore a simplified version of the short lived, tan white and chrome yellow. A launch was held at Chatsworth Park in early 1985, and to back up the new image, several Dennis Dominators were also painted into Coachline promotional livery (2184, 2195, 2199, 2278, 2419, 2421). In addition, a number of buses had been painted into the livery of the former constituents of the PTE, with 1737 in Sheffield, 1640 and 2160 in Rotherham and 1797 and 2214 in Doncaster, and they also formed part of the Coachline fleet.

Above

The coaching inheritance was strong with contributions from Doncaster and Sheffield, with Dearneways, giving the PTE a presence in Rotherham's coaching market.

Clockwise from Top Left

The Coachline fleet also had a number of heritage, and specially painted vehicles at its disposal, all fitted with Tachographs.

904 was a former Sheffield Leyland PD3 that had been restored by apprentices. 1640 and 1737 were Roe bodied Atlanteans, and 1797 with Alexander body, were all painted ready for the opening of Rotherham garage.

Dominator 2160 was painted in the final form of trolleybus livery worn in Rotherham, whilst 2214 was painted in a version of Doncaster's former tram livery.

All districts had a number of Dominators advertising Coachline, as seen on 2195.

Clockwise from Top Left

The Dorchesters were delivered in the new livery, in a style that had been neatly designed by Plaxtons.

The PTEs paintshops, however, seemed to take great relish in painting all different types of vehicle, in a variety of versions.

To be fair, the original coaching livery was tan, white and chrome, and where no diagrams existed, that's how they were outshopped.

75 is seen in Sheffield, 17 at Tinsley, 1026 in Doncaster, 1092 on a private hire for Rotherham and 99 at East Bank garage.

COACHLINE
EXCURSIONS

The best day trips around

July 1992

Initially, Coachline was split around the three districts, with a small pool of drivers at each garage, but this was ineffective, and SYT pooled all the vehicles together at Leadmill at deregulation. In early 1987, the instruction went out to repaint all the vehicles in Coachline and heritage livery, not based at Leadmill, into standard fleet colours. This left Coachline with three Dorchester's, five Dominators, two Tigers, one Olympian and two refurbished Leyland Leopards.

Drivers had been paid standard rates of pay, but this was uneconomic in the coaching sector and a special coaching rate was negotiated and applied from 1987. The Dominators had seen little use and were soon repainted and allocated away (although they could be used by Coachline as required), leaving a small dedicated fleet of buses and drivers to operate a large package of holidays, private hires and excursions, which included, for two seasons, holiday express work to local seaside destinations.

Extra vehicles were bought to increase the fleet, with Javelins, more Tigers and B10Ms joining over the years, together with oddments such as the former Compass Bova. Some National Express contract work had been taken on and a Volvo B10M 'Expressliner', had been added to the fleet. In an odd twist, they weren't the only private hire operation in the company. Each garage, being a cost centre, could also bid for private hire work, and they did, and they sometimes beat Coachline on price. It was a bizarre situation.

Doncaster branched out with its Premier Coaches operation on the purchase of that business, and a revised fleet livery for Coachline had been devised to give it a fresher, sharper feel for the new decades ahead. In order to control costs, it had been merged into the SUT/Sheafline fleet, before finally returning to its spiritual home at Leadmill, and then Rotherham.

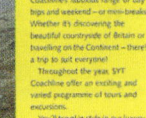

The biggest problem with a bus company running coaches is that the costs are not shared equally. The standing costs of garaging the fleet (that is heat, light, rates etc.) are borne by the main fleet, with coaches normally only taking the variable costs (pay, fuel etc.), and invariably, vehicle replacements also come from the main vehicle replacement budget. Doubts had also been expressed about fleet utilisation, the running joke being that Olympian 100 was called 'The Olympic Torch', because it never went out.

Matters came to a head, when due to yet another disappointing years' figures for the unit, the Board looked at either closing Coachline down altogether, slimming the fleet to a bare minimum or sale to a third party. The latter course of action was taken and Coachline was sold to Glen Harrison, who had formed a new South Yorkshire Coachline Limited company. Drivers were given the option of moving into the new company, or returning to service work with Mainline, which a number chose to do. Mainline would only have one true coach left, the recently purchased Volvo B10M, 1000, based at Doncaster, and from now on would only hire standard buses, although that market was limited.

That didn't stop the company from operating special services when conditions were right, and an open day at Tinsley Railfreight Depot, in the east of Sheffield, provided the opportunity to prove this. A fleet of buses were required to transport over 10,000 people to and from the event, over a twelve hour day.

The much heralded Supertram network was in desperate trouble, losing upwards of £6 million per annum. Mainline, however, saw this as a potential for development, and had started studying how they could, possibly, integrate the system into the network. Adverts had appeared in the financial press inviting suitors to operate the network as a franchise from April 1997, and Mainline decided to enter the bid process.

The latest batch of Volvo B10Ms started arriving in March, although it would take until the late summer for them all to arrive. These differed to earlier deliveries in having a revised chassis, with further refinements to braking, and a reversion to the Voith gearbox. Internally, they were fitted with Callow and Maddox seats, to a new, individual design, trimmed in the 'Red Caterpillar' moquette. Yellow handpoles, and a revised, darker flooring material completed the look. Externally, they were fitted with tinted glass, to avoid temperature build up, and the first eight, destined for service X78, were fitted with double glazing and dual purpose seats.

Above

Bus 1021 was nominally part of the training fleet, but unusually it had been fitted with a large internal cage, and was available for fishing club hires, both externally and within the company.

Seen at Greenland, it wore this unusual livery of primrose and red.

Supertram was in dire straights and Mainline decided to bid to run the system. Some early sketches were done for livery design, and also to include as part of the bid process.

Right

Heavy investment in more Volvo B10Ms involved the complete rebranding, and timetable makeover, for service X78.

While operated from Doncaster, it also provided a welcome boost for Rotherham's network. 745 is seen on Chantry Bridge, while Peter Sephton, and representatives from Alexanders and Volvo, launch the new buses at Doncaster Racecourse.

These were a real step change in quality and also had improvements for drivers, being fitted with an improved heating system, newly designed cab seats and improved cash handling drawers (which became standard). These were the last B10Ms ordered, and the fleet of these now stood at 180, with those delivered over the previous six years.

Those for the X78, were for Doncaster, for a revised timetable linking Doncaster to Rotherham, Meadowhall and Sheffield. A complete branding package was developed which marketed the route as 'Xcellent', 'Xtra value' and the like. The improved daytime frequency of every 20 minutes, was a 30% improvement in what had gone before, and was a real challenge to improved train services and car use. On a Sunday, the service was extended to the Yorkshire Outlet just beyond Doncaster town centre, although this later gave way to a dedicated service.

A further six buses were also allocated to Doncaster from this batch, to act as back up the dedicated X78 buses, but also to bolster the attack on Wilfreda Beehive, who were slowly but surely consolidating their position within the town.

The rest of the batch, 26 in all, were allocated to Olive Grove (initially, the last three were due to go to Greenland, but in an effort to reduce spares capacity at different garages, this wasn't followed through) and the majority were given branding for services 81 to 84 on the Ecclesall to Stannington corridor, fiercely competing, and protecting market share, against Supertram.

Above

The Ecclesall to Hillsborough corridor received a welcome boost with the arrival of 26 B10Ms into Olive Grove.

Most of the batch carried branding, as seen on 755 on Ecclesall Road, but they were delivered 'naked', as seen on 760 at the garage.

The last three were fitted with standard fleetnames and could be seen all over the city, whilst in the evening, and on Sunday, the branded buses could also be found on services to Stocksbridge.

Above and Below

Luckily, accidents are rare, but when you're driving something as heavy as a double deck bus, the damage caused on impact is going to be immense.

1824 has managed to come into contact with Fife Street railway bridge, 1700 has done the same on Darnall Road and 1805 has picked a fight with a cherry picker. After recovery, a one way visit to Greenland garage for component recovery, followed by a trip to the scrapman beckoned for these veterans.

All these new arrivals finally provided a cascade process that removed the final Leyland Atlanteans from the fleet, which had recently been gathered together at Greenland for schools work and Leyland Nationals, which were struggling to purvey the right image. It also meant the first Dennis Dominators could be placed on reserve. The Atlanteans were in good order and easily found buyers.

The commercial unit was having another productive year, with refurbishments ongoing for GM Buses North, East Yorkshire and, former rival, North Western. Repaints had also started for the former Yorkshire Rider companies, who now went under names as diverse as Kingfisher and Calderline. The turnover of the unit had provided a profit of over £150,000 that went directly into the Mainline business.

Mainline had also been looking long and hard at its fleet of dual purpose seated Dennis Dominators, now coming up to ten years of age. Structurally sound, having had their rear ends rebuilt a few years earlier, their interiors required work to update the image for the coming millennium. The refurbishment to these vehicles, initially carried out at Rotherham, with some buses being dealt with at Olive Grove, saw a completely new interior.

This included new flooring, sidewall panels and dual purpose seats in the red moquette, although for those allocated to Halfway, low back seats were specified in the upper saloon. Handpoles were also removed, and powder coated in yellow, followed by full body refurbishment and repaint.

The first batch of Volvo B10Ms, used on service 52 in Sheffield, were coming up to six years of age, and the grey interiors were starting to look dowdy, and a refurbishment programme, costing £150,000, was commenced on getting these vehicles looking modern again. The fleet of 25 buses, had clocked up some 350,000 miles each, and structurally were in great condition, although the decision was taken to fit them with new radiators.

A small team of new recruits to the commercial unit were sent to Greenland garage, to set up a mini production line within the garage, and work commenced on returning them to sparkling condition. This included replacing the floor from the first step to just beyond the first axle, replacing all handpoles, refurbishment of seats and squabs into the new red material and a revised drivers cab, incorporating the new cash drawer.

The commercial unit's work can be broken down into two categories; planned and collision damage repairs. For planned work, the requirements of the customer, either external or within Mainline, would be determined by them and arrangements made to cost up the necessary time and materials. This is then relayed to the Bodyshop Supervisor who then decides which member of the relevant team (Bodymakers or Service Assistants) would be required.

Generally, all seats would be removed, floor removal would take place whilst an Engineering Fitter would disconnect any heating pipes, especially if the lower saloon floor was to be removed. Once removed, any rotten floor bearers would be replaced and a report sent back to the customer, as many unseen defects can be found at this stage. Once the lino is removed from the upper deck, sanding of the plywood floor can take place, to make the surface as good as possible to accept the replacement floor covering.

External panels that require repair or replacement, would be marked up for attention by the Bodyshop Supervisor, and a team would set about those tasks. This could entail a full or partial repanel, new or repaired front dome, fibreglass corners and anything else that could hinder the repaint process, would be dealt with at this stage. Any external or internal corrosion, snapped pillars or historical accident damage would be dealt with. In the case of some London area operators, they would send a diagram showing what items they wanted dealing with and how.

Once the seat cushions were removed from the vehicle, and depending on workload within the unit at the time, the squabs and backs, would either go to the trim shop on site, or be collected by a contractor. Externally most body panels would be cut and fitted by the Bodymaker doing the task, but more intricate panels, or steelwork would be made by the unit's Sheetmetal Engineer, with a contractor being used if a large batch of a certain item were required.

Above

The unit 52 Volvos were approaching their sixth birthday, and it was time for some TLC.

601, seen on Greenland's top park, has had the treatment, and has been freshly painted in Mainline livery, ready for another punishing shift on this busy service.

Note the wheelhub covers. Expensive, but the chrome look gives an air of quality, far above the competition.

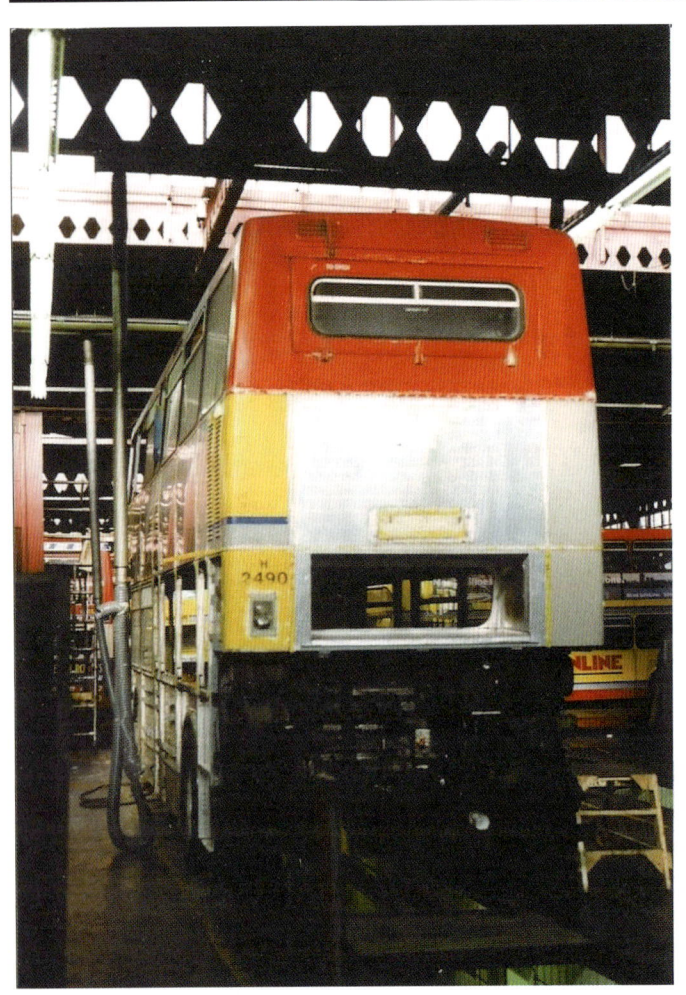

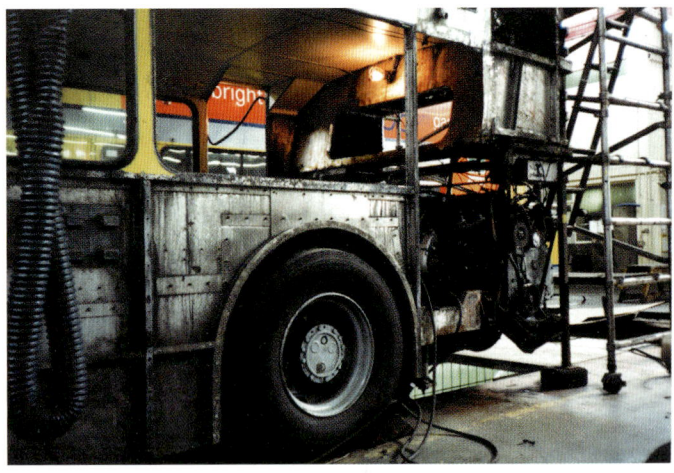

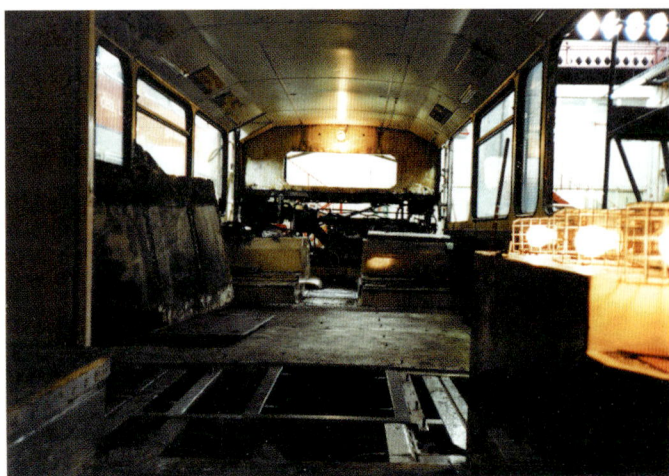

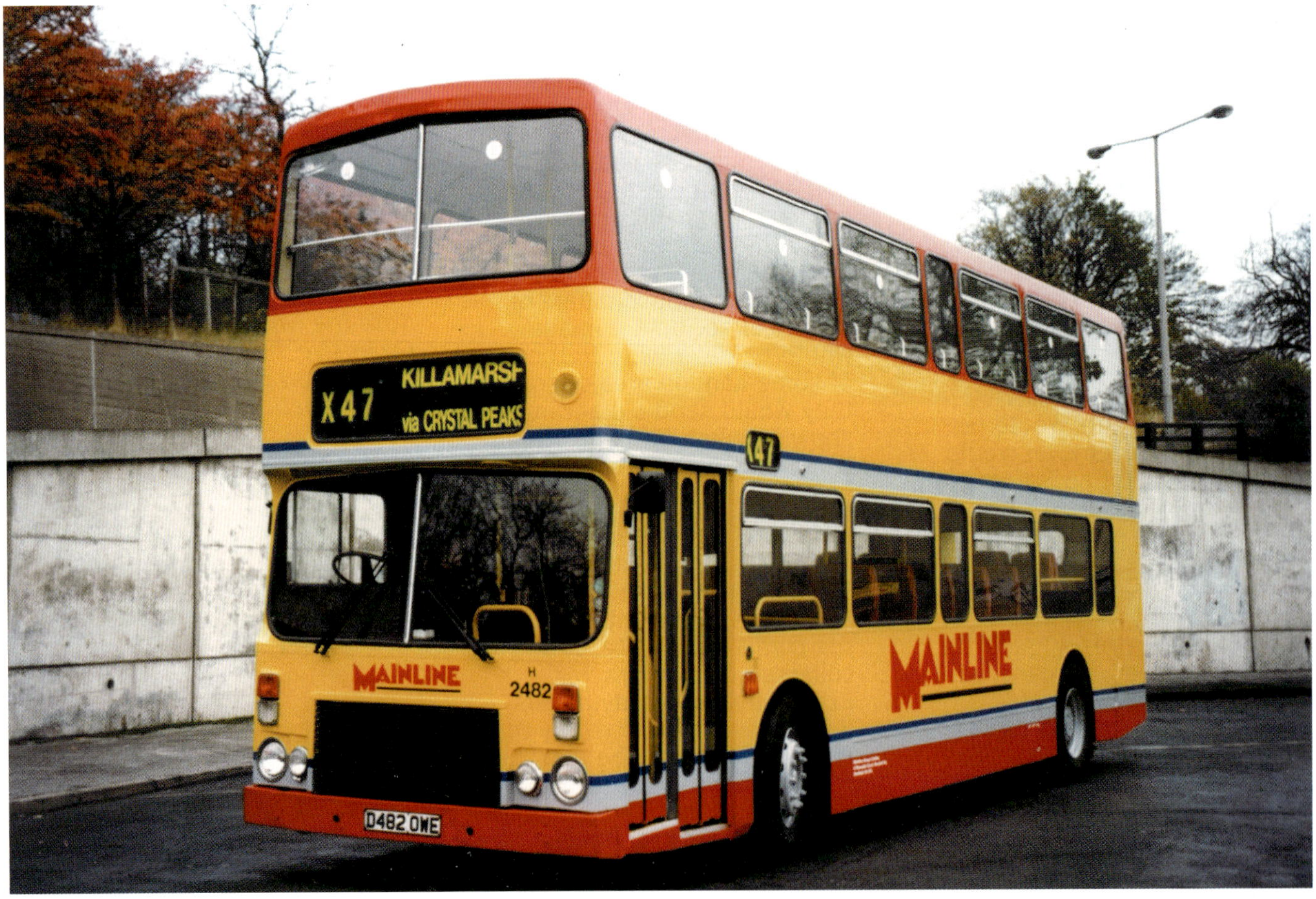
X47 KILLAMARSH via CRYSTAL PEAKS
X47
MAINLINE
H
2482
MAINLINE
D482 OWE

In some cases, involving hard to find fibreglass items, or a collision repair required new items to be made, the fibreglass shop at Greenland garage would be called on to assist, both in skill and timesaving for the unit.

Once all stripping had been completed, both internally and externally, a new plywood floor would be installed and a new floor covering laid, which in some cases included new side walls. Heaters would be refitted and plumbed in, and seat frames, which had either been repainted, or in most cases powder coated along with handrails by a contractor, would be fitted and generally the vehicle completed as each team finished their task.

In house painting was carried out by using the traditional brush painting method using a separate paint preparation area. Each vehicle would be dealt with by a two person team, using machine sanders. In the case of Routemasters from London, such was the thickness of the paint around the windows, a partial paintstrip would be required, but generally a vehicle would have a machine sand and wash.

Most vehicles in the commercial unit would be dealt with in the Greenland or Rotherham paintshops, where on average, two painters would set about masking up and undercoating the vehicle, which would generally take a week to complete, including fitting of vinyls. On completion, the vehicle would go back to the bodyshop to have a variety of finishing tasks carried out, seat squabs refitted, lights wired in, new mirrors, and any other snagging work, before a final inspection and clean ready for return to the vehicle.

The traffic control measures introduced to Doncaster, had caused a drop in patronage of 8%, and was out of step with the rest of the business, which was now stable, or in growth. That had economic consequences for Dunscroft garage, which was to close by the end of October, moving its operations into Doncaster. The site, now released back to SYPTA Properties, was sold for housing.

This garage had long been treated like a family business, and it was with some regret that conditions outwith Mainline's control, had forced its demise.

Further service changes had been planned for the autumn. Powells, an operator which had generally kept to schools and private hire work, had entered the fray, with a competitive service to Dinnington via Whiston. Mainline responded by registering service 129 in front of the interloper. Service 143 in Rotherham, only recently introduced to serve the huge Kimberworth Park estate and connect it with Meadowhall, was strengthened with a new timetable. A new X46 was registered in competition with Yorkshire Terrier, a newcomer called Aston Express, on the Killamarsh corridor, via Woodhouse, which would eventually become a bigger network via the Mosborough Parkway.

Service 13 in Sheffield was extended across the city centre to Heeley Green, Meersbrook and Hollythorpe Rise, replacing double deck service 38, and giving a low floor service to the area. This reduced the overall frequency of services 13/14 to but there had been a drop in patronage due to Supertram. This was also part of a plan to deal with the old 34/8/9 combine, which was a heavy loss maker.

Opposite and Above

The refurbishment of the dual purpose Dominators was more than just a cosmetic change.

Seen in the workshops at Olive Grove, 2474 and 2490 are receiving major structural repairs, which included a new rear end frame as well as flooring. This was in addition to new seats and complete interior refit.

2482, allocated to Halfway, is seen in the 'as finished' state, and was effectively, a new bus.

Olive Grove engineering also undertook accident repairs that didn't warrant a visit to the Commercial Unit.

2240 is seen being given a new front end on the 'long' pits.

Above

New entrants were never extravagant on vehicle policy, but it could be said that Powells was going for the lowest common denominator.

A pair of Leyland Nationals await further competitive activity in Rotherham Interchange.

Aston Express entered the fray with this quaint AEC Reliance. To the enthusiast, this was a great opportunity to ride a vintage vehicle, but did it really further the goals of public transport? Eckington Bus Station is the location.

The most profitable part, to Hollythorpe Rise, had been incorporated into the 13, but the individual 'legs' of the remainder of the combine, required a complex pattern of route diversions. Some areas, such as Firshill Crescent, got a better level of service, increaseing from every 30 to every 20 minutes with revised services 33 and 34, but some dropped to hourly. No area was left unserved, but the inevitable outcry was loud, and carried enthusiastically by the local press.

A valiant attempt to run the remnants of Sheffield's works special services commercially was also cut back to a remaining rump numbered 469 and 470. Although a Saturday service, and frequency enhancements had been tried, there just wasn't enough business to sustain anything but a peak hour operation.

In Doncaster, a new service 75 was commenced to the Yorkshire Outlet from the town centre, providing a daily service, replacing service X78 on Sunday. To operate this, a further two Volvo B6LEs (451 and 452) were purchased, fitted out to the same specification as previous buses of this type, but were painted in an overall advert for the centre. Lakeside was now a growing shopping, business and residential area of the town, and services were to be expanded through it, over the coming years.

Wayfarer III ticket machines were rolled out to Sheffield and Rotherham from October, finally catching up with Doncaster, who'd had them for two years already. This time, however, no magnetic card readers were purchased, and those fitted to the buses used on service 60 and 97 were removed. Mainline, as part of its bid to operate Supertram, had mooted integrated ticketing arrangements, and didn't want to specify a product that wouldn't be able to be integrated to both modes of travel. Doncaster continued to use their card readers.

The Director's made it known to the Board that two things should be provided. Firstly, a Credit Union should be provided for all employees. Secondly, a new pension scheme should be set up to mirror the former LGPS, since new employees were now unable to join that.

Each was achieved. Transave (the Credit Union) has continued to this day, with over 14000 members, and is the fifth largest in the UK. This scheme is also now available to members of the Police, NHS and other businesses. The driving force behind that was Dave Edwards and Charlie Clark.

The Mainline pension scheme continued until the takeover by FirstGroup and was absorbed as an exemplary scheme.

Another year of improvement had seen passenger numbers finally start to rise in some areas and helped produce a profit, in the year ending April 1996 of £2 million. That's not bad, but still not good enough for the banks and finance houses, that were looking at nearer £8 million.

Clockwise from Top Left

Hello and goodbye. To launch new service 75 in Doncaster, a further pair of Wright bodied Volvo B6s were purchased. Seen here at the Yorkshire Outlet, John Swann, and assorted guests, do the obligatory photo call.

Several marques of chassis left the fleet during the year. The final Atlantean, National and Iveco were taken off fleet strength.

1773, nominally a school bus vehicle, is seen in Flat Street, Sheffield. Nationals 27 and 881 are seen in Sheffield Interchange and Waingate and Iveco 257 is seen in Hyde Park, Doncaster.

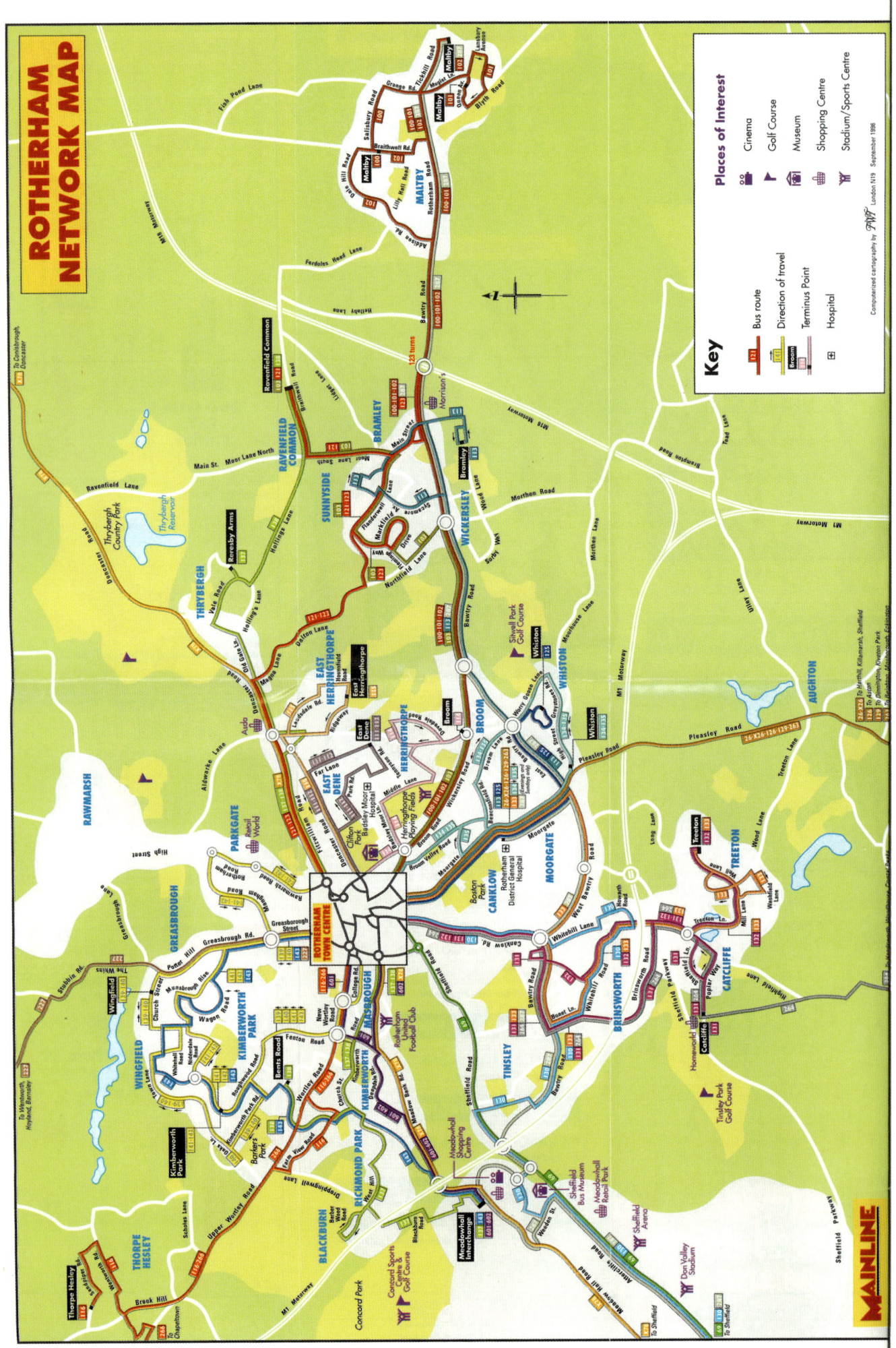

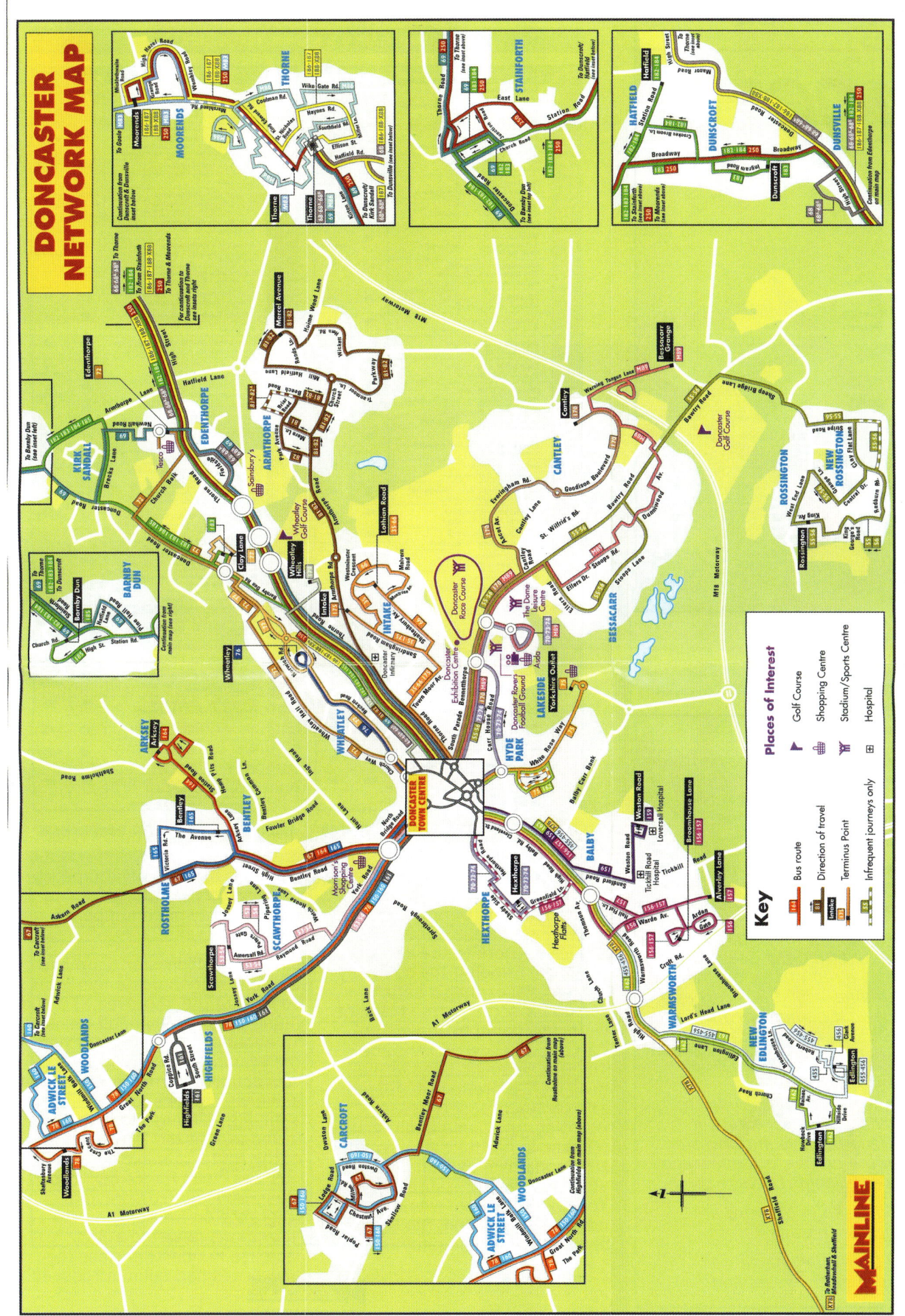

Chapter 12

1997

Above

The Don Valley licence had been used for a potential competitive battle in Ipswich, but was mainly known for low cost tendered operation in Sheffield.

Efforts were made to modernise the fleet, and get it looking similar to the rest of the group.

Mercedes 75, which had been inherited from the Beenak days, carries a red variant of the fleetname, whilst 228 carries a somewhat homemade looking variant in green. Both pictured in Sheffield's former markets area.

The licence was next used to purchase the operations of Wilfreda Beehive in Doncaster. With the purchase, came some modern Dennis Darts.

506 is seen in the yard at Doncaster garage.

The Don Valley name was phased out by years end.

The competitive battle in Doncaster was finally coming to a conclusion. Wilfreda Beehive, who had been scaling back their operation, under severe competition from Mainline, indicated that it wanted to go back to being a premium coach, and holiday, operator.

Mainline made an offer for the services and eight, modern, Plaxton bodied, Dennis Darts. With it came a substantial service network to the north of the town, bringing the company back to places that it hadn't served for some years. Mainline were now going to serve all of Carcroft, Skellow, Askern and Toll Bar. Also included in the deal, were a group of tendered and commercial services in Barnsley, and some additional mileage in north Nottinghamshire. Handily, this also increased pressure on Yorkshire Traction, who were now, via acquisition, the largest competitor the company had.

The change was scheduled for March, but a further service change would be required in the summer to review the competitive network that had built up, and tailor it accordingly.

Powells had also decided to throw the towel in on services around Rotherham, and was also planning to come off competitive journeys in the spring, leaving them with a small number of tendered routes.

Mainline's Doncaster team had also invested in passenger surveys of the improved X78 and found surprisingly good results. To enhance the service further, the evening and Sunday service was doubled in frequency, and in a similar practice to the railways, a mobile valeting service was introduced at the Doncaster end of the route, to make sure each bus was clean for its next trip. This also included spraying fragrance on the vehicle. The alterations reflected a 33% increase in ridership since the new buses had been introduced.

A fly in the ointment was Aston Express. This company, which had been created by two former members of the Yorkshire Terrier management, had folded, but had been rescued, reformed, and had now decided to compete against Mainline and Stagecoach on a small number of routes. In Sheffield, they targeted the 75, 76, 81 and 253, whilst also operating a 99 between Crystal Peaks and Chesterfield. Mainline responded by setting up a special 'hit squad' of buses and drivers to run on top of their services.

Mainline was still awaiting the results of the competitive tender to operate Supertram, but was now enlisting its advice to a group bidding to operate a similar service in Nottingham, teaming up with McAlpine and Ansaldo. In the event, the tender went to a group headed by Nottingham City Transport.

Above

Effective advertising for the X78 targeted car users, as seen on 745 and 747, was so successful, the timetable required constant improvement to cope with loadings.

The service wasn't an express, but good marketing gave that impression. Eventually, the frequency maxed out at every 10 minutes.

Above

Aston Express was reformed and after a while running niche minibus services, it then, after a change of ownership, moved onto frequent city services, which required the use of the 'hit squad'.

One of Aston's, Alexander bodied S56s is seen in Eckington Bus Station while 'hit squad' Dominator 2106, also carrying an advert livery for Talking Pages, is seen in Sheffield.

Two final Volvo B6 low floor buses arrived for the opening of Millhouses Tesco. Funded by the supermarket, in later life they would see service with other operators.

454 is seen in the newly constructed bus stop at the centre.

A further two Volvo B6LEs with Wrightbus bodies (454 and 455) were ordered for a new 'Park and Ride' service, based on the new Tesco superstore, at Millhouses. In the peaks, this would operate to and from the city centre. Between the peaks, these buses would operate on a network of free bus services to the store, from surrounding areas. The buses were delivered with standard Mainline interiors, but were painted allover blue, with red and white Tesco lettering, as they owned them. This mini network was provided for with a small, dedicated pool of drivers, who after a while, noticed that people were also using the service for the nearby Sainsbury's store as well.

A similar free bus, operated with Renault S56s had operated for Morrisons' new store in Ecclesfield, but after a short period, they withdrew funding, and used the money to advertise on ASO buses, whose garage was virtually next door to the store.

Further work on the Bawtry Road corridor had been undertaken, and was now at an advanced stage, with both road and other infrastructure improvements, planned and costed. The £3 million scheme would also enable real time information to be provided and traffic light priority to be given. However, legal wrangles meant that at best, work couldn't actually start 'on the ground' until the spring of 1998. Mainline signed a Quality Corridor agreement with SYPTE, initially promising to allocate Volvo B10Ms to the Maltby corridor, and potentially ordering low floor buses for the route, as and when the work was completed.

A trial also took place with an LPG powered, Northern Counties, bodied DAF. This was proposed as one form of bus for the Quality Corridor, and was used for three weeks to demonstrate Mainline's commitment to the project. At the time, new technology was expensive to operate and purchase, and if gas buses were to be introduced, a sizeable Government grant would be required to install the specialist fueling and servicing equipment at Rotherham garage.

The biggest ticket launch for some time occurred in February. The '60 minute Switcha' (which very quickly entered the local lexicon as plain 'Switcha') was a new transfer style ticket, modelled on continental practice. The ticket, once purchased, allowed as many journeys as possible within an hour (that's from the time the journey started, rather than the total duration), by simply showing it to the driver, to check validity. The enthusiast fraternity boasted about how many different buses they could board within the 60 minutes.

To raise awareness, a major promotion drive was undertaken, with buses being fitted with vinyls, news boards and for the initial few days, balloons were also fitted inside the buses. Backed up with press and radio advertising, using local celebrity Tony Capstick, it was an instant success. The launch price was £1, and this effectively capped the maximum fare, meaning the very ends of the network were recipients of a fare cut. By the end of the first sales period, they were selling at a rate of 45,000 a week, and by June they were at 64,000.

Hot on the heels of the 'Switcha' was a new 'Group All Day Saver'. Any four people could now travel together, all day, for just £4. Again, instantly successful, both of these tickets helped the company gain additional market share from its competitors.

A new promotion was also launched for concessionary passengers called 'Collect and Travel'. In an era where free travel is now the norm, at that point in time, concessionary fare holders still had to make a contribution to their journey. By collecting bus tickets, the applicant could exchange these for free 'Saver' products, ranging from one day to one month.

Engineering's initiative was called 'Business Process Re-engineering'. That mouthful was shortened to 'Pit Stop'. This was a new way of dealing with servicing, inspecting (VEX) and annual testing (MOT) vehicles.

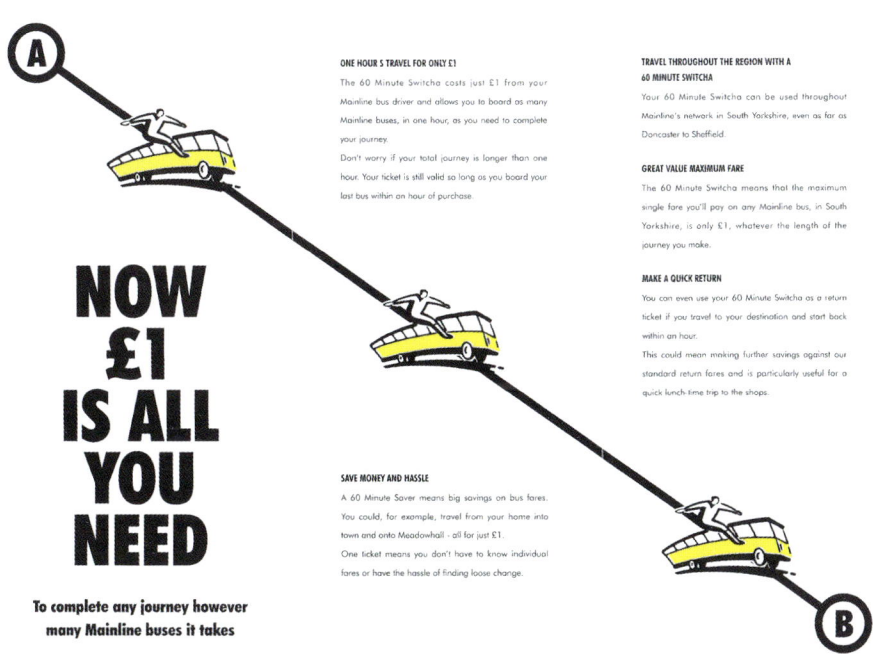

Above

The Bawtry Road improvement works finally commenced and thoughts were given about the type of vehicle to be used on it.

This Northern Counties bodied, LPG fuelled, DAF, was exhibited and used in service on the busy Maltby corridor, but costs for conversion were prohibitive.

Above

The 52 was a busy service, but passengers were not normally encouraged to ride on the roof!

619 was outshopped in this attractive livery for Sheffield Children's Hospital, and is being launched by Peter Sephton and representatives for the charity involved.

A good relationship had been built up with the Go Ahead group, and the company won a major order for the refurbishment of Go North East's fleet of Leyland Nationals.

Fresh out of the workshops, this example shows off its new 'split step' at Rotherham garage.

The principle was based on Formula 1 techniques, where following an inspection, vehicles stayed in service until parts and labour were in the right place to do the job. The engineers had spent quite a lot of 1996 working out what would be required to get a trial up and running. Surveying all grades of staff, they made changes to stores holdings and facilities to cope.

The initial trial was to be held at Greenland, and an area beside the MOT testing bay was identified and suitably equipped, which included new lighting, tools, lifts and heating. Three engineering fitters volunteered to be part of the trial. Using this technique, a vehicle fault could be identified, parts ordered, the correct grade of staff allocated and space made available, at the most effective time, most likely, a bus working a part day duty.

In the past, individual craftsman had to find their own tools, order parts and fill in paperwork. This had now been swept away, with specialist members of administration staff now doing those roles, leaving the craftsman to get on with the job in hand. The plan, if it worked, would enable the company to reduce its spare margin, which would significantly lower costs, meaning a better return on investment.

The final Unit 52 Volvo B10M (619) came out of the refurbishment programme, being specially painted in an overall advert for the Sheffield Children's Hospital Appeal. As the service passed the front door of the building, a large 'Get Well Soon' was painted on the roof of the vehicle. This bus differed from the rest, as the seats were clad in a new, vinyl version, of the 'red caterpillar' moquette. It also had slightly orange hand poles, in an effort to cure reflections at night, in the cab.

The commercial unit had won a significant contract to refurbish and repaint all Go North East's fleet of Leyland Nationals. Work included, new floors, new wiring and a complete repanel and repaint. They had also won a contract, from FirstBus owned, Centrewest, to refurbish and repaint 31 minibuses that would eventually move to Glasgow.

Service changes were made in the spring, seeing the first proper withdrawal of Dennis Dominators out of the fleet, except for accident casualties or the examples sold to Capital Citybus three years earlier. Most of these went for further use, with three going to sister company Northern Bus, one to Isle Coaches, but a significant number making the trip to Scotland to work for Allison Coaches in Dunfermline.

At the same time, a large cut was made to the number of minibuses required in Doncaster, as some services were converted back to single/double deck operation, as the integration process from the Wilfreda services take over worked through.

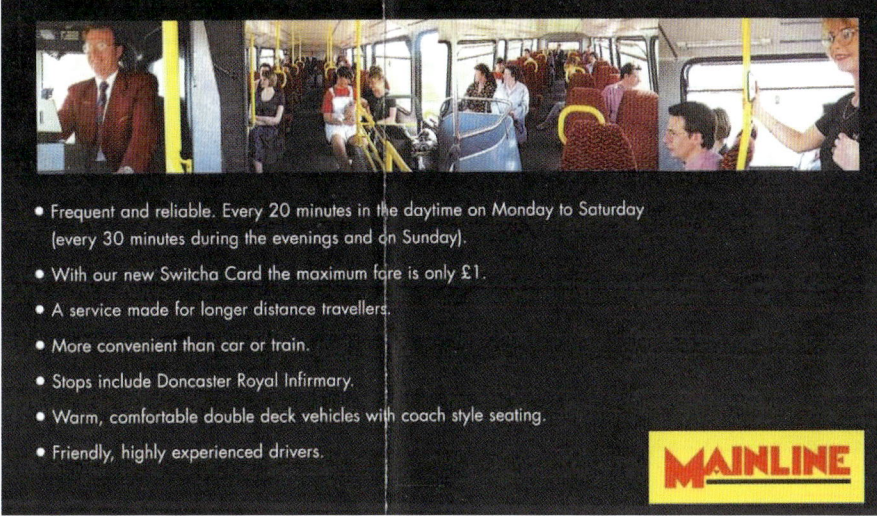

The ex Wilfreda services were operated on the Don Valley Buses licence. This being seen as a requirement, should the MMC or OFT object to this course of action. Initially, the seven Darts were numbered 4000 to 4007, but some were renumbered in the 500 series.

Doncaster also took the opportunity to try the 'Xpress' concept on service X88 to Goole. Five, new refurbished, former Fastline, Dennis Dominators, and two Volvo B10Ms, were given special branding, and fares offers, including 'Switcha' were available.

The Doncaster change contained the now, seemingly annual, pattern of alteration to services on the Thorne Road corridor, which led to changes to services 179 and services 175 and 176 being replaced by new service 35 and alterations to service 66. These were now operated by a combination of minibuses and Volvo B6s released from the Armthorpe services, by converting those to single/double deck operation. Part of the Rossington service was diverted via West Bessacarr at all times, replacing service 171, which had previously been the case in the evenings and on Sundays.

Wrapped up around this change, one of the largest since deregulation, was a free, public holiday service on the Spring Bank Holiday Monday. Buses were free from start of service until 1600hrs on that day, within the borough, in association with local traders and the Council. Loadings were up by 36%, compared to a normal public holiday, and a prize draw was held for gifts and experiences in the town.

Above

The X88 was relaunched with refurbished Dominators and nearly new Volvo B10Ms.

Aiming to replicate the success of the X78, this was also part of a rationalisation scheme, now that Mainline's biggest competitor in the town had gone.

2472 is seen in Hatfield on its way to Sandtoft Trolleybus Museum, whilst 750 is seen resting in the town.

The refurbished Dominators in Doncaster differed from those for Sheffield in retaining high backed seating in the upper saloon.

Above

Swansong for the Tigers, as two of the former Sheafline Leyland's were reactivated from reserve.

62 was sent to Rotherham to operate service 400, seen departing Meadowhall with a load which was quite normal, and hence uneconomic, for this service.

1001 went to Greenland to operate educational tours.

This was all part of a scheme to attract passengers to visit Doncaster again, after the somewhat negative reaction to its traffic management scheme. It was so successful, that it was repeated on the August bank holiday.

Rotherham introduced a new service 400 between Meadowhall, Swallownest and Crystal Peaks, also serving the new Sheffield City Airport, built on the site of the former Tinsley Park steelworks.

The Whiston network was also revised, with further changes taken to make the network here more viable.

Services 501 and 502 in Sheffield had seen a drop off in patronage, due to competition with tram and from the revised service X78, which despite serving the same stops, was seen as being faster. In order to stop the rot, and increase the number of passengers travelling (to the south, the route was in competition with ASO service 72 to Jordanthorpe and Batemoor), new vinyls were fitted, and the service was branded 'Meadowhall Shuttle', playing on its ten minute frequency. This was the swansong for the Leyland DAB articulated buses, as they were now showing signs of age, and parts availability was expensive. On Sundays, the service operated with conventional single/double deck vehicles.

A special fares promotion was also introduced, which made it significantly cheaper than Supertram.

Once the work on the Unit 52 Volvos had finished, thoughts were turned to the final 14 original B10Ms based at Greenland. The rest of the 1990 batch, based at Doncaster, had been spruced up with new moquette and repaints, but something special was planned for twelve of the Sheffield buses (626 to 638); 639 was refurbished in a normal style to act as a spare.

Passenger research had been carried out for a long time by bus companies, and Mainline was no different. Some companies, like Trent Barton, had slavishly followed the views of existing and potential passengers, and had tailored their network accordingly. They were slightly different, as they weren't the major operator in Derby and Nottingham, but provided vital links into these centre's from towns and villages surrounding them. That approach only partially worked in a metropolitan area.

Service 51 had long been a stalwart of the company, and had been upgraded to Mainline status in 1990. A fresh look at the timetable, based on customer needs, recognized that later journeys would be desirable and that they would welcome more leg room and on bus entertainment.

The mini refurbishment unit at Greenland got to work modifying the buses used on service 51. They were given a full exterior makeover, which included a new front bumper, alloy wheels, new livery and route branding, with a greater use of black than before. Internally, as well as being refloored, the buses had new Callow and Maddox seats, a standing pen as well as greater space for luggage. A radio system was fitted and tinted glass was placed in the windows. To finish the whole job off, new yellow hand poles and grab points were fitted. The investment was in the region of £120,000.

The whole treatment was referred to as 'Silver Service' and a marketing plan put in place, promoting the new look service.

Posters, press advertising and leaflet drops gave the new service a high profile.

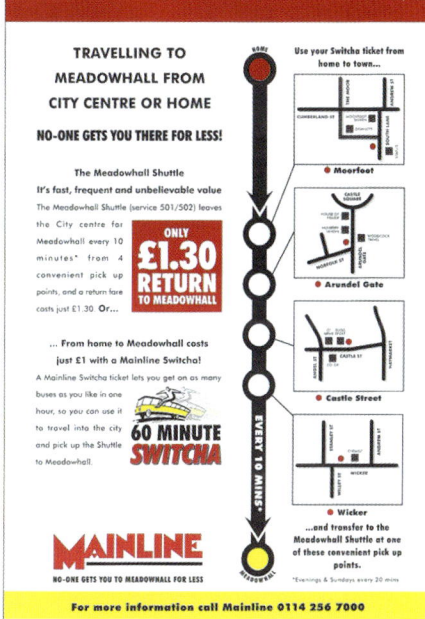

This was also backed up with reports on BBC's 'Look North' and Yorkshire Television's 'Calendar' magazine programmes, as well as free journey vouchers for the first month of the new service.

It certainly got the travelling public talking, and the figures for the service gradually increased. The radio system, however, proved to be a problem. Initially tuned to BBC Radio Sheffield, some staff had found ways to retune the radios to more 'robust' output, playing dance and house music, which wasn't particularly appreciated by the good burghers of Crosspool. It also had a tendency to latch on to electrical interference coming from the Supertram catenary, and was eventually turned off.

Above

The final rebrand for services 501/2 took the form of these pleasing vinyls attached during the year.

2007 is seen leaving the bus station at Meadowhall. Mainline had looked at refurbishing these buses for longer life, but after the takeover by First, these buses quickly became obsolete and were withdrawn.

Above

The refurbished Volvos for the 51 were completed in house, and the striking new look was completed using parts from Alexander, East Lancs and specially fabricated units from Mainline's central engineering facility. 626 is seen at Greenland garage.

First did not see the value of 'Silver Service' and relegated the buses to standard service. 636 is seen at a very frosty Olive Grove. The doors being left open can't have done anything for the ambience inside, for the customers.

In Rotherham, Mainline had kept a presence on the routes to Mexborough and Conisbrough from the town, right through the heart of Yorkshire Traction territory. The 298 was now extended from within Mexborough to the former Manvers Colliery site, which was now developing into a shopping and office park. Strengthening on service 143 between the Kimberworth estates and Meadowhall had seen the end to Northern Bus service 44 (which had been started by Richardson's way back in 1986) and a new service 230 was introduced between Meadowhall and Barnsley via Chapeltown and Birdwell, in direct competition with Yorkshire Traction. This was a former Tom Jowitt service.

Evening student travel had become big business, especially on Ecclesall Road in Sheffield. One of the main campus locations was Collegiate Crescent, roughly 1.5 miles from the city centre. In the evenings, and on Sunday, Mainline provided a bus every ten minutes along the corridor, but, the taxi trade had spotted a gap in the market. They had set up an illegal rank, a matter of yards away from a legal one, at the bottom of the street, frequently blocking the bus stop box. Ten minutes might not seem a long time to wait, but if theREs a group of students, then the cost is shared, making a taxi journey a viable option.

In response to this, three, former Aston Express Metroriders, were taken into the commercial unit and were prepared for a brave new experiment in bus travel. Bus Zero, aimed to be an extension to the night time experience. All the seats had been placed around the perimeter, and 'disco' style lighting was installed. The walls were covered in a chequerplate style material, and the windows were given a smoked glass effect using vinyl. Externally, the buses were painted overall silver with a simple '0' as a fleetname. No mention was made of Mainline, except in the legal lettering.

Controversially, which garnered many headlines in the local press (no publicity is bad publicity), they were also fitted with a contraceptive machine.

The headlines screamed about how Mainline was corrupting the youth and promoting promiscuity, but you could argue that Mainline was simply promoting good health practices. Considering most of the writers of these headlines had been brought up in the 'swinging sixties', the sense of irony was not lost.

Top

3011 was one of the MCW Metroriders that were converted for 'Bus Zero' use. They were additionally used on special services for walkers, as the floor covering could be easily cleaned of mud.

Below

The B10BLE was another cracker from Volvo, and Mainline took delivery of ten in late 1997, ordering 20 more for 1998.

They needed some modifications to the seating layout prior to entry into service.

786 is seen at Moorhead, Sheffield in spring 1998. Everything in these photos has been swept away for redevelopment.

The timetable and route was simple. From Hunters Bar, it operated via a loop serving West Street and the majority of the city centre's pubs and clubs. For a 50p fare, it was significantly cheaper than taking a taxi, and a small band of drivers were specially picked to operate this every night from Wednesday to Saturday. Initially, the 'Helping Hands' squad was brought in to distribute publicity, although on launch night, the company managed to get actor Stephen Lewis, who had played 'Blakey' in LWT's 'On The Buses' television programme to help out.

The drivers, amongst themselves, worked out tactics to outflank the taxi trade, by sometimes sitting an extra minute or two at the best stops, or encouraging people to board the bus instead of any taxi.

Whilst a novel idea, it was difficult to compete with the flexibility of the taxi trade, and Mainline did look at investing in a fleet of taxis for its own use.

As part of a continuing theme, albeit a separate contract, Mainline also took on a new night bus network from the 'Pulse' and 'Vogue' entertainment centre that had recently opened on Attercliffe Common. Sheffield's nightlife was booming, with people coming from as far afield as Nottingham, Derby, Bradford and Leeds for a night out. This new club complex was some way outside of the central area, and it was quickly realised by its management, Rank Leisure, that its success would not be assured, unless it had decent transport links. Getting to the venue wasn't a problem during 'normal' hours as services 69, 130 and 287 passed the door, with Supertram not being far away, but when it as early hours of the morning, there was nothing.

Initially the contract was for twenty buses, but this was quickly increased, with buses being used to go to Doncaster etc. A volunteer group of drivers were used, and a number of buses were fitted with stereo systems and loudspeakers. At the same time, measures were taken to refresh the night bus network in the city, usage of which had dropped dramatically in the face of deregulated taxi competition.

On 1 December, Mainline learned that it had been unsuccessful in its bid to operate the Supertram franchise. The winning bidder had been Stagecoach, who had offered to take on the network, without subsidy, which was not something Mainline had offered. Immediately, nothing changed, although it was anticipated that Stagecoach would want to operate competing services, or offer feeders to make Supertram profitable, or at least, cover its costs. The winning bid only covered the rights to operate the system, with the infrastructure being retained by the PTE.

The only new buses of the year arrived in December. Ten, Wrightbus bodied, Volvo B10BLEs arrived at Olive Grove. Initially they were destined for the Maltby corridor in Rotherham, but as that was nowhere near being ready, they were sent to Sheffield instead.

They arrived in a modified version of Mainline livery, incorporating elements of the 'Silver Service' livery from service 51. Internally, they were decked out in the, by now standard, grey, red and yellow style. They did require a number of alterations prior to entering service, mainly around seat pitch, and spent most of December being prepared for service. They were placed into service on route 60 in Sheffield and on the 3 and 4 Millhouses circular services, although in the evenings and on Sunday they could also be seen on service 50 to Dore.

Vinyls were late being delivered, so for the first week of operation, they did so without fleetnames. A small problem was encountered on Springfield Road in Millhouses, as the new buses tended to ground, due to a hump in the road. Drivers were instructed to use the 'ferry' lift at this location. They were also retrofitted with the same stereo system as on service 51, but the same problems were encountered, and it was eventually turned off.

These buses were powerful, and quickly became firm favourites of the driving staff. A deal had been negotiated, if for any reason Mainline had become unable to keep up with the finance payments on these buses, they would pass to FirstBus, although that would become a moot point, within seven months.

The year ended with a sense of quiet anticipation as to what Stagecoach would do with their new acquisition. It had been a year where Yorkshire Traction had become the main focus for attack, and it seemed like Mainline was winning. The year ended April 1997 produced a profit of £685,000, although lower than the previous year, reflected high fleet investment and consolidation purchases, which improved the balance sheet.

Above

Bus adverts were still big business, and in the days before vinyl, were painted on. 2232 is in Olive Grove; 2276 & 2358 in Doncaster.

Chapter 13
1998

This Page

Rear end transfers had been removed from vehicles to enable the space between decks for advertising (Mainline used Decker Media, co owned with Nottingham City Transport).

A yellow vinyl, fitted above the rear window was trialled on a number of buses, but it was discontinued.

A study of rear ends at Olive Grove garage yard has bus 2245 in our focus.

A bizarre by product of the Mainline ESOP, was some of the covenants that been added to the sales process. Some of these were standard fare that had also been levied on other former PTA owned bus companies. These included a guaranteed level of service, fleet size, network coverage etc. They also included clawback clauses on extra profits the company made.

The PTA had also included a clause which limited the amount of money the company could borrow to replace its fleet. This benefitted the PTA, as the majority of the fleet was leased from it, but negatively affected the age profile for the company and its passengers. Mainline had realised that it had to replace a significant proportion of the Dennis Dominator fleet in the coming years, and just using profits, and existing loans alone, would equate to just 30 buses per year.

Mainline requested that the PTA removed this covenant, making the company able to secure finance to replace the fleet at a more acceptable level (around 80 to 100 buses per annum).

Being good business sense, it would also reduce the age profile of the fleet, and provide a better customer environment, as well as lowering engineering costs. The PTA decided, in their wisdom, to refuse this request, claiming that Mainline would use this ability to get additional finance, to compete with Supertram.

The PTA had now been left with the debt for building the tram network, and this was causing significant headaches for the authority, which was now looking at options on refinancing (in the event, the Government wrote off £80 million worth of costs, leaving a small fraction to be paid by the local councils). This is outwith the scope of this book, but it did have an effect on Mainline as the PTE was now applying pressure to the company to take more work on commercially, or the PTE would withdraw the tenders the mileage it was based on. In addition, the PTE raised the concessionary fare to 35p per single journey, which caused a small decrease in passengers.

Above

Over a third of the fleet was made up of Dennis Dominators built between 1981 and 1986.

Although well maintained, they were beginning to show their age, and withdrawals started in earnest in 1998.

2168 is climbing up one of Sheffield's seven hills towards Commonside, 2292 is at Sheaf Square and 2433 is pictured at Meadowhall, with the famous Tinsley Towers visible in the distance.

It had been proven that when the fleet had been invested in, passenger numbers had risen. Service 51, which was now operated with refurbished Volvo B10Ms, was showing a rise in patronage of 6% in the first six months of the new timetable being in place, with up to a 12% increase in evening passengers. The buses on the 51 had now been fitted with Garmin GPS tracking systems, to enable real time information to be collated and used to plan improvements. The 51 only competed with Supertram on a small corridor of the route, so these additional customers had come from other operators or from car users attracted back to using the service.

A small batch of, Plaxton bodied, Dennis Dart SLFs had been received on loan from FirstGroup (as it had now been renamed), to test the viability of these vehicles in Sheffield service. Painted in overall red (they were initially meant for Glasgow), they had recently seen service in York, and carried fleet numbers in the 3000 range, used by First's, Yorkshire Rider, operation.

They were fitted internally with the new First corporate scheme of purple, grey and turquoise, which was pleasing on the eye. They were used throughout the operating patch, mainly at Greenland and Halfway. They were the precursor to the arrival of a trial Dennis Dart SPD (Super Pointer Dart) which was a full length version of the model.

Above

Innovations such as that on service 51, brought a renewed sense of optimism, and proved to the Board, that continued investment, brought passenger growth.

Steve Arnold, Mainline's Marketing Manager, shows off the refurbished interior, being rolled out on service 51. The radios were soon removed.

The first evidence of help from outside came with these Plaxton bodied, low floor Dennis Darts.

They stayed for a short time, but operated from Halfway and Greenland garage. 3315 is seen in the company of 2459 in

Anybody wishing that PTEs, and the like, had their hands on the operation of bus services, may like to take note, that no thought was placed on how these actions would affect the well being of the average passenger.

Before Stagecoach took on the franchise, the tram operating company was losing between £4.5 and £6 million a year on direct operations, not all of that could be laid at the door of Mainline. Legal advice, and action was being considered by the company at the start of the year, but in the meantime, there was still competitive battles to be won, and fleet enhancements to be made.

The silver prototype operated on service 51, and had a restyled front end, which made the design more modern for the new millennium. If a bus can survive service 51, it can survive anywhere, and the company ordered a batch of 20 for early delivery. This fleet of buses was earmarked for operation on the Rotherham to Maltby corridor, but the Quality Corridor still hadn't been finished, meeting with considerable public opposition in the Broom and Wickersley areas.

In addition, an order was placed for a batch of 16, Plaxton bodied, Mercedes Vario midibuses, as an effort to rid the fleet of some of the aging fleet of Renault S56s.

The Varios were used to remove conventional buses from the 70, 71 and 711 group of services by reforming it as two different routes. Supertram, and the removal of the tower blocks at Norfolk Park, had a detrimental effect on the finances of this group of services.

The section of service 711 between the city centre and Parson Cross was withdrawn, replaced by frequency enhancements on service 97. The section between the city centre and Darnall, via Attercliffe, was replaced by a new service 6, which then continued via the Bowden Wood and Littledale estates, in a loop back to Darnall. The section between Darnall and the city centre was replaced by a new service 7 which was now the main service from Prince of Wales Road to the city via Norfolk Park.

Some overcrowding was experienced in the peaks, and conventional single deck buses had to be substituted on to service 7 after a short while, displacing the Varios on to service 64, which now operated to Manor Top and Herdings, being displaced by service 51 in Charnock.

The Varios, which started to be delivered in April, looked good, bedecked in the usual Mainline livery and internal specification. However, the bodies were somewhat heavy for the chassis, and this led to problems with cracks appearing in stress plates and members. Throughout their life with the company, significant programmes of repair and rectification were performed to get a satisfactory lifespan out of the vehicles.

Clockwise from Top Left

The new Dennis Dart SPD was trialled and ordered by Mainline. The demonstrator, seen here in Rotherham garage, was later used on service 51.

The Mercedes Benz Varios looked the part, but continuing bodywork issues caused problems throughout the vehicles life.

132, and colleagues are seen for an official photo shoot and 133 is seen running light in the Wicker, Sheffield.

Above

Now you see it, now you don't.

The purchase of Charlotte Road garage was made in the early part of the year after the original purchaser failed to get planning permission.

The site was levelled, but what was the purpose of buying the land? All would be revealed to the workforce as the year progressed.

In Sheffield, a new bus gate had been opened in Heeley on St. Ann's Road. This short thoroughfare, behind Heeley City Farm, had been fitted with bollards, that could be lowered by transponders fitted to buses 400 and 441 to 449, operating on service 13. In the past, this area had been covered with terraced houses, but had been bulldozed in the 1970s for a motorway project that never actually (thankfully) got off the ground. Some redevelopment had taken place, and in the peaks, it become a bottle neck for traffic.

The bollards were part of a wider traffic management plan for this area, and the high profile service 13, with its quality vehicles, was seen as being key to persuading more people out of their cars. As with all new technology, things didn't go exactly to plan. The bollards would occasionally stay in the upright position, meaning buses then had to reverse out into oncoming traffic. Despite signs, yellow lines and lights, some motorists took the bollards to mean that the street was closed, and often parked in front of them. In addition, the steering lock on the B6s wasn't the best, and it took some effort to rejoin the main carriageway when leaving the road.

An effort was made to restore some sense of order to the north Doncaster network as competition with Yorkshire Traction was scaled back. A new coordinated network was now offered, although without combined ticketing. The new network worked for both companies, as it reduced their respective PVR requirements.

Yorkshire Traction withdrew from operating on the hospital corridor. In later years, the whole network would be abandoned by Yorkshire Traction after being purchased by Stagecoach, leaving virtually all Doncaster's buses in the hands of one operators.

One idea, that was progressed so far as to have vinyls and publicity produced, was a special promotion on 'Saver' tickets. There was now a number of special promotional seven day versions in circulation across the operating territory. As the company still didn't know what Stagecoach had got planned for Supertram, and to best protect its revenue and passenger base, a new £4.95 ticket was to be introduced, in each area, from the end of February. This would sweep away all the promotional offers, but for travel across the local authority areas, a 'super' version would still be required.

In the event, this never actually took place. Negotiations were opened with Stagecoach, who at this time wanted to collaborate with Mainline, rather than compete. In order to cement the deal, the 'Switcha' product was now made available on both operators services, with each partner keeping the revenue they took for selling it. This had the same effect on Supertram as it did on Mainline, effectively capping the maximum fare. It was a Mainline product, and therefore, and price changes would be made by the company. The price on announcement of the deal was £1.25.

On the back of their purchase, and similar to what they had done with other bus operations they had purchased, Stagecoach reduced the price of their Supertram weekly ticket to £4.95. That made Mainline's, all encompassing ticket seem expensive at £8.95, although the network reach was much wider. This was also competed for by ASO/Yorkshire Terrier's 'Bus Card' at £5. At this time it was decided to continue to offer discounted tickets on certain routes, but the option to roll out a full weekly ticket, for less than a fiver, was still actively available for deployment.

Two purchases had been made by the company during the start of the year. The first involved bricks and mortar in the shape of Charlotte Road garage. The former SUT site had been sold to a developer, but when they couldn't get planning permission to develop the site, it reverted to SYPTA properties.

The second involved Northern Bus. In May, the fleet of buses required for general service work would be absorbed by Mainline, leaving a smaller company that would operate school buses and supply engineering services to other bus companies.

Above

The purchase of Northern Bus reunited former members of the Mainline fleet, as well as bringing in an assorted bunch of Nationals and Metroriders, the former staying only briefly.

Dominator '2115' is leaving Meadowhall, National 29 is seen at Halfway, and a gaggle of Metroriders find solace in the top park at Olive Grove.

Above

We are the management. The new owners of Mainline quickly replaced the existing management team, and installed a refreshed Board.

From left to right we have Bernard Keane, Martin Wilson, Ray O'Toole and Ian Davies.

Only Bernard and Ian had survived from the previous Mainline Board.

This company was to be called MASS, and would eventually morph into the largest school bus operator in the county using ex Mainline Dennis Dominators and London Leyland Titans.

Mainline took on all the Northern Bus network, bringing the company back to Dinnington, and also gaining territory to places it hadn't operated in a long time such as Holmesfield, Huddersfield, Penistone, Worksop and Leeds. Mainline took a few vehicles with the purchase, including the Dominators only recently sold to them. The fleet was split between Olive Grove, Rotherham, Halfway and Greenland. The Dominators were destined for the training fleet, having been converted to Gardner engines at Northern Bus. A few elderly Nationals were placed in service at Rotherham and the minibus fleet of Metroriders went to Olive Grove for Inner Circle services 8 and 9.

Northern Bus had also ordered eleven Dennis Dart SPDs, and these were added to Mainline's batch at Plaxtons, having their specification altered to match accordingly. Part of the Northern Bus batch was supposed to relaunch the X32 service to Leeds. The service was instead subcontracted to be operated by First Leeds instead.

Only the Metroriders ever made it into Mainline livery, as it was announced in June, that Mainline had received an approach to purchase the company, by FirstGroup, in an offer that valued it at £44.2 million. That was split into £24.7 million in FirstGroup shares, £5 million in cash and £14 million to go to SYPTA to release Mainline from all its existing caveats and liabilities, including leasing agreements. That offer was accepted by the shareholders in Mainline Partnership Limited and was formally completed on 10 July 1998, although launch day was the 13th.

The previous board of Mainline departed, with Peter Sephton and Mike Pestereff opting to take early retirement. Ian Davies and Bernard Keane were reappointed as Directors for the new Mainline operating unit, within FirstGroup, as Managing Directors for Sheffield and Rotherham/Doncaster respectively, joined by a new Finance Director, Martin Wilson. A new Engineering Director, Andy Campbell, also joined from West Yorkshire. Mainline was now part of a new, Yorkshire, regional structure which was overseen by Ray O'Toole. To many people, it looked like it had been taken over by the old Yorkshire Rider.

There were also changes at garage level with Gary Nolan returning from Stagecoach as General Manager for Olive Grove (although he quickly became Managing Director for the entire company as Ian Davies was despatched to become Regional Director for Yorkshire and Bernard Keane left for Volvo). Bert Middleton went to Halfway, Bob Hamilton went to Greenland (he had previously joined from Northern Bus), Graham Willis went to Rotherham with John Swann at Doncaster. Peter Sephton's former P.A., Barbara Bedford became Divisional Marketing and Development Manager, eventually going on to group level, being the driving force behind the FTR project.

There was some disquiet about the new management, especially Mr O'Toole, and some employees were now wondering if sale was the correct course of action.

New 'buzzwords' were entering the company dictionary such as 'dynamic', 'demanding' and 'thriving' to describe certain managers. Mainline management was all of those things before, just more subtle about it, only shouting about their actual achievements.

In the days of the emerging 'supergroups', it would be inevitable that Mainline would have fallen to one of them. The level of profit generated by the company wasn't enough to satisfy finance houses, and in order to reach the required 15% margin, vast swathes of the network would have had to be axed, or facilities consolidated (which happened anyway). Consolidation was the only real option. The bitter pill was that Trevor Smallwood, who was the joint Chief Executive of FirstGroup, with Moir Lockhead, had 'retired' from the business, just after Mainline had been absorbed. He was a 'nuts and bolts' busman, who hailed from Rotherham, and understood the area. It was he who had been key on getting the workforce to accept the takeover bid, and now he was gone.

In preparation for the takeover, buses that had been repainted since June had left the shops with no fleetnames. Bus 1943, which had been refurbished in a similar fashion to the Dennis Dominators, was treated to a revised red and yellow livery, with no bands of grey or blue. One of the final repaints to include the blue and grey stripes was overall advert bus 2304, which entered service with an advert for Don Valley Centertainment.

The new Dennis Dart SPDs (508 to 539) started to be delivered just after FirstGroup had taken over. The buses were delivered in standard Mainline 'Silver Service' livery, as on 781 to 790, with First logos replacing that of Mainline. The first 11 came with a different axle and gearbox setting, as these were the Northern Bus ordered examples. Later deliveries, in common with buses being painted in general from this time, were to a slightly different paint specification, eliminating the grey and blue lines.

Greenland received the first of the new deliveries, placing them into service on the 22 between Nether Edge and Southey Green via the city centre. Rotherham's were next for the highly anticipated Bawtry Road Quality Corridor. Doncaster got the final examples, going on to the Rossington and Cantley services.

Above

The new 'First' logo quickly appeared on buses, as and when they were due for 28 day examination.

Metrorider 3004 is seen at Meadowhall coach park, 2189, on the first day of the new ownership, is seen in Sheffield Interchange and brand new Dennis Dart SPD 509, is seen being 'run in' on the East Dene circulars in Rotherham.

Below

Together with the new logo, the main fleet livery was simplified to plain red and yellow.

2479 is seen freshly outshopped at Sandtoft Trolleybus Museum.

These new buses were certainly an upgrade on the vehicles they replaced, and this enabled further batches of Dennis Dominators to be withdrawn. This also enabled a cascade to be started within the garages to upgrade some secondary services and deal with the Northern Bus integration process.

Drivers were issued with a new 'f' pin badge to replace their partnership one, which was no longer to be worn. Buses generally started to receive the new fleetname as stocks were available, which meant for a while some buses only operated with a very small 'Mainline' logo on either side of the bodywork. The new fleetname looked smart, although modest, and was of such a size to make advertising on the sides of single deck buses permissible.

The first major service change under First was a complete redesign of the Dinnington network. From Sheffield, new services X5 and X6 provided new links, sweeping away a whole range of slower services. A peak hour X2 provided a link to Thurcroft and Laughton, via Meadowhall. The 208 was replaced by a new X8 and a new off peak link between Meadowhall and Dinnington was provided by service 261. From Rotherham, a new 129 provided a link between the two towns via Whiston, but the direct corridor via Thurcroft was left to Stagecoach, who had boosted the frequency of their service 19 to four buses per hour.

The new network was operated by Greenland and Rotherham garages, and was operated primarily by Volvo B10Ms. The new network quickly increased passenger loadings.

A number of company roadshows were organised for the new management team to be introduced to the employees. One was organised for each district, but it was the one at Royal Victoria Hotel in Sheffield which caused the biggest surprise and upset. At this meeting, it was announced that Greenland garage was to close in 1999, and the fleet would be divided up between Halfway, Rotherham and the newly acquired piece of land on Charlotte Road. Work would take place at Olive Grove to enable it to operate nearly 400 vehicles (although the allocation never really got beyond 350), Halfway to increase the fleet size to nearly 100 and Rotherham would take on the work of the articulated Leyland DABs, Dinnington and parts of the Beighton network.

There was a fierce debate that night about how this wasn't the direction the employees had envisaged when FirstGroup took over, but, the deal had been done, and this was the new commercial reality of bus operation in South Yorkshire. Heated words were exchanged with some of the new First regional management, which ensured that future roadshows were never attended to such a high level again.

Also announced that night was a new, blue, uniform to replace the Mainline maroon, white and grey, and a batch of 23 new Volvo B10BLEs for service 52, ironically operated from Greenland. Twenty of the Volvos had been ordered by Mainline prior to FirstGroup purchasing the company. Another 100 had been promised for 1999.

Certainly, First saw South Yorkshire as being an area in which they could exploit the new strategy of quality services, developed as 'Showcases'. Service changes, which involved the Dennis Dart SPDs involved a package of measures designed to increase ridership. In Rotherham, the Quality Partnership finally got underway, with over 15 new bus stops and miles of bus priority provided.

In Doncaster, the new image was launched with 'teddy bears' in a slightly intriguing 'if you go down to the woods today' style promotion, which gave teddy bear toys away in exchange for bus tickets. This enabled more modern single deck buses to be used to start the replacement process of further Renault S56s. The services to Rossington were recast, with a new service 58 reintroducing the separate service to West Bessacarr, leaving the 55 and 56 to the main Bawtry Road.

Schools services were also ripe for renewal and a former Eastern National Leyland Tiger (79) entered the workshops at Rotherham to be converted into a high capacity schools bus. The conversion included dual purpose seats, three point belts and a complete retrim in the vinyl 'red caterpillar' moquette. It was painted in an overall yellow livery, with large black school bus signs adorning the sides. It was meant to be the first of many, but was overtaken by events, which saw First commit to purchasing new school buses, and it became a solitary example.

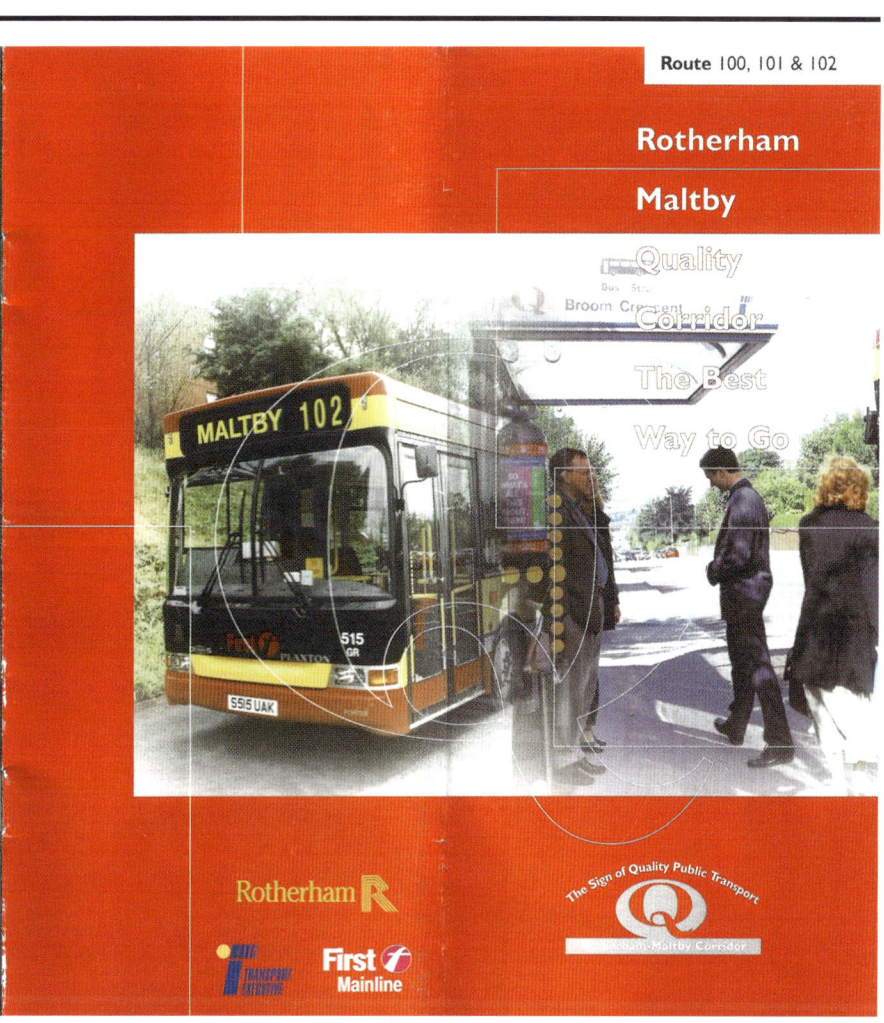

Right

School buses were seen as being a good market to return to again. Tiger 79 was refurbished as a trial.

From now on the commercial section became more of a central works for FirstGroup, and did less and less work for outside companies, or other bus groups. It now specialised in rebuilding accident damaged buses throughout the group as well as refurbishments and repaints. Its talents spread far and wide, and there wasn't one of the group's companies that didn't use the services provided. Mainline had also proposed spending £600,000 refurbishing its fleet of Leyland DAB articulated vehicles, but this was placed on hold by the new owners, and indeed the buses left service the following year.

The new buses for service 52 (791 to 813) entered service in November in the new FirstGroup scheme of mist grey, rubine red and reflex blue. Fitted with standard First interior, they were all allocated to Greenland, replacing the B10Ms to other work, allowing further Dennis Dominators to exit the fleet. They originally came fitted with 'First Sheffield' fleetnames, but these were changed after a couple of months to 'First Mainline'.

They also introduced a new timetable, lowering the frequency from every five to every six minutes, but introduced a new 24 hour element, operating every 30 minutes on the Crookes side of the route, with hourly extensions to Woodhouse. These night journeys were charged at normal fares, a break from tradition.

Above and Right

The commercial engineering team effectively became the central works facility for FirstGroup, after acquisition, with nearly all group companies using the facilities.

Two Greater Manchester Metrobuses undergo overhaul in Rotherham, beside a similar London General machine.

The new First livery made it on to the streets in the autumn, with a relaunch of service 52.

791 is seen on the first day at Woodhouse Station and 795 is awaiting fitting out at Greenland.

To most people, the old Mainline died on that night at the Royal Victoria Hotel. Some familiar faces were there, but the ethos had changed. This is a convenient point to stop telling the story. First Mainline continued on after 1999, becoming First South Yorkshire, but that's another story, for somebody else to tell. The last financial accounts posted by Mainline showed for the year ended March 1998, a profit of £2.9 million (twelve months later, after hefty cuts in services, facility consolidation and another round of redundancies, FirstGroup managed to triple that amount). Not bad. Not bad at all. A good company. A damn fine company.

Above and Right

It was going to take some time for the new simplified livery to be rolled out, and buses ran for some time with grey and blue bands.

305 is seen advertising Adecco and 400 is seen heading for Loxley, both in Sheffield Interchange, whilst former Wilfreda Dart 4005 is in Duke Street, Doncaster.

Mainline had planned to start renewing the training fleet, by replacing Atlanteans with Dominators, converted by MASS. Two were done, outshopped in Mainline livery, but delivered to First. 9109 and 9111 are seen in Rotherham.

They were high quality conversions and the buses were fitted with Gardner engines, in place of their Rolls Royce units.

Chapter 14

The Service Fleet

Above

From humble vans, to trucks and snowploughs, the company had a vast array of service vehicles at its disposal.

M32 was a Ford Transit, and is seen here freshly painted into the new SYT livery, at Rotherham in 1985.

M57 was a Leyland PD2, which served as a treelopper, as well as a recovery wagon, seen here assisting an Atlantean at Meadowhead.

M1 was known as 'Duggy'. Leadmill was responsible for city centre recovery, and its assisting a forlorn Rotherham Dominator in Fitzalan Square, Sheffield.

SYPTE had spent considerable amounts of money, building up a healthy fleet of miscellaneous vehicles. SYT inherited around 100 ancillary vehicles at deregulation, ranging from the more commonly seen Driver Instruction Vehicles (DIVs) to recovery vehicles and service vans There were also general use pick ups, head office cars, fork lift trucks and even a fuel tanker.

The service, or ancillary fleet, as it was referred to in corporation days, used various codes to denote vehicle types. For example, a small van would be referred to as a (VS) or lorry (L) but this had been simplified, by the PTE, in 1977, with all vehicles falling into that category, being renumbered in a fairly haphazard way, and sometimes reusing previous numbers, preceded by an 'M' prefix.

When the fleet moved to SYT, some vehicles gained the same red vinyl stickers worn by the bus fleet, whilst a number of Transit vans were painted into SYT livery. The fleet remained broadly intact, apart from the odd accident damaged vehicle being written off, until new vans started to arrive in 1988.

Each garage had their own Leyland PD3 recovery vehicle, and most garages repainted theirs, well before a decent portion of the bus allocation was, in SYT livery, but the last one, and possibly the last vehicle in the fleet to retain PTE livery, was Dunscroft based M52, still awaiting its SYT repaint in 1990.

In April 1986 a number of these Leyland PD3s, gave up their 'dateless' registrations for the Coachline fleet. These were M3 (475 HDT), M4 (476 HDT), M10 (3913 WE), M16 (819 CWW), M20 (477 HDT), M52 (4475 WE) and M53 (3910 WE). The recovery vehicles gained 'OWJ/A' registrations in return. A more controversial swap, much later was M5 (220 AWY) which was on the preserved, former, Rossie Motors Daimler, which would thankfully revert back to its original registration, prior to leaving the company. Around this time M12 (388 KDT) had been renovated by Doncaster garage staff into DCT condition.

In 1986, former Volvo Ailsa 430 (the only MkII Ailsa built) was converted by PTE apprentices, for use as a new Road Show bus, becoming fleet number M11, This would replace M6, which had been converted in 1983,although it sat at Meadowhall HQ for a number of years before finally leaving the fleet.

Other vehicles existed such as a fuel tanker M79, which was purchased in the late 1970s, with the prospect of fuel strikes looming. The PTE, like others at that time, were taking no risks with fuel supply, so purchased this vehicle in order to distribute fuel stocks around the garages. The tanker saw little use, and despite being allocated to the Driving School, sat idle at Meadowhall, until placed into store at East Bank, prior to disposal.

Meadowhall HQ also became home to two more, semi long term residents, which were treelopper M57 (which had also been used as a spare vehicle covering mot preparation/long term breakdowns for the recovery fleet), and recovery vehicle M17, which having been displaced from Halfway garage by replacement vehicle M10, performed a period of recovery training, but eventually, both vehicles would be sold for scrap. Other vehicles, of interest, that had been lurking at Meadowhall for many years, were the former Sheffield Transport Comet lorry M2 and Fordson tractor M47 which were placed on long term loan to the Sheffield Bus Museum.

With central stores being based at Meadowhall since 1987 it would also become home to many other types of the company vans including the two, former, Dodge cash vans (with a very similar chassis to the Dodge S56) and a fairly unusual Dodge 'curtainsider' van (M80).

SYT had also inherited 4 elderly, but capable, AEC Matadors that were adept at performing heavy winching and suspended tows. These vehicles dated from between 1939 to 1951, and were originally gun tractors built for the war department. When they were acquired, they were heavily rebuilt for recovery work.

Above

The recovery fleet was also known as 'Snow Emergency Vehicles', and could also be used for gritting purposes, being fitted with internal grit bins.

M3, seen in Ecclesfield and M10, seen in Fitzalan Square, Sheffield, are assisting in getting vehicles moving in truly awful conditions.

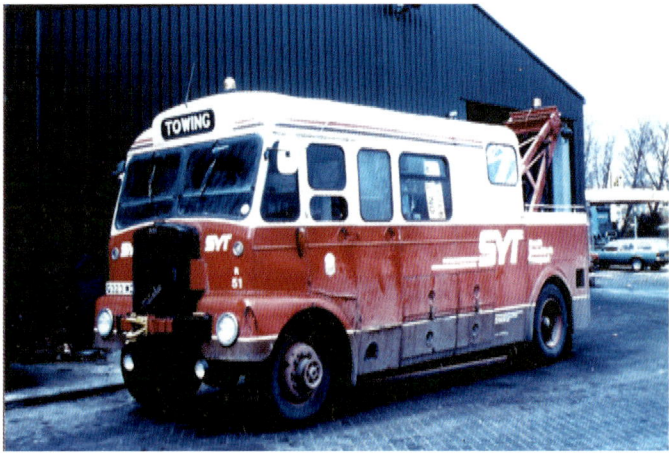

Above

Cash movement was undertaken by Dodge vehicles such as M78, seen at Herries. In later years this task was undertaken by private contractors, and the cash van fleet was moved on to stores work.

Heavy recovery was also undertaken by SYT, and a fleet of AEC Matadors were kept on strength. Built between 1939 and 1951, mainly for World War two service, it was a remarkable testimony to their builder, they survived into the 1980s.

R51 is seen at Halfway and M48 is seen on the Dairy Park at Herries.

Three of these vehicles were inherited from the three constituent corporations, with a fourth being acquired secondhand from SELNEC (the predecessor to Greater Manchester PTE) and put into use at Halfway. By 1988 the rules on operating vehicles with trade plates was subject to a change, and these plates were not permitted for use on recovery vehicles any longer, which meant that M49's former registration of 'EDT 644J' would become valid again, with M48, M50 and M51 having to be registered for the first time. They gained, in order, 'Q' prefix registration plates Q325/324/323 WDT.

In April 1989 the decision was taken to dispose of all four Matadors that the company owned, selling them to Isle Coaches of Owston Ferry, who would go on to be a regular buyer of redundant vehicles from the SYT/Mainline fleet, as the years went by.

Three of the Matadors were in SYT livery when sold, but M50 still retained its Rotherham Corporation livery, albeit without fleetnames, and never carried a fleet number, with all three SYT liveried vehicles, carrying their pre 1977 'R' (Recovery) fleet numbers, only being 'numbered' M on paper.

From 1988 SYT took delivery of a variety of vans, pick ups and cars, in addition to a Ford cargo lorry, for the unit repair section at Rutland Way, to start replacing older stock. Over time, the new Mainline livery would be gradually applied to the 'M' fleet, although just like every overlap of livery, the fleet would never be completely repainted, such was the every day useage requirements of the fleet. In 1992, Greenland's PD3 M18 (BWW 654B), received a unique version of the former SYT livery, using black for the skirt instead of brown, and gained the nickname 'The Boss', which was displayed on a plate attached to the front of the vehicle. After a while, using a degree of Yorkshire accent, it would be renamed 'The Hoss'. Leadmill, not to be outdone, decided to name their truck M1 (DUG 167C) 'Duggy the Dinosuar'.

For many years SYT/Mainline on occasions provided recovery for rivals Andrews and Sheffield Omnibus a practice that lasted in the Yorkshire Traction era. The company was also the on call recovery agents for South Yorkshire Police, removing blockages from key junctions, if called into help.

By 1989, the fairly elderly driver training fleet was mainly made up from vehicles from the late 1960s and early 1970s, was replaced by a batch of surplus, Roe bodied, Leyland Atlanteans (these being former fleet numbers 1611/24/27/30/31/49). Most of the conversions were undertaken at Rotherham, but a couple were processed by engineering apprentices at Meadowhall. They were converted by the addition of a Instructor's seat, additional mirrors, sealed up staircases and fitment of a separate heating supply. They were repainted in bold new livery of brown, white, red and yellow (designed by Copy and Concepts) with huge L plates vinyl's. An additional pair of Leyland Leopards were also acquired for use by the training school, and former coach 1021, which also doubled as the 'fishing coach', having a large metal cage fitted amidships for tackle boxes and the like. When not in use for training, this vehicle was made available for hire to both external and internal clients, and as Yorkshire has a large fishing fraternity, it was in regular use.

Despite many new purchases of new vans over the years, the tax payers of South Yorkshire could consider that their money had been well spent, with at least one MKII Ford Transit (M27) passing into privatisation. Whilst in Mainline ownership, allocated to Olive Grove, it operated briefly with Mainline stickers over its SYT fleetnames. New Ford Transits delivered since 1994 had appeared in all over white, with Mainline fleetnames, until space in the paintshops could be made to deal with them.

Just like the introduction of the SYT livery, some garages would waste no time repainting their recovery vehicle into the new Mainline livery. During early 1990, Leyland PD3 904, which was restored by the PTE in 1984, was used for special events and hire, but would see occasional use with the Driving School, fitted with temporary 'L' plates. From June 1994, it would, on paper, be renumbered as 9904 and would continue in this role of show bus/driver trainer until 2001.

Above

The company owned two roadshow vehicles, Ailsa 430 (now numbered M11) and Atlantean M8, seen here in Hillsborough Park.

M7, seen outside Greenland garage, was used by the company as a mobile Santa's Grotto.

Seen with Instructor Dickie Byrne, Leyland PD3 trainer M100 is in the somewhat uninspiring, former PTE training livery, with SYT vinyls.

Land Rover's have always featured heavily in the company's service fleet. Halfway garage's M99 is seen in Sheffield's old Central Bus Station.

Above

M18 was called 'The Boss' which was changed to 'The Hoss', and was given a unique black skirted version of the SYT livery, seen here in Attercliffe, assisting an Andrews Fleetline.

M53 is seen in Sheffield Omnibus' Ecclesfield garage, nursing a poorly looking Atlantean back home. Normally, South Yorkshire Police would ask the company to recover vehicles, if it assisted in getting traffic moving.

Flatbed lorries and vans were also an essential part of the mix. Ford Cargo M72, new in November 1986, is seen in Doncaster and Transit M37, which had been restored to this unique livery by the company's apprentices, is entering East Bank garage.

A surprise addition to the fleet, was an AEC Mercury recovery vehicle, becoming part of the fleet as part of the integration process from Sheafline in July 1993, and was allocated to Greenland and numbered M7. It would spend a couple of years there, retaining Sheafline livery, before disposal to Isle Coaches. An interesting acquisition took place in July 1993 when a former, Ministry of Defence, Bedford MJ lorry, was purchased for potential use as a replacement recovery truck. Taken to Herries garage, its rear body was rebuilt by the craftsmen there as a mobile workshop, using Alexander body parts. This was meant to be the first of the Leyland PD3 replacements, and was numbered M6. It was smartly painted in post office red, with yellow Mainline fleetnames, but wasn't a huge success, due to weight and low power issues. After moving to Olive Grove, upon the closure of Herries, it would transfer to Greenland. M6 was swapped with M52 from Doncaster, leaving M6 to enjoy an easier life in the flatlands of Dunscroft.

Its poor handling lead to an accident, whilst performing a recovery in the summer of 1996, and it was subsequently disposed of.

Company cars were no new thing, be it a head office or managers car. These all had 'M' numbers allocated, but in the 1990s the only thing that made these stand out, was the fact they had gained registrations from the former Coachline fleet. When that business had been sold, registrations such as 3913 WE, 4475 WE, 819 CWW etc. were retained by Mainline.

In June 1994 a new fuel issuing system was introduced which couldn't deal with alphanumeric fleet numbers. The 'M' fleet was renumbered into the 9000 series, so M1 would become 9001 and so forth. Leyland PD3 M18 (9018) came to grief, when it collided with Volvo B10M 696 on Commercial Street in 1995 and was withdrawn immediately, being sold to Isle Coaches.

In late 1995 Alan Hull, Engineering Manager at Olive Grove thought it was time his fleet of service vehicles was smartened up, but he was not a fan of the Mainline livery, once describing it as looking like 'something from a circus'.

He ordered the vehicles in the garage to be painted overall red. Leyland PD3 9001 received Eager Beaver 'signal red', with no fleetnames, while the two Ford Transit pick ups received Mainline 'post office red', just leaving the service support Transit (M28) in standard livery.

By 1996 the Driving School fleet was ready for a refresh, and an amended style of Mainline livery was used with the lower half being Post Office red, with a broad yellow between decks band, but the two Y type Leopards gained full Mainline livery, with Leopard 1021 gaining a and red livery, although not part of the 'M' fleet numerically it was still available as a driving school vehicle.

In August 1997 Greenland applied some light hearted lettering to the upper panels on one side of Leyland PD3 9052, calling themselves 'Greenland Road Engineering, The fifth emergency service' a tongue in cheek comparison to the AA's adverts of the time, as they were claiming that they were the 4th emergency service.

In 1998 the driving school was looking to upgrade the fleet and two Dennis Dominators, latterly with Northern Bus (former Mainline 2112/5) were converted by Northern Bus, on behalf of Mainline as DIVs, and appeared with First Mainline fleetnames, arriving just after the take over. They joined former Mainline 2114, that had also come via Northern Bus, which was also in the training fleet, but mainly used for type training, as it still carried Northern Bus livery, and didn't have a secondary handbrake. Gradually the Leyland Atlanteans would be moved out of the fleet as Chief Instructor, Alan Hawcroft, desired to improve the quality of the training fleet.

Above

M6, a former military Bedford was converted at Herries into a recovery vehicle, the intention being to buy a fleet of these to replace the venerable PD3s. It wasn't a success, and the plan was shelved. It's seen here under conversion at Herries and at the Rotherham open day in 1993.

Matching the bus fleet, it would take time to get vehicles into the Mainline livery, and vinyls were used to remove the former SYT identity.

M1 is seen assisting an errant Renault on Flat Street in Sheffield, while M53 is tooled up for winter, having been fitted with its snow plough, at Herries garage.

At the same time Leyland Leopard 9107, was converted to semi automatic transmission by Northern Bus on Mainline's behalf. During the summer of 1998, Greenland's Leyland PD3 9052, had suffered an engine failure, and it was thought that it would be withdrawn. It was out of use for some time, with workshop staff placing a wreath on its front end, proclaiming 'RIP'. However, it would receive a reconditioned engine, and repaint into Post office red when Alan Hull moved to Greenland with First Mainline fleetnames in yellow, being completed in August 98. Its reprieve would not last long, as it would be sold for scrap in March 1999, together with a number of scrap buses, left in Greenland when that garage closed.

Land Rovers had featured throughout the years, with at least ten different ones being part of the PTE fleet. Gradually the number was reduced, with examples being sold by the early 1990s, but one did remain, M62 (RCP 357X) which was based at Herries for many years. This vehicle had fallen out of use at some point in 1997 and Malcolm Woodward, who was by now Training Manager for the company, claimed 'you cannot run a bus company effectively without a Land Rover'. M62, by then renumbered as 9062, would be restored by Autoservices at Greenland, being recommissioned, and then be repainted overall Post Office red, with yellow First fleetnames. This vehicle could also be fitted with a snow plough and was often used to clear external parking areas of the company's garages.

Above and Right

As time was available, each garage repainted their recovery vehicle. Greenland's M52, Doncaster's M16 and Rotherham's M4 are seen freshly outshopped in Mainline livery.

An unusual battery tug (M69) was kept at Doncaster, but by the time of this photo, had been out of use for some time.

Clockwise from Top Left

M62 was nicknamed the 'Bertmobile' after Olive Grove's Garage Manager, Bert Middleton. It was used to check out hilly routes after snow, and was also used as a snowplough, clearing ice from within the garage, and its environs.

A familiar sight from 1989, was the service support van (M28), know as '92' after its radio call sign. Seen at the bottom of the Moor, dealing with minor accident damage on Leyland DAB 2009. M52 was retired with an engine fault, but was soon resuscitated at Greenland. The fitters have given it a wreath, as it was thought it couldn't be saved.

After the Matadors left the fleet, really heavy recovery was undertaken by outside contractors. An MCW Metrobus has come to grief at Owler Bar, and requires rescue from a field.

M1 (9001) and M62 (9062) were repainted into this overall red livery at Olive Grove.

Chapter 15

Blinds

In today's world of dot matrix, LED's and even 'smart paper' destination indicators, for nearly 100 years, the best way of letting someone know where your bus was going, was a destination blind.

On the formation of SYPTE, each constituent fleet had their own design of blind, and method of showing route numbers. In Sheffield, a standard had developed based on a three track number blind with two destination blinds. This was repeated on the side and rear, although the distinction between number and destination blinds varied, according to bus type.

In Rotherham, a single destination blind, with a two track number blind had become standard, generally with a destination repeater on the side, although this was normally unused. In Doncaster, they went for a single piece blind that simply spelled out the destination in huge letters, often only showing numbers for joint workings (such as Sheffield).

The PTE decided to standardise on the Sheffield system, modifying other district's blinds, where possible. In the case of Rotherham, they shoe horned in an additional number on the first track of the numeric blind, but for Doncaster, the existing blinds were reissued, with numbers now present.

As the years went on, the number of buses retaining non standard displays dwindled, and a program was put in place at Doncaster, to update buses that had been absorbed from local independents, fitting them with standard PTE style displays.

Single deck vehicles generally had their own displays, normally for the routes they were restricted to, although in Doncaster, they simply reissued the upper destination blind for single deck buses.

The PTE had redesigned their blinds in 1983 for each district, in upper case, and generally they had no more than 70 destinations on each blind, arranged in a haphazard order, but matching route groups.

Lower case blinds were ordered for Rotherham and Halfway in 1985, but the program was never completed in Rotherham. Red blinds had been ordered for Fastline and Nipper vehicles, which required blue bulbs to be fitted later. This was the situation SYT inherited in 1986. There were still plenty of older blinds in circulation, but the majority were from 1983 or later.

It would be impossible to list every single blind that was ordered between 1986 and 1998. What follows is a snapshot of destination blinds in use during that period. A new set of blinds was issued for Rotherham and Halfway in 1988, to cope with services moving from East Bank. Doncaster completely replaced theirs in 1990 and Sheffield in 1991. A further issue was started in 1995/6 to change over to 'dayglo' blinds, with each area receiving a full set, with Halfway finally admitting it was in Sheffield and adopting that.

The lists are presented in area order, by date. Inserts are not included.

Lists should be read downwards, from left to right.

A '*' equates to a blank.

Top and bottom blinds are separated by a line.

Below

The PTEs standard style of display was inherited by SYT. Generally, the blinds were set up to display singularly in each aperture, or could be used together to show via points etc.

Doncaster had a curious distinction, where the outer and inner terminal were generally shown at the same time, although this would cease under SYT.

Daimler Fleetline 1572 shows this peculiar situation to good effect in Doncaster town centre.

Sheffield 1983 — Double Deck vehicles — Printed white on black, Tyvek

*
PRINCE OF WALES RD
WISEWOOD
LOXLEY
SHIREGREEN
WINCOBANK
STANDON ROAD
UPWELL STREET
SANDSTONE ROAD
CHANCET WOOD
HOLLYTHORPE RISE
GRAVES PARK
NORTON
MEADOWHEAD
WOODSEATS
SCARSDALE ROAD
SHEFFIELD LANE TOP
SHIRECLIFFE
HEMSWORTH
HERDINGS
JORDANTHORPE
GLEADLESS
LODGE MOOR
WYMING BROOK
*
CITY
GREYSTONES
GREENHILL
BRADWAY
LOW EDGES
PARSON CROSS
FOX HILL
HILLSBOROUGH
YEW LANE
WORDSWORTH AVE.
SOUTHEY GREEN
LONGLEY
NETHER EDGE HOSP.
BATEMOOR
DRONFIELD
CHESTERFIELD
HOLMESFIELD
GOSFORTH

CHARNOCK
BIRLEY
DYKE VALE ROAD
HALLAMSHIRE HOSPITAL
*
SHEFFIELD
FASTLINE (logo)
BEIGHTON
HACKENTHORPE
WESTFIELD
WATERTHORPE
HALFWAY
MOSBOROUGH
ECKINGTON
KILLAMARSH
SPINKHILL
HARTHILL
DINNINGTON
KIVETON PARK
SWALLOWNEST
ASTON
SOUTH ANSTON
NORTH ANSTON
TREETON
DONCASTER
ROTHERHAM
MALTBY
BRINSWORTH
BAKEWELL
CASTLETON
*

*
HEELEY
INFIRMARY ROAD
WALKLEY (TINKER LANE)
INTAKE
COMMONSIDE
ELM TREE
RIVELIN DAMS
COLDWELL LANE
CROSSPOOL
BUS STATION
CRIMICAR LANE
FULWOOD
NETHER GREEN
RANMOOR
BROOMHILL
*
RUSTLINGS ROAD
MALIN BRIDGE
ROSCOE BANK
MARCHWOOD
RINGINGLOW
BENTS GREEN
ECCLESALL
MIDDLEWOOD
EWDEN VALLEY
FIRTH PARK
MARGATE DRIVE
MILLHOUSES
BEAUCHIEF
DOBCROFT ROAD
TINSLEY (HIGHGATE)
TOTLEY BROOK
TOTLEY
OWLER BAR
DORE
CITY
TEMPLEBOROUGH
VULCAN ROAD
ATTERCLIFFE
DARNALL
BRIGHTSIDE
NORFOLK BRIDGE

SHEPCOTE LANE
WYBOURN
STRADBROKE
WOODTHORPE
HANDSWORTH
WOODHOUSE
BALLIFIELD
CROOKES
CROOKES (SCHOOL RD)
*
SHEFFIELD
FASTLINE (logo)
BARNSLEY
CHAPELTOWN
ECCLESFIELD
GRENOSIDE
GREENGATE LANE
HIGH GREEN
STOCKSBRIDGE
OUGHTIBRIDGE
STANNINGTON
DUNGWORTH
BRADFIELD
CIRCULAR
FOOTBALL
SCHOOL
GARAGE
SPECIAL
*

Sheffield 1981 — Single Deck vehicles (left), Coaches (right) — Printed white on black, Tyvek

*	GARAGE	*	TEMPLEBOROUGH
SHEFFIELD	SPECIAL	ASTON	SHEFFIELD LANE TOP
BRADFIELD	*	SWALLOWNEST	SHIREGREEN
STOCKSBRIDGE	MOORFOOT	KIVETON PARK	CITY
FIRTH PARK	BUS & RAIL STATIONS	SOUTH ANSTON	CIRCULAR
TEMPLEBOROUGH	*	DINNINGTON	HEELEY
BAMFORD		WORKSOP	INFIRMARY ROAD
GLOSSOP		RETFORD	COLLIERY
GAINSBOROUGH		GAINSBOROUGH	SCHOOL
RETFORD		SHEFFIELD	
WORKSOP		CHAPELTOWN	
HALIFAX		HIGH GREEN	SPECIAL
HUDDERSFIELD		WORTLEY	PRIVATE
PENISTONE		PENISTONE	*
GREAT HOUGHTON		HUDDERSFIELD	
HEMSWORTH		HALIFAX	
WOMBWELL		WOMBWELL	
CHESTERFIELD		UPTON	
ECKINGTON		BARNSLEY	
MARSH LANE		LEEDS	
GLEADLESS		WAKEFIELD	
HALLOWES		DEWSBURY	
SHEFFIELD		BARDFORD	
*		SHEFFIELD	
MANOR PARK		BAMFORD	
NORFOLK BRIDGE		CASTLETON	
INFIRMARY ROAD		DERWENT	
HEELEY		GLOSSOP	
CIRCULAR		MATLOCK	
PARSON CROSS		CRICH	
BLACKBURN		HATHERSAGE	
HERDINGS		BAKEWELL	
JORDANTHORPE		*	
BRADWAY		BARROW HILL	
LOW EDGES		CHESTERFIELD	
SHEFFIELD LANE TOP		SHEFFIELD	
BRINSWORTH		BRADFIELD	
TOTLEY		MANCHESTER	
LOWER WALKLEY		DONCASTER	
BUS STATION		ROTHERHAM	
CITY		*	
CROOKES CIRCULAR		BLACKBURN	
COLLIERY		DARNALL	
SCHOOL		FIRTH PARK	

Sheffield 1991   Double Deck vehicles   Printed white on black, Tyvek

*
CITY AND MOORFOOT
CITY
CITY VIA STANDON RD
MEADOWHALL CENTRE
FIRTH PARK VIA S. RD
FIRTH PARK
WOODHOUSE
WOODHOUSE VIA S. RD
BALLIFIELD
CROOKES
SHIREGREEN
HEMSWORTH
HERDINGS
WYMING BROOK
LODGE MOOR
CROSSPOOL
GLEADLESS
CRYSTAL PEAKS
HALFWAY
HACKENTHORPE
BEIGHTON
PRINCE OF WALES RD
DARNALL
MANOR TOP
BATEMOOR
JORDANTHORPE
MEADOWHEAD
WOODSEATS
LOW EDGES
BRADWAY
ECCLESFIELD
HIGH GREEN
CHAPELTOWN
SHEFFIELD LANE TOP
CITY
*
HALL PARK HEAD
BENTS GREEN
FULWOOD
MIDDLEWOOD
ECCLESALL
RINGINGLOW
EWDEN VALLEY

STANNINGTON
DUNGWORTH
MARCHWOOD
MALIN BRIDGE
HUNTERS BAR
WINCOBANK
HILLSBOROUGH
CITY
MILLHOUSES
TOTLEY
TOTLEY BROOK
PARSON CROSS
SOUTHEY GREEN
NETHER EDGE HOSPITAL
INTAKE
WALKLEY
CRIMICAR LANE
NETHER GREEN
TRANSPORT I.CHANGE
RANMOOR
HALLAMSHIRE HOSPITAL
LEEDS
SHEFFIELD
DINNINGTON
ASTON
STOCKSBRIDGE
DONCASTER
ROTHERHAM
WORKSOP
CIRCULAR
PRIVATE
NOT IN SERVICE
GARAGE
*

Note: Top blind also used on Volvo B10M vehicles.

*
WISEWOOD
LOXLEY
OUGHTIBRIDGE
DEEPCAR
STOCKSBRIDGE
WORDSWORTH AVE
SHIRECLIFFE
LONGLEY
ATTERCLIFFE
WYBOURN
WOODTHORPE
NORFOLK PARK
MANOR LANE
SHEPCOTE LANE
PARKWAY MARKETS
TINSLEY
BRINSWORTH
TREETON
CATCLIFFE
SWALLOWNEST
DINNINGTON
TODWICK
KIVETON PARK
SOUTH ANSTON
CASTLETON
BAKEWELL
HATHERSAGE
BASLOW
FOX HOUSE
HOPE
KILLAMARSH
MEADOWGATE LANE
MOSBOROUGH
ECKINGTON
CHESTERFIELD
DRONFIELD
HALLOWES
SHEFFIELD
*
DORE
BIRLEY
CHARNOCK
PARKHEAD

HEMSWORTH
GRENOSIDE
FOXHILL
COLDWELL LANE
INFIRMARY ROAD
HEELEY
NORTON
GRAVES PARK
TRANSPORT I.CHANGE
MEADOWHALL I.CHANGE
ABBEYDALE GRANGE SC
NORTON COLLEGE
ECCLESFIELD SCHOOL
PARSON CROSS COLL.
ATHELSTAN SCHOOL
HERRIES RD. GARAGE
VIA MEADOWHALL
VIA STANDON ROAD
VIA HILLSBOROUGH
VIA GREYSTONES
VIA CRYSTAL PEAKS
VIA THE PARKWAY
VIA BARNSLEY
VIA CITY CENTRE
CIRCULAR
PRIVATE
NOT IN SERVICE
FASTLINE
LIMITED STOP
PARK AND RIDE
SCHOOL
RAIL REPLACEMENT
CITY AND MOORFOOT
CITY
MEADOWHALL I.CHANGE
FOOTBALL
*

Sheffield 1991   Artic & SD vehicles (left), Minibuses (right)   Printed white on black, Tyvek

Artic & SD vehicles		Minibuses	
*	KING ECGBERT SCHOOL	*	DARNALL
BUS AND RAIL STATIONS	ABBEYDALE GRANGE SC.	PARK 'N' RIDE	CARTERKNOWLE RD
CITY AND MOORFOOT	ALL SAINTS SCHOOL	CITY CLIPPER	DARNALL CIRCLE
MEADOWHALL I.CHANGE	RANMOOR	EARLY BIRD	TINSLEY HIGHGATE
CITY CENTRE	*	PRIVATE PARTY	WOODHOUSE
SHEFFIELD GARAGE		NOT IN SERVICE	HANDSWORTH
SCHOOL SERVICE		SPECIAL	CUTTHROAT BRIDGE
SPECIAL SERVICE		SCHOOL	RIVELIN DAMS
NOT IN SERVICE		MEADOWHALL CENTRE	RIVELIN P.O.
CIRCULAR		TRANSPORT I.CHANGE	HIGH BRADFIELD
PRIVATE		MOORFOOT	CATCLIFFE
*		*	STOCKSBRIDGE GV
HERDINGS		WYBOURN CIRCLE	HILLSBOROUGH
WYMING BROOK		NORTON LEES	*
LODGE MOOR		WYMING BROOK	BATEMOOR
CROSSPOOL		HACKENTHORPE	JORDANTHORPE
PRINCE OF WALES RD		MOSBOROUGH	NETHER GREEN
DARNALL		BEIGHTON	BEAUCHIEF
WOODHOUSE		SOTHALL	DORE
CROOKES		NORFOLK PARK V. M'H	HALLOWES
BALLIFIELD		CRYSTAL PEAKS	DRONFIELD CIVIC CEN
THORPE HESLEY		ASTON	CHESTERFIELD
SHARDLOWS WORKS		SWALLOWNEST	SHEFFIELD
PARKWAY MARKETS		BROOMHALL	GOSFORTH
HACKENTHORPE		SHIREGREEN V.M'H	COAL ASTON
CRYSTAL PEAKS		SHEFFIELD	CALOW ROYAL HOSP.
MEADOWGATE LANE		SHARDLOWS WORKS	APPERKNOWLE
BEIGHTON		THORPE HESLEY	MARSH LANE
INTAKE		CITY CENTRE	NETHER EDGE HOSP.
ELM TREE		CHARNOCK	LODGE MOOR HOSP.
SHEFFIELD		GLEADLESS	*
*		*	TRANSPORT I.CHANGE
DINNINGTON		MANOR PARK CENTRE	LOWER WALKLEY
KIVETON PARK		WOODTHORPE	OUGHTIBRIDGE
PENISTONE		SHIREGREEN	WARREN
ASTON		SANDSTONE ROAD	GRENOSIDE
ROTHERHAM		FIRTH PARK	CHAPELTOWN
BATEMOOR		SOUTHEY GREEN	MEADOWHALL
JORDANTHORPE		ATTERCLIFFE	HERRIES GARAGE
MEADOWHEAD		SHEPCOTE LANE	FOXHILL
FOOTBALL		ELM TREE	SOUTHEY GREEN
TRANSPORT I.CHANGE		PARKWAY MARKETS	TEMPLEBOROUGH
		SHEFFIELD LANE TOP	PARSON CROSS
		ECCLESFIELD	*

Sheffield 1991/5 Eager Beaver/Volvo B10M Printed white on black, Tyvek/Yellow on black, plastic

*	FIRTH PARK	MALTBY	MILLHOUSES
FISHPONDS	FIRTH PARK via S'don Rd	CEDAR DRIVE	WYBOURN
TRANSPORT I.CHANGE		LOW EDGES	DORE
SHIREGREEN	WOODHOUSE	BRADWAY	CASTLETON
FIRTH PARK	WOODHOUSE via S'don Rd	WOODSEATS	BAKEWELL
WOODHOUSE		HIGH GREEN	GLOSSOP
CROOKES	CROOKES	CHAPELTOWN	BUXTON
CROOKES SCHOOL ROAD	BALLIFIELD	ECCLESFIELD	CRICH
BALLIFIELD	SHIREGREEN	SHEFFIELD LANE TOP	HOLMESFIELD
DARNALL	HEMSWORTH	HALL PARK HEAD	RINGINGLOW
HANDSWORTH	JORDANTHORPE	BENTS GREEN	SHEFFIELD
CITY	HERDINGS	FULWOOD	HIGH STORRS SCHOOL
BROOMHILL	LODGE MOOR	MIDDLEWOOD	DON VALLEY STADIUM
MOORFOOT	WYMING BROOK	ECCLESALL	SHEFFIELD ARENA
BIRLEY	CROSSPOOL	STANNINGTON	CIRCULAR
CHARNOCK	CHARNOCK	DUNGWORTH	PRIVATE
ELM TREE	GLEADLESS	MALIN BRIDGE	NOT IN SERVICE
GLEADLESS	CRYSTAL PEAKS	HILLSBOROUGH	PARK AND RIDE
BASE GREEN	HALFWAY	HERRIES ROAD	SCHOOL SERVICE
MARKETS	CITY AND MOORFOOT	WISEWOOD	RAIL REPLACEMENT SVC
*	MOSBOROUGH	LOXLEY	TRAM REPLACEMENT SVC
LOXLEY	KILLAMARSH	WORRALL	
MALIN BRIDGE	MEADOWGATE LANE	OUGHTIBRIDGE	FOOTBALL
WISEWOOD	ECKINGTON	STOCKSBRIDGE	*
SHIRECLIFFE	SPINKHILL	CITY CENTRE	
CITY	HARTHILL	SHEFFIELD I.CHANGE	
FULWOOD	BEIGHTON	*	
HERRIES GARAGE	ROTHERHAM	TOTLEY	
HUNTERS BAR	DONCASTER	TOTLEY BROOK	
MONTENEY ROAD	BARNSLEY	PARSON CROSS	
HILLSBOROUGH	DINNINGTON	SOUTHEY GREEN	
LOWER WALKLEY	ASTON	NETHER EDGE	
OUGHTIBRIDGE	BATEMOOR	DARNALL	
TRANSPORT I.CHANGE	GRENOSIDE	MANOR TOP	
*	FOXHILL	BASE GREEN	
NOT IN SERVICE	SHIRECLIFFE	BIRLEY	
PRIVATE	*	DYKE VALE ROAD	
*	HEMSWORTH	INTAKE	
	GRAVES PARK	CRIMICAR LANE	
	CHANCET WOOD	RANMOOR	
	SANDSTONE ROAD	NETHER GREEN	
	MARGATE DRIVE	HALLAMSHIRE HOSPITAL	
	HOLLYTHORPE RISE	CARTERKNOWLE RD BTM	
	UPWELL STREET		
	MEADOWHALL		

Sheffield 1995   Double Deck vehicles   Printed yellow on black, plastic

*
MEADOWHALL CENTRE
FIRTH PARK
WOODHOUSE
CROOKES
SHIREGREEN
HEMSWORTH
HERDINGS
LODGE MOOR
CHARNOCK
CRYSTAL PEAKS
HALFWAY
CITY AND MOORFOOT
KILLAMARSH
MEADOWGATE LANE
ECKINGTON
SPINKHILL
BEIGHTON
ROTHERHAM
PRINCE OF WALES RD
DARNALL
BATEMOOR
MEADOWHALL I.CHANGE
JORDANTHORPE
GRENOSIDE
FOXHILL
SHIRECLIFFE
CITY CENTRE
SHEFFIELD I.CHANGE
*
COLDWELL LANE
GRAVES PARK
CHANCET WOOD
SANDSTONE ROAD
MARGATE DRIVE
SCARSDALE ROAD
UPWELL STREET
MALTBY
CEDAR DRIVE
LOW EDGES
BRADWAY
HIGH GREEN
CHAPELTOWN

ECCLESFIELD
SHEFFIELD LANE TOP
HALL PARK HEAD
BENTS GREEN
FULWOOD
MIDDLEWOOD
ECCLESALL
STANNINGTON
MALIN BRIDGE
HILLSBOROUGH
WISEWOOD
LOXLEY
CITY CENTRE
SHEFFIELD I.CHANGE
*
OUGHTIBRIDGE
STOCKSBRIDGE
TOTLEY
TOTLEY BROOK
PARSON CROSS
SOUTHEY GREEN
NETHER EDGE HOSPITAL
BASE GREEN
DYKE VAKE ROAD
INTAKE
WALKLEY
CRIMICAR LANE
RANMOOR
HALLAMSHIRE HOSPITAL
PLUMBLEY
WYBOURN
CASTLETON
BAKEWELL
DORE
SHEFFIELD CITY CENTRE
SHEFFIELD I.CHANGE
*

*
DEEPCAR
WHARNCLIFFE SIDE
MOSBOROUGH
NORWOOD
HARTHILL
HEATHLANDS
MARSH LANE
NETHERTHORPE
CHESTERFIELD
DRONFIELD
HOLMESFIELD
WORDSWORTH AVE
HERRIES ROAD
HOLLYTHORPE RISE
GRIMESTHORPE
BALLIFIELD
HANDSWORTH
WYMING BROOK
CROSSPOOL
BIRLEY
NORTON
GLEADLESS
MANOR PARK CENTRE
MANOR TOP
HACKENTHORPE
*
MEADOWHEAD
WOODSEATS
CARTERKNOWLE RD BT
MILLHOUSES
HUNTERS BAR
NETHER GREEN
OWLER BAR
RINGINGLOW
HATHERSAGE
FOX HOUSE
HEELEY
HIGHFIELD
LOWFIELD
ARBOURTHORNE
UPPERTHORPE
WARREN LANE
DUNGWORTH

WINCOBANK
CANKLOW
TINSLEY
DINNINGTON
ASTON
CATCLIFFE
SWALLOWNEST
TODWICK
KIVETON PARK
SOUTH ANSTON
DONCASTER
BARNSLEY
WORKSOP
ECCLESFIELD CO SCH
ATHELSTAN SCHOOL
ST MARIES SCHOOL
WORRALL
LEES HALL ROAD
YEWLANDS SCHOOL
HIGH STORRS SCHOOL
HINDE HOUSE SCHOOL
NOTRE DAME SCHOOL
ASTON COMP SCHOOL
WALES SCHOOL
ECKINGTON SCHOOL
WESTFIELD SCHOOL
HALFWAY GARAGE
GREENLAND GARAGE
*
Via WOODHOUSE
Via STRADBROKE
Via HARTHILL
Via MEADOWHALL
Via STANDON ROAD
Via HILLSBOROUGH
Via GREYSTONES
Via CRYSTAL PEAKS
Via THE PARKWAY
Via WOODSEATS
Via HUTCLIFFE WOOD
OUTER CIRCLE
CIRCULAR
PRIVATE
LIMITED STOP

Halfway 1985/8	Double Deck Vehicles	Printed white on black, Tyvek	
*	*	*	*
Sheffield	Football	Sheffield	Via Gleadless
Halfway	School	Dyke Vale Road	Via Woodhouse
Killamarsh	Fastline (logo)	Holbrook	*
Hallowes Estate	Whitwell Colliery	*	Kiveton Park Colliery
Eckington	Renishaw Park Colliery	Harthill	Renishaw Park Colliery
Green Lane	Kiveton Park Colliery	Spinkhill	*
Dronfield	High Moor Colliery	Elm Tree	High Moor
Westfield	Private Charter	Sheffield	Marsh Lane
Mosborough	Garage	Halfway	Eckington School
Beighton	Circular	Killamarsh	Wales School
Swallownest	Not in Service	Crystal Peaks	Netherthorpe
Hackenthorpe	*	Eckington	*
Harthill		Ballifield	Woodall
Spinkhill		Darnall	Harthill
Sheffield		Woodhouse	Clowne School
Rotherham		Westfield	Belph
Eckington		Beighton	Portland School
Clay Cross		Beighton Circular	Shireoaks
Hillsborough		Westfield Circular	Birley
Rother Valley Park		Westfield	*
*		Mosborough	Fastline
		Swallownest	Private Party
		*	Circular
		Rotherham	School
		Eckington	Not in Service
		Crystal Peaks	*
		*	
		Dronfield	
		Coal Aston	
		Gosforth	
		Sheffield	
		Chesterfield	
		Holmesfield	
		Plumbley	
		Sheffield City Centre	
		Holbrook	
		Sothall	
		Beighton	
		Meadowgate	
		Rother Valley Park	
		*	

Rotherham 1983	Double Deck Vehicles	Printed white on black, Tyvek
*	KILLAMARSH	*
BAWTRY	HALFWAY	CONANBY
DONCASTER	ROTHERHAM	TEMPLEBOROUGH
SHEFFIELD	TREETON	TINSLEY
CONISBROUGH	CATCLIFFE	FLATHERS WORKS
MEXBOROUGH	BRINSWORTH	HOYLAND
RAWMARSH	SILVERWOOD	BARROW COLLIERY
ROTHERHAM	THRYBERGH	IZAL FACTORY
MALTBY	RICHMOND PARK	ULLEY
HELLABY	WINGFIELD	OAKWOOD
BRAMLEY	MUNSBROUGH	WORRY GOOSE ISLAND
WICKERSLEY	STUDMOOR ROAD	BRECKS
FLANDERWELL	ROTHERHAM	STAG
FAR LANE	*	CANKLOW
TENNYSON ROAD		NURSERY DRIVE
DOVEDALE ROAD		THREE MAGPIES
EAST HERRINGTHORPE		WAVERLEY VIEW
*		*
ROTHERHAM		ROTHER VALLEY PARK
HIGH GREEN		EASTWOOD TRADING EST
CHAPELTOWN		ASDA
THORPE HESLEY		COLIN CAMPBELL
SCHOLES		MOWBRAY STREET
BLACKBURN		FULLERTON HOTEL
SHARDLOWS WORKS		PARK HOTEL
SUNNYSIDE		QUEENS HOTEL
CEDAR DRIVE		TENTER STREET
MOOR LANE		VIA CONANABY
RAVENFIELD		VIA MOWBRAY STREET
BRAITHWELL		VIA OLD DENABY
BARNSLEY		VIA RICHMOND PARK
SITWELL PARK GATES		VIA TRADING ESTATE
WHISTON		VIA WESLEY AVENUE
COWRAKES LANE		CIRCULAR
*		LIMITED STOP
ROTHERHAM		SCHOOL SERVICE
WORKSOP		PRIVATE
THURCROFT		SPECIAL
DINNINGTON		SHOW
HARTHILL		GARAGE
KIVETON PARK		*
ASTON		
SWALLOWNEST		
ECKINGTON		

Rotherham 1983/8   Single Deck/Minibus Vehicles   Printed white on black, Tyvek

*	SHARDLOWS	*	Not in Service
DONCASTER	ALSING ROAD	Greasbrough	Private
CONANBY	TREETON	Darnall	School Bus
BAWTRY	CATCLIFFE	Elm Tree	Works Service
SHEFFIELD	BRINSWORTH	Intake	*
THURNSCOE	THRYBERGH	Crane Road	
GOLDTHORPE	SILVERWOOD	Henley	
WATH	PARK HOTEL	Brampton	
ROTHERHAM	RICHMOND PARK	Ulley	
MALTBY	KIMBERWORTH PARK	Hoyland	
FLANDERWELL	DOVEDALE ROAD	Wentworth	
BRAMLEY	TEMPLEBOROUGH	Scholes	
BRECKS	ROTHERHAM	Rotherham	
WORKSOP	CHESTERFIELD	Bramley	
THURCROFT	CIRCULAR	Flanderwell	
DINNINGTON	SCHOOL SERVICE	Wickersley	
HARTHILL	PRIVATE	Silverwood	
KIVETON PARK	SPECIAL	Ravenfield	
ECKINGTON	SHOW	Braithwell	
KILLAMARSH	GARAGE	Maltby	
ROTHER VALLEY PARK	*	Dovedale Road	
SWALLOWNEST		East Dene	
HALFWAY		Aston	
ASTON		Ballifield	
ULLEY		Crystal Peaks	
ROTHERHAM		Killamarsh	
SITWELL PARK GATES		Halfway	
WHISTON		Worksop	
COWRAKES LANE		Treeton	
OAKWOOD		Catcliffe	
BRAITHWELL		Brinsworth	
RAVENFIELD		Rotherham	
CEDAR DRIVE		Meadowhall	
SUNNYSIDE		Whiston	
BARNSLEY		Thorpe Hesley	
HOYLAND		Chapeltown	
WENTWORTH		Rotherham Hospital	
BARROW COLLIERY		Sheffield	
ROTHERHAM		Kimberworth	
HIGH GREEN		Blackburn	
CHAPELTOWN		Parson Cross	
THORPE HESLEY		Cowrakes Lane	
SCHOLES		Greystones	
BLACKBURN		Midland Road	

Rotherham 1988	Double Deck Vehicles	Printed white on black, Tyvek
*	South Anston	*
Greasbrough	Intake	Templeborough
Doncaster	Parson Cross	Tinsley
Sheffield	Elm Tree	Izal Factory
Conisbrough	Totley	Brecks
Mexborough	Owler Bar	Canklow
Rotherham	Rotherham	Sheffield
Maltby	City	Rotherham
Bramley	Darnall	Three Magpies
Brecks	Sheffield	Eastwood Trading Est
Flanderwell	Thurnscoe	Asda
East Dene	Goldthorpe	Park Hotel
Dovedale Road	Wath	Tenter Street
East Herringthorpe	Wentworth	Greystones Road
Rotherham	Dinnington	Rotherham Hospital
High Green	Harthill	Rotherham
Chapeltown	Kiveton Park	Wincobank
Thorpe Hesley	Aston	Firth Park
Scholes	Ulley	*
Blackburn	Not in Service	Norton
Not in Service	Circular	Upwell Street
Cedar Drive	Special	Sandstone Road
Ravenfield	Private	Chancet Wood
Braithwell	School Special	Scarsdale Road
Barnsley	*	Hollythorpe Rise
Hoyland		Graves Park
Whiston		Longley
Cowrakes Lane		City
Rotherham		Woodseats
Worksop		Via Mowbray Street
Thurcroft		Via Richmond Park
Eckington		Via Trading Estate
Killamarsh		Sheffield
Woodhouse		Rotherham
Halfway		Limited Stop
Crystal Peaks		Fastline
Rotherham		Circular
Treeton		School Special
Catcliffe		Special
Brinsworth		Football
Thrybergh		*
Richmond Park		
Kimberworth Park		
Kimberworth		

Rotherham 1996   Double Deck Vehicles   Printed yellow on black, plastic

*	ROTHERHAM	ULLEY	SOUTH ANSTON
DONCASTER	SHEFFIELD	TEMPLEBOROUGH	NORTH ANSTON
RAWMARSH	NOT IN SERVICE	TINSLEY	DARNALL
SHEFFIELD	PRIVATE	BRECKS	GOLDTHORPE
CONISBROUGH	SCHOOL SPECIAL	CAKLOW	WATH
MEXBOROUGH	*	GREYSTONES ROAD	WENTWORTH
ROTHERHAM		WINCOBANK	LIMITED STOP
MALTBY	*Note: This blind was also used in B10M buses.*	FIRTH PARK	SCHOOL
BRECKS		*	FOOTBALL
FLANDERWELL		CIRCULAR	BRITISH RAIL
EAST DENE		Via THREE MAGPIES	*
DOVEDALE ROAD		Via RICHMOND PARK	
EAST HERRINGTHORPE		Via ARENA AND STADIUM	
ROTHERHAM		Via TEMPLEBOROUGH	
CHAPELTOWN		Via ROTHERHAM HOSP	
THORPE HESLEY		Via MEADOWHALL	
HIGH GREEN		Via BRINSWORTH	
MEADOWHALL		Via TINSLEY	
THRYBERGH		Via KIVETON PARK	
RICHMOND PARK		Via THURCROFT	
KIMBERWORTH PARK		Via DINNINGTON	
KIMBERWORTH		Via KILLAMARSH	
ROTHERHAM		Via CRYSTAL PEAKS	
CEDAR DRIVE		Via ROTHERHAM	
RAVENFIELD		Via MEXBOROUGH	
BARNSLEY		Via HOYLAND	
*		*	
HOYLAND		CLIFTON SCHOOL	
WHISTON		ST BERNARDS SCHOOL	
COWRAKES LANE		ASDA	
ROTHERHAM HOSPITAL		GALA BINGO	
WORKSOP		HELLABY	
ECKINGTON		GREASBROUGH	
MOSBOROUGH		FIRBECK	
CRYSTAL PEAKS		WOODSETTS	
ROTHERHAM		TODWICK	
TREETON		BRAMLEY	
CATCLIFFE		BLACKBURN	
BRINSWORTH		BRAITHWELL	
DINNINGTON		ELSECAR	
HARTHILL		THURCROFT	
KIVETON PARK		KILLAMARSH	
ASTON		HALFWAY	
WALES			

Doncaster 1983	Double Deck Vehicles	Printed white on black, Tyvek
*	TOWN CENTRE	*
ARKSEY	*	DONCASTER
BENTLEY	DONCASTER	TOWN CENTRE
SCAWTHORPE	ARMTHORPE	ADWICK SCHOOL
KENDAL ROAD	BARNBY DUN	BALBY CARR SCHOOL
HIGHFIELDS	DUNSCROFT	DON VALLEY SCHOOL
WOODLANDS	GOOLE	DANUM SCHOOL
ASKERN	HATFIELD	HUNGERHILL SCHOOL
BURGHWALLIS	LINDHOLME	THE McAULEY SCHOOL
SKELLOW	MOORENDS	*
SPROTBROUGH	RAWCLIFFE	VIA ASKERN ROAD
DONCASTER	SYKEHOUSE	VIA THE AVENUE
*	THORNE	VIA WOODLANDS
EDLINGTON	*	VIA WOODLANDS EAST
ROSSINGTON	SCHOOL SPECIAL	VIA CONANBY
BAWTRY	RACE SPECIAL	VIA WEST BESSACARR
WEST BESSACARR	FOOTBALL SPECIAL	VIA CENTRAL DRIVE
CONANBY	WORKS SERVICE	VIA RADBURN ROAD
CONISBROUGH	SPECIAL	VIA WEST END LANE
ROTHERHAM	PRIVATE	VIA BECKETT ROAD
SHEFFIELD	GARAGE	VIA HATFIELD
DONCASTER	*	VIA HAT. WOODHOUSE
INNER CIRCLE		VIA LINDHOLME
FINNINGLEY	*Note: This blind was also used in single deck vehicles.*	VIA SOUTH COMMON
WROOT		VIA STAINFORTH
MISSON		*
*		EASTFIELD ROAD
ALVERLEY LANE		MERCEL AVENUE
BROOMHOUSE LANE		WICKETT HERN ROAD
BALBY		OWSTON PARK
BECKETT ROAD		SILVER JUBILEE CLOSE
CANTLEY ESTATE		CIRCULAR
HEXTHORPE		NEW ESTATE
HYDE PARK		LONG LANDS LANE
RACECOURSE		INT. HARVESTERS
WHEATLEY HILLS		PILKINGTONS
INTAKE		PEGLERS
LOTHIAN ROAD		SPECIAL
FLORENCE AVENUE		PRIVATE
HOWBECK DRIVE		GARAGE
ST. PETERS ROAD		*
CLAY LANE		
EDENTHORPE		
WESTON ROAD		

Doncaster 1990 — Double Deck Vehicles — Printed white on black, Tyvek

*

GARAGE
NOT IN SERVICE
PRIVATE
WORKS SERVICE
SCHOOL BUS
HIGH MELTON COLLEGE
WAKEFIELD
ACKWORTH
SOUTH ELMSALL
HAMPOLE
DONCASTER

*

SKELLOW
OWSTON PARK
ARKSEY
BENTLEY
DONCASTER
SCAWTHORPE
WOODLANDS
HIGHFIELDS
ANSTEN CRESCENT
BESSACARR GRANGE
CANTLEY
TOWN CENTRE
BALBY
BROOMHOUSE LANE
ALVERLEY LANE
WESTON ROAD
TOWN CENTRE

*

INTAKE
LOTHIAN ROAD
SILVER JUBILEE CLOSE
CLAY LANE
TOWN CENTRE
ARMTHORPE
EDLINGTON
ROSSINGTON
OLD CANTLEY
WEST BESSACARR
DONCASTER
TICKHILL
CONANBY

SHEFFIELD
MEADOWHALL
ROTHERHAM
THE DOME LEISURE CENTRE
RACE COURSE
HYDE PARK
HEXTHORPE
TOWN CENTRE

*

BECKETT ROAD
EDENTHORPE
WARMSWORTH
FLORENCE AVENUE
TOWN CENTRE
GOOLE
MOORENDS
THORNE
DONCASTER

*

CLAY LANE
DUNSCROFT
BARNBY DUN
HATFIELD
LINDHOLME
HATFIELD WOODHOUSE
KIRK SANDALL
STAINFORTH
SCHOOL BUS
WORKS SERVICE
PRIVATE
NOT IN SERVICE
GARAGE

*

*

VIA SOUTH BUS STATION
VIA DONCASTER R.INF
VIA BECKETT ROAD
VIA BENTLEY
VIA WEST BESSACARR
MERCEL AVENUE
VIA CONANBY
VIA ROTHERHAM
LONG LANDS LANE
NEW ESTATE
CIRCULAR
GARAGE
DUPLICATE

*

BALBY CARR SCHOOL
DANUM SCHOOL
EDLINGTON SCHOOL
THE McAULEY SCHOOL
ADWICK SCHOOL
DON VALLEY SCHOOL
WOODLANDS FIRST SCH
WOODFIELD MIDDLE SCH

*

CROMPTONS
PEGLERS
CARR HILL IND ESTATE
WHEATLEY HALL IND EST
KIRK SANDALL IND EST

*

VIA SOUTH COMMON
VIA BRICKYARDS
VIA LINDHOLME
VIA HAT. WOODHOUSE
VIA STAINFORTH
VIA HATFIELD
VIA BRECKS LANE
VIA WHEATLEY HALL RD
HUNGERHILL SCHOOL

HATFIELD HIGH SCHOOL
STAINFORTH MIDDLE SCH
THORNE GRAMMAR SCH

*

Doncaster 1996   All Vehicles   Printed white on yellow on black, plastic (single aperture)

Sorry
Not in Service

GARAGE

PRIVATE

WORKS SERVICE

SCHOOL BUS

DONCASTER
Harworth Bawtry

BAWTRY
Ranskill Harworth

BAWTRY
Lound Everton

MISSON
Lound Bawtry

RETFORD
Harworth Ranskill

RETFORD
Everton Lound

HALLCROFT

SKELLOW

CARCROFT
Woodlands Owston Park

CARCROFT
Bentley

DONCASTER
Woodlands North Bus Stn

ARKSEY
Bentley

BENTLEY

TOLL BAR
Bentley

SCAWTHORPE

WOODLANDS
Highfields

HIGHFIELDS

DONCASTER
North Bus Station

BESSACARR GRANGE
West Bessacarr

ROSSINGTON
West Bessacarr

WEST BESSACARR

DONCASTER
West Bessacarr

DONCASTER
South Bus Station

BALBY

CANTLEY

DONCASTER
Town Centre

WESTON ROAD

BROOMHOUSE LANE

BROOMHOUSE LANE
Alverley Lane

BROOMHOUSE LANE
Hexthorpe

BROOMHOUSE LANE
Hexthorpe Alverley Lane

DONCASTER
Hexthorpe

INTAKE
Sandringham Road

LOTHIAN ROAD

DONCASTER
Town Centre

WHEATLEY HILLS
Hospital

CLAY LANE
Beckett Road

WHEATLEY
Beckett Road

DONCASTER
Town Centre

ARMTHORPE
Hospital Mercel Avenue

ARMTHORPE
Hospital Parkway

TICKHILL

EDLINGTON
Balby Road Roberts Road

EDLINGTON
Balby Road Hill Top

EDLINGTON
Howbeck Drive

DONCASTER
Ten Pound Walk

DONCASTER
South Bus Station

CONANBY

DENABY

MEADOWHALL
Conanby Rotherham

SHEFFIELD
Rotherham Meadowhall

DONCASTER
Meadowhall Rotherham

WHEATLEY PARK

LAKESIDE
The Yorkshire Outlet

LAKESIDE
Bennetthorpe The Dome

LAKESIDE
Yorkshire Outlet The Dome

DONCASTER
Lakeside

DOME LEISURE PARK
Town Centre Hyde Park

DOME LEISURE PARK
Town Centre Bennetthorpe

HEXTHORPE
Hyde Park Town Centre

Doncaster 1996   All Vehicles   Printed white on yellow on black, plastic (single aperture)

HEXTHORPE
Bennetthorpe Town Centre

DONCASTER
Town Centre

RACECOURSE

EDENTHORPE
Wheatley Hall Road

EDENTHORPE

THORNE
Edenthorpe Hatfield

THORNE
Edenthorpe Stainforth

DONCASTER
Stainforth Edenthorpe

MOORENDS
Stainforth Thorne

DONCASTER
Hatfield Edenthorpe

GOOLE
Rawcliffe

MOORENDS
Rawcliffe

THORNE
Rawcliffe

HATFIELD
Edenthorpe Dunscroft

DONCASTER
Stainforth

DUNSCROFT
Barnby Dunn

DUNSCROFT
Stainforth Westfield

BARNBY DUN

DONCASTER
South Bus Station

MOORENDS
Hatfield Thorne

DONCASTER
Thorne Hatfield

STAINFORTH

THORNE
Town service

HATFIELD

Sorry
Not in Service

GARAGE

PRIVATE

WORKS SERVICE

SCHOOL BUS

KIRKHOUSE GREEN

NORTON

BELLE VUE

KIRK SANDALL

ADWICK

ASKERN

FINNINGLEY

CARLTON

DUNSCROFT

CAMBLESFORTH

SCAWSBY

MEXBOROUGH

CUSWORTH

GooleTown Service
NORTH STREET

Goole Town Service
OLD GOOLE

Goole Town Service
FAIRFIELD

Goole Town Service
HOSPITAL Grange Road

Goole Town Service
HOSPITAL Grosvenor Avenue

Goole Town Service
NORTH STREET

Goole Town Service
WORKERS SERVICE

Chapter 16

The Garages

Greenland (GR)

Built in 1958, Greenland, or, to give its Sunday name, Greenland Road, was located in the east of the city at Darnall.

Constructed as part of the modernisation plan for tramway removal and built with a simple steel framework, covered in metal and glass sheeting, the design saved enormous amounts of weight and materials, which was still a consideration after the second world war.

Surrounded by a dwarf brick wall, to one end was a spacious engineering workshop, that could undertake all tasks associated with the smooth running of day to day operation, but could also undertake heavier work if so desired.

Three large, undercover bays, enclosed bus parking and associated workshops for tyres, batteries etc. A mechanical bus wash was also fitted and a steam cleaning bay was provided.

A large administrative block was at the opposite end of the building which housed the time house, paying in facilities and ticket rooms. In addition, a large canteen could accommodate upto 200 diners at the same time.

A large yard, which overlooked the main garage, was also provided. Such was the rush to get the garage into service, the yard, which could accommodate 100 buses, was brought into use before the main building was finished.

A number of portable buildings were placed on the top yard to facilitate operation whilst the accommodation block was finished, and these went on to be the base for the Sheffield Transport's driver training school, which moved over from Herries garage.

This enormous site, could accommodate 300 vehicles (buses were thinner and shorter back then), and was an important part of the day to day operation of the company.

There was also a side yard, which was mainly for staff parking (few staff owned motor vehicles), but could be used for about 20 buses overnight.

The training school moved to Meadowhall in 1979 and between 1982 and 1983 a large extension was built at the rear of the main garage, extending it by about a third. Measures were also undertaken to stabilise the top park.

As part of the extension, a new steam cleaning bay was built, MOT facilities and additional pits, taking over part of one of the original bays.

At deregulation, the paintshop, trimmers, plant maintenance and the glass fibre shop moved over from Central Works, and the garage took over the responsibility for heavy accident repairs for the district.

As the years went by, further alterations were made to the garage which included 'the tent' which was used for hywema jacks and for the pit stop programme. Driver training moved back in 1987 and they were accommodated in Portakabins erected on the side yard.

As well as the 'Beaver Hut', when Meadowhall head office closed, a separate set of Portakabins were erected to house the finance and computer services section. At its largest, the garage accommodated 250 buses on site.

The garage was closed by First in 1999 and the site was subsequently sold to B&Q for a warehouse store, which has subsequently closed.

Above

Greenland was home to the majority of the company's articulated buses over the years.

2001 was painted in this special advert for 'The Star' in 1987.

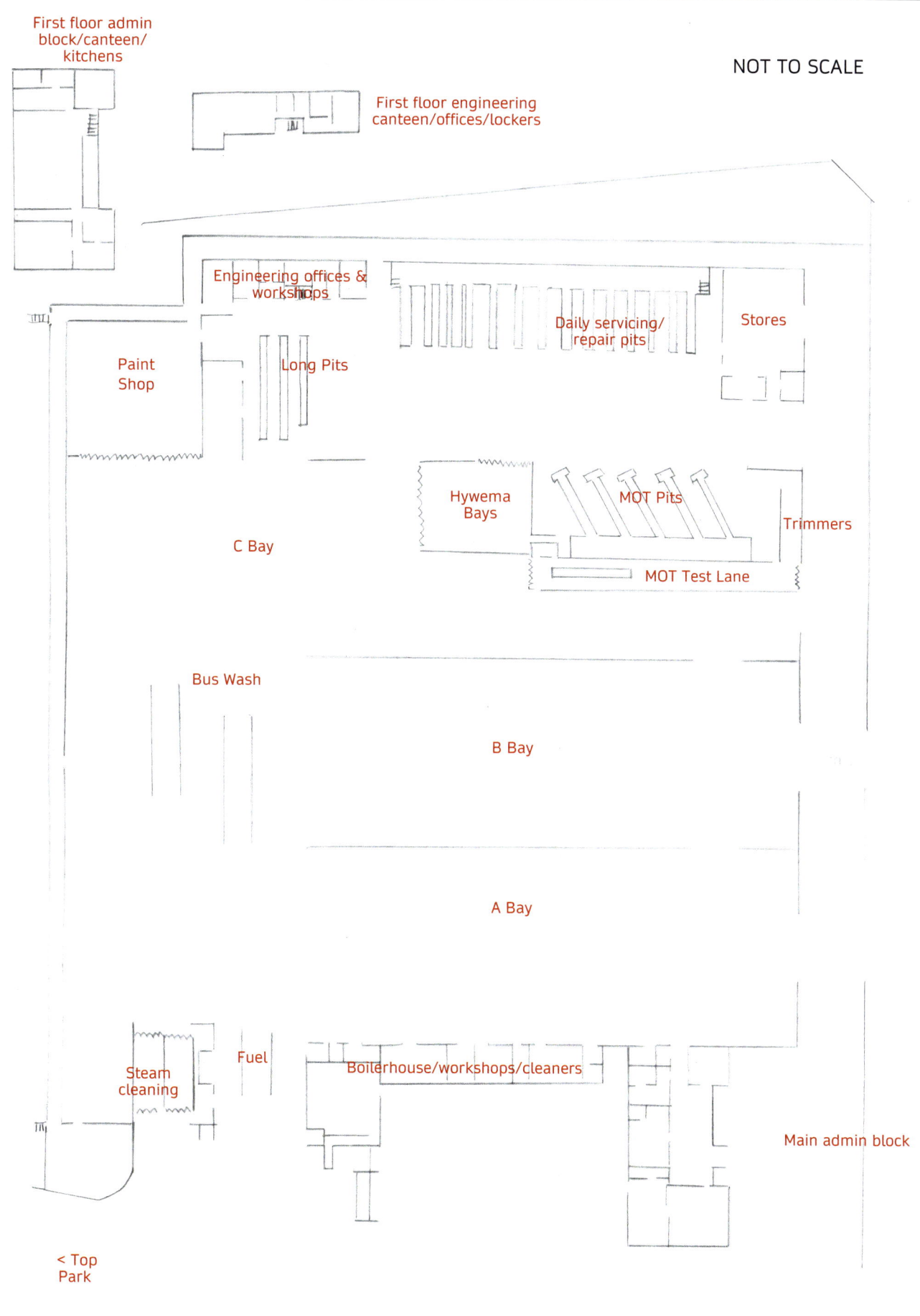

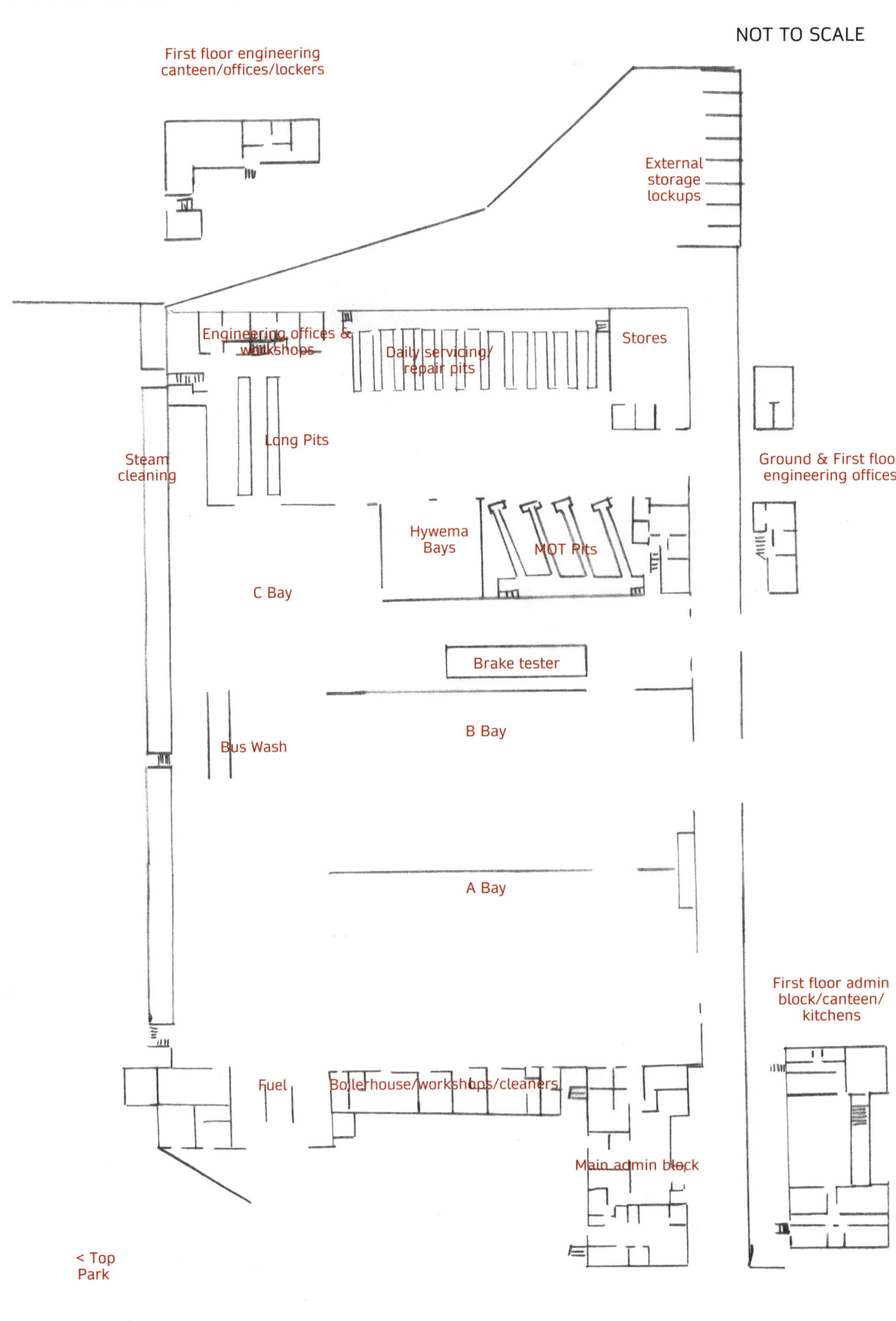

East Bank (EB)
Olive Gove (OG)

Left

Bus 693 managed to collide with the wall within the engineering bays of the garage late one night. The bodybuilders are seen here getting to work fitting a new front end to the bus, over one of the two 'artic' pits installed in the early 1980s.

Built in 1961, this was the final garage to be constructed by Sheffield Transport as part of the tramway withdrawal programme.

A virtual carbon copy of Greenland, it was slightly smaller and had a smaller top park for parking of buses.

Built on the site of allotments and playing fields, it followed the same pattern of three bays for parking, an engineering section and administration block. The plans from this garage were used by Leeds City Transport to construct Middleton and Bramley, under a Yorkshire Improvement committee, which also saved Leeds from having to pay architect's fees.

As with Greenland, during the early 1980s work was undertaken to modernise the garage with additional pits and the fitment of a brake tester. East Bank was also home to the district engineers and new office accommodation was built for them in addition to facilities for the emergency crews, who manned the city's Matador recovery vehicle.

More pressing, however, was the need to secure the back of the property, which was slipping on to the main building below.

After heavy rain, buses were forbidden from parking near the garage, on the top park, for fear they would simply roll down the bank.

A substantial amount of money was spent building a perimeter wall around the site, raising part of it by six feet and underpinning the building. A new warm air, automatic door system was also fitted in the fuelling bays.

The garage was initially closed by SYT in 1988 and was used by an indoor karting company called Trax. They tarmaced over the majority of the interior parking bays, but left the workshops untouched.

As they couldn't make that business work, they eventually left, and although still owned by SYPTA, the building suffered some vandalism.

Purchased by the new Mainline in 1994, the garage had to have significant money spent on it again to restore it to a functioning location. This included removal of all the tarmac, restoring the drains, making good all vandalism and refurbishment of the accommodation block.

Under First, the adjacent Charlotte Road garage was also brought into the site.

Plans to buy Olive Grove Road, which is in front of the garage, to make one complete facility, came to nought, so the site is still split in two.

Further remedial works were required on Charlotte Road, as it suffered some subsidence (the entire area was quite marshy in the past, and is riddled with coal mine workings), and a new fence was erected around the site.

Further works have been undertaken on site, which now has a new inspection bay, new bus washes, and has received work on the roof.

Currently the only garage in Sheffield, the former canteen facility is now in use as offices, with all staff changeovers occurring in the city centre.

As well as the day to day running of the operation, the garage can undertake all kinds of rebuilding jobs and chassis work. Two hywema bays were built in PTE days, and these are still used to day for engine changes and other jobs for which a pit, or hardstanding, are impractical.

The garage is located in the south of the city, about a mile from the city centre in Arbourthorne.

Herries (HE)

Right

The 1950's heritage is plain to see in this photo taken just prior to the garage's closure. To the left of the Leopard, a small paintshop had been installed in 1986, and two painters turned out one bus per week, in addition to those painted centrally.

The first of the new garages to be constructed by Sheffield Transport for the tramway replacement programme, this garage, built in 1952, was constructed on marshland, within a stone's throw of Sheffield Wednesday's Hillsborough stadium.

Due to restrictions after the war, the garage was constructed using brick and reinforced concrete, as there was a national shortage of steel (somewhat ironic for a city with the greatest concentration of steelworks in the UK).

The plans were originally based on a London Transport design, and consisted of three separate elements. The first was an engineering block that housed pits and stores facilities. A separate, covered, three lane fuelling/wash station, was also part of this block.

The second element was a three bay parking garage, which also included workshops for electrical and bodymaking disciplines. Such was the shortage of building materials, the third bay was constructed slightly later than the other two.

The third element was an accommodation block. Again, due to material shortages, this was initially not built, and wooden huts were used for a number of years until bricks and concrete could be sourced for its completion.

The garage was fiercely independent, and was known by most crews as the 'Hillsborough Bus Company'. It was, however, a friendly place.

During 1979 it was recognised that the workshop area required modernising, and the garage in general was brought upto modern standards.

A new, five pit, engineering block was built on the land in front of the current workshop and new fuel tanks were installed. In addition, a new wash bay was built, and a secondary facility was provided inside the garage.

To the rear of the garage, the parking yard was refurbished and the newly modernised facility could hold about 160 buses, although the parking situation was tight.

Land was acquired just after the rebuilding of the engineering bays, on a plot adjacent.

The Dairy Park allowed breathing space and the allocation eventually settled at around 170.

At deregulation the tinsmiths and blacksmiths moved to a small building at rear of the canteen, and the former driving school buildings at the rear of the main building were repurposed as a snooker hall and welfare facilities.

An extension, formed out of portable buildings, was added to the accommodation block, to house the additional clerical staff made homeless by the closure of the area office on Arundel Gate.

Closed by Mainline in 1994, it required further modernisation to bring it up to modern standards.

The site was bought by Hillfoot Steel, who occupied adjacent premises, and is currently in use by them for warehousing purposes. They have made numerous modifications to the frontage of the site, but it is still recognisable to this day.

The former workshops were sub leased to a high end car dealership, but this has now ended. South Yorkshire Police were regular visitors to the canteen on site, as it was it was said the food was better than at their Niagra training base, less than a mile away.

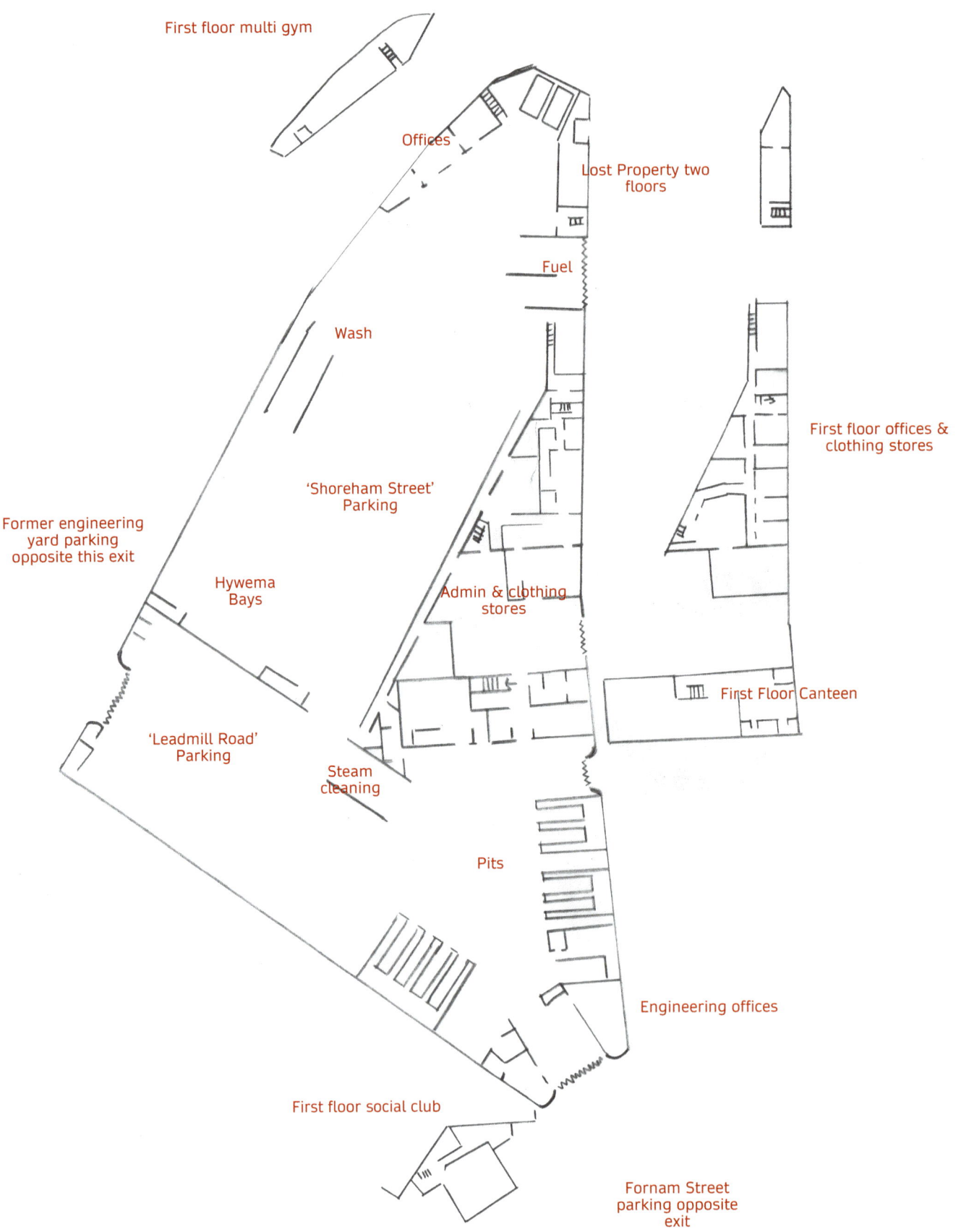

Leadmill (LE)

Left

The entrance to the fuel pumps was hardly ideal, and led to buses queuing on the street to enter the building, which could be difficult if bands were playing in the adjacent Leamill nightclub.

2183 and 2217 are being fuelled and oiled at the end of another evening peak.

Leadmill was the oldest garage in the system, and the one that continually seemed to have a cloud hanging over it.

A former tram depot, the garage had been converted in 1960 to accommodate 125 buses and the associated workshops to go with it.

Two buildings in one, Shoreham Street tram depot backed on to Leadmill bus garage, which was an extension built on in 1938.

When they were combined, a hole was knocked through to permit through running of buses.

The former tram entrance was blocked up, somewhat crudely, and the fuel tanks were located in the space. The tram tracks were removed and new roadway built over the top. This left an enormous void under the garage, which was used to store all the corporation's archive, a facility also used by the PTE and latterly, Mainline.

The original Leadmill had small pits for bus servicing and was also home to the conductor training school.

The size and shape of the garage hampered modern operation, and as early as the 1970s the PTE was on the lookout for a new location for the allocation.

As slum clearance took place in the late 1960s and early 1970s around the garage, which also took into account plans to build an urban motorway to the south of the city, additional parking land was acquired on the adjacent Fornham Street.

Initially, this was rough ground and as the buses were simply parked there, it had been known for vehicles to be stolen or rough sleepers to make use of the vehicles. In PTE days, a secure fence was built, making the compound available for about 30 buses.

A yard was also acquired on Shoreham Street, which allowed a further 30 buses to be parked in the open.

The PTE could never find suitable land to build a replacement, despite even considering building on top of the central bus station, and the garage was subject to light modernisation which included further pits, a new chassis wash and the creation of a lifting bay.

The garage housed the company's uniform store for Sheffield and the districts cash counting facility.

Being within walking distance of the city centre, many crews made use of the canteen facility here.

When Mainline was privatised, the lease deal for Leadmill was very short, as the land was in a prime development zone.

The lost property section closed and became the responsibility of the individual garages and cash counting moved to Rotherham.

After the allocation moved to Olive Grove, it was used as general storage, even featuring in the film 'The Full Monty', as the rehearsal rooms for the band.

The garage was listed at one end, and that survives today. The rest of the main site was sold for student housing, and was swiftly demolished. The land on Fornham Street was also used for that purpose, but additionally houses a small supermarket.

The land on Shoreham Street was sold to the BBC, who built new studios for BBC Radio Sheffield.

A friendly garage, that coped remarkably well with its Edwardian surroundings, no job was too small for the engineering team on site.

The office block also housed the Coachline unit for many years, and its long, winding passages resounded to laughter, emanating form all parts of the building.

Halfway (H)(HA)

Right

Formerly the main exit of the garage, after the closure of the 'new' pits, this area became the hywema bay.

Bus 2474 is undergoing an engine change, with a brand new Gardner six litre, turbo charged, unit being installed.

This small, 1960s built garage, was acquired by the PTE with the business of Booth & Fisher (Motor Services) Limited.

Unusually, the PTE kept the name going for a few years after acquisition, and also operated the adjacent fuel filling station as well.

Located at the very south eastern boundary of Sheffield, it was a stone's throw from the Derbyshire boundary, and the towns of Killamarsh and Eckington were within walking distance.

Despite its location, it was allocated to Rotherham district for engineering purposes, and shared in their practices and routines.

It was in an ideal location for the new Mosborough 'townships' being developed for the expansion of the city in the early 1970s, and was beside the new Waterthorpe estate.

Inherited as part of the operations were a vast quantity of contract operations for the National Coal Board and numerous school services in northern Derbyshire. Over time, these would be expanded and turned into stage carriage operations.

The building was fairly simple in construction, being built of brick and metal sheeting. In the main shed was servicing pits for buses and coaches, and a bus wash.

A fairly large accommodation block was also on site, with offices and canteen facilities.

Under the auspices of the PTE, new engineering pits were built across the road from the garage on Old Lane, and hardstanding was acquired at the rear and front of the site.

The exit incorporated a steep slope, and certain types of bus were forbidden from exiting the garage this way. The MCW Metrobus was banned from the building, although evidence suggests that they could fit.

The garage was another that was constantly under threat. The closure of colleries had taken a huge chunk out of the revenue, and it was a constant battle to keep the garage open and solvent.

In 1990, the new pits were rented out and the on site facilities were downgraded.

The staff bent over backwards to keep the garage afloat.

With the closure of Greenland, the garage got a new lease of life, and the garage was renovated, with the new pits being brought back into use.

It was the location for the first Wright Gemini buses purchased by FirstGroup and the batch could regularly be seen pounding the streets of service 41.

A small amount of Derbyshire contract work remained, but the diminishing returns on school work saw that that part of the operation eventually fold.

As part of the general milage reduction by First, the garage was closed and sold to TM Travel, who still operate it today.

The garage can be found on Station Road, Halfway. At its maximum, it accommodated around 100 buses.

Over the years, as new roads have opened, the need for smaller satellite garages has diminished, with operators preferring to concentrate operations on larger sites.

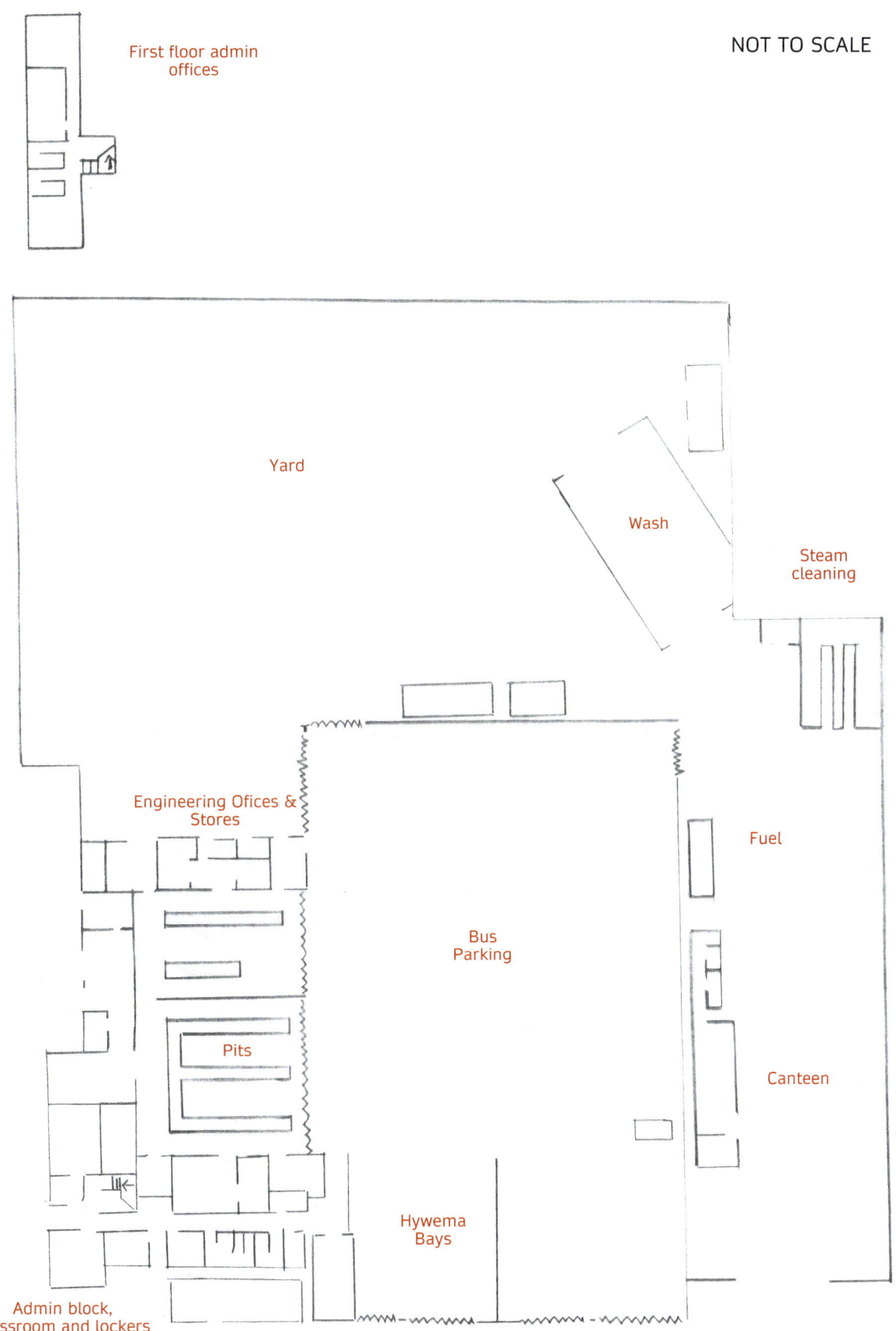

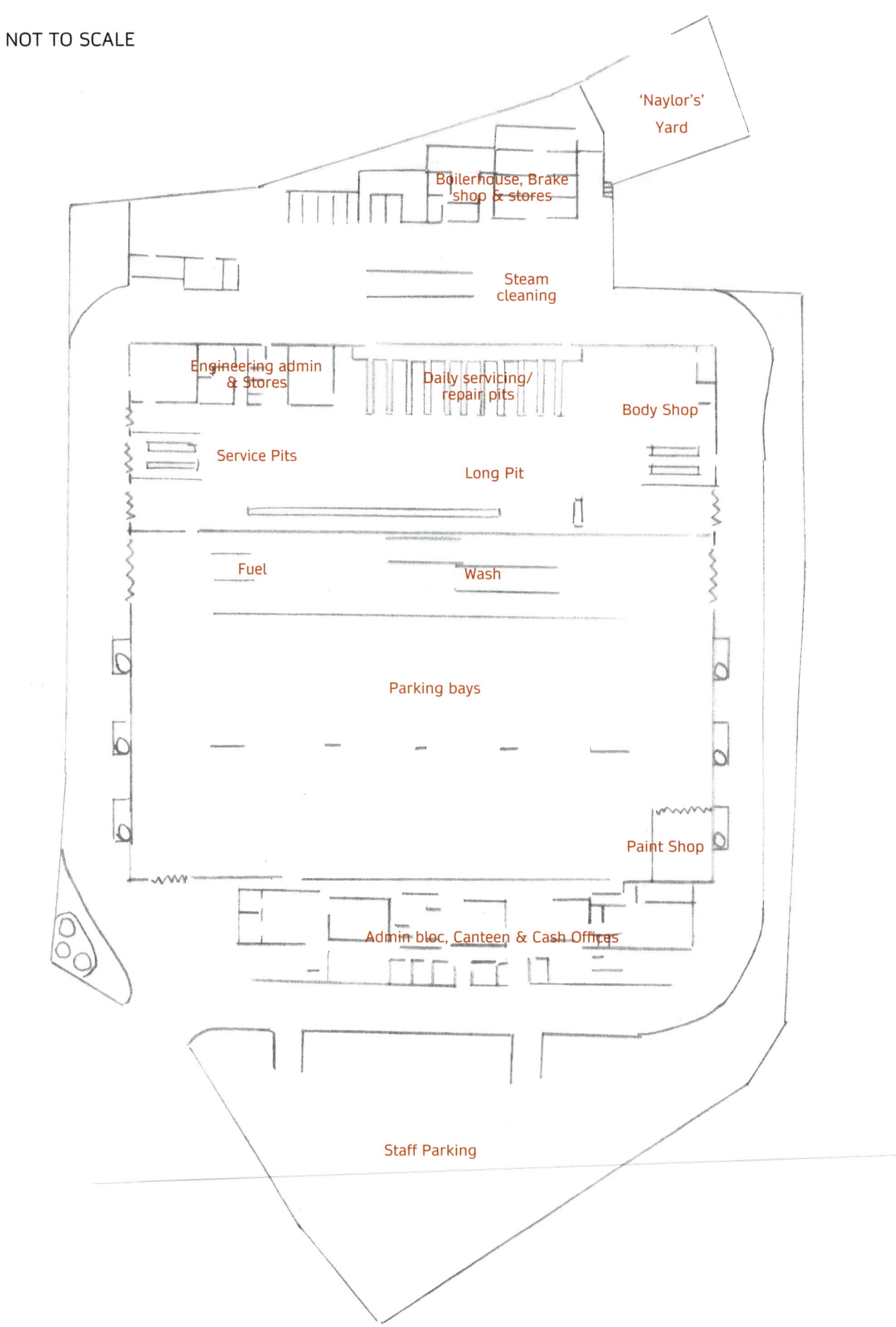

Rotherham (R)

Left

A new, two bay paintshop was constructed inside the garage in 1989, boosting the amount of capacity that could be used.

2267 and 2413 are undergoing repaint, by brush, in 1991.

Serious toolbox action going on with Dominators 2423 and 2434 in the remote pit section of the garage.

Much has already been said about the garage in this book.

Completed in 1982, the garage was part of SYPTEs expansionist policy for the county. Built on the site of a former ironworks and quarry, the design was a slightly modified example, based on general principles, from Greater Manchester's Tameside facility in Ashton.

Hardstanding, all undercover, provided accommodation for 160 buses, and two bus washes were also installed, together with fuel lanes. Unusually for the PTE, buses were going to be block parked, in rows, the normal pattern being herringbone style.

A large accommodation block was built to house the district's engineering and operational management and a canteen was also provided.

Two sunken gardens were also provide for staff use and cash counting facilities were installed. These facilities would be in addition to those provided in Rotherham town centre.

An engineering section consisted of over 20 pits and a MOT testing facility was also provided. This was also going to be the district's works facilities, so, a body shop was also added.

Externally, a perimeter road was constructed, allowing off road parking for vehicles, and a 200 space car park was built for staff.

A degrease bay was built and a facilities building, with separate stores for flammable goods, was also provided. Two coal fired boilers, built to support local industry, were maintained to provide hating throughout the site.

Sadly, the expansion never came, and from deregulation onwards, the building resounded to echoes of what might have been.

As mentioned earlier, plans were made to vacate the premises, but a new life was found for the garage, sharing the operational duties with the commercial section.

Gradually, the engineering facilities were put to their full use, and buses from all over the UK could be found under the roof, rubbing alongside native stock.

Once Meadowhall head office closed, some functions moved here, with the Training School relocating from Greenland.

Once Greenland closed, additional work was brought into the building, and it very nearly reached its peak capacity.

Under FirstGroup ownership, the garage would seem to have a more secure future, as it effectively became the defacto central works for the group, with buses being sent here for refurbishment, accident repair and repainting.

However, general malaise in the town, and the ongoing reduction in miles worked by the company, saw the garage closed in 2017, with staff and vehicles moving to Sheffield and Doncaster.

The garage is currently standing empty and has recently been used as a vaccination centre and also used as a training facility for South Yorkshire Police.

It is located on Midland Road in the Masbrough area of the town, about a ten minute walk from the Interchange.

Doncaster (DR) (DO)

Right and Below

The new engineering building was built between 1982 and 1984 and replaced cramped facilities inside the main garage.

In this 1995 shot, buses are undergoing routine exam and two new Volvo B6s are undergoing preparation for service.

2362 bore this livery for JWE Phoneshops, and is seen in the spacious garage yard.

The former garage and engineering workshops of Doncaster Transport were acquired by the PTE in 1974.

Located on Leicester Avenue, a stone's throw from the famous Doncaster Racecourse, these premises had been home to the town's buses and trolleybuses for many years.

The frontage incorporated the entrance and exit to the building, framed by offices on either side and above.

Entry through the front door was greeted by a small reception area, with a palatial staircase to the offices above.

The radio room and traffic offices were located here, as was the district's operational management. A canteen was also on site, which it was reputed, made the best chips in the region.

The main garage had the usual bus wash and fuelling facilities, with workshops on either side of the building, including a full bodyshop and paintshop.

As part of the general modernisation programme carried out by the PTE, proposals were made for a brand new engineering block to be built on the rear yard of the premises.

This new building necessitated the removal of the former shed that was on site, and for a time buses were parked on the racecourse site.

This new workshop had the full suite of facilities that were now required, including MOT facilities. Some tasks were maintained in the older workshops, like painting, but the older portions of the garage were used for storage, especially preserved vehicles.

Part of the garage site was sold in 1993, and operations consolidated on the new workshop site, with most parking now being on hardstanding.

A small portion of the old garage was repurposed as a fuel and wash facility, and the opportunity was taken to remove all the electrical substation equipment fitted as part of the PTEs 'Electroline' trolleybus experiment.

Office accommodation was moved to Doncaster town centre, although some staff remained in the garage, now sharing facilities with the engineering section.

Doncaster was renamed Leger Way, and this is the name is still carries today.

The garage suffered a spate of vehicle thefts, mainly minibuses, and additional security measures were introduced, which included new fencing.

The workshops have been used as an overspill for vehicle refurbishment when Rotherham was operating at full capacity, and with its relative isolation, has been used to test out various ideas before being committed company wide.

Under First, for a time, the garage was also linked to York, and vehicles from their allocation could be seen on site undergoing work and rectification.

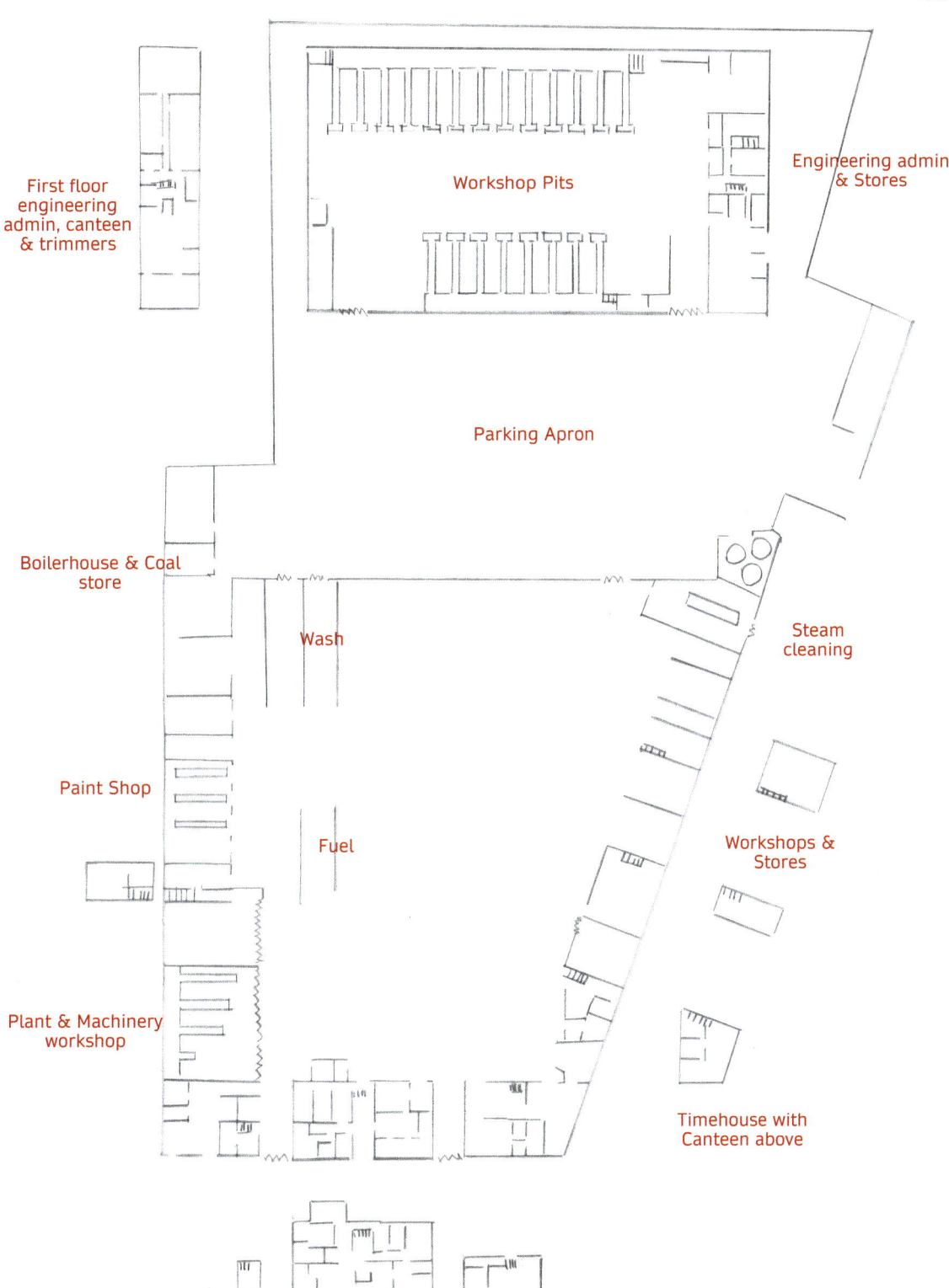

NOT TO SCALE

Dunscroft (DT)

Left and Below

Anybody want to buy an Atlantean?

The vast grass field at Dunscroft was used for storage when East Bank had to be cleared. In this 1991 scene, this is the front row of three lines of buses on site.

All these buses would go onto to have further lives, some of them were barely ten years old.

1780 and 311 stand on the pits in its last year.

The smallest garage with the company, Dunscroft, or Bootham Lane, had been acquired by the PTE with the business of T.Severn & Sons.

It was retained as a satellite garage to Doncaster, and maintained an allocation of about 35 buses, mainly operating services from Doncaster to the former pit communities of Hatfield, Stainforth, Dunscroft, Thorne and then onto the villages of the East Riding, eventually ending up at Goole.

It also handled quirky services to the villages around Sykehouse, which operated in different directions at different times of the day.

At deregulation, very little changed, with the trunk routes to the north east being its bread and butter. A small amount of 'town' work was taken on, with the operation of service 172 to Clay Lane and additional vehicles were brought in when SYT purchased Premier Coaches, forming a small, district coaching and private hire operation.

The facility consisted of two small sheds, which incorporated two pits and a bus wash/refuelling facility.

Very few buses were parked under cover, with the majority of the fleet being housed in a yard at the front of the garage.

A vast field occupied part of the site, and this became quite famous, locally, as the dumping ground for buses that were for disposal, or for long term storage.

Upto 80 vehicles could be stored on the land, and large swathes of Atlanteans, Dodges, Nationals and Metrobuses made their way here for onward disposal or sale.

The garage was also a handy place to 'blood' new managers, being the starting place for many a member of senior management, over the years.

Changes to the road pattern in Doncaster had caused a drop in patronage in the town, just as the company was ridding itself of competition locally, and cost savings required that the garage be closed in 1996.

The garage's allocation had been quirky from the start, and had oddments from former independents allocated to it from time to time, although the allocation had settled to be mainly AN68 Atlanteans, some Dennis Dominators had been allocated just prior to closure.

After closure, the site was quickly cleared and a small housing estate was built on the remains.

The garage's allocation was moved into Leger Way.

A friendly garage, it was noted for the number of family members that worked there, either as mother and daughter, father and son or husband and wife. It was that kind of town, and the garage was still referred to locally as Severn's, long after that name had been consigned to the history books.

Top and Right

Rotherham could turn its hand to anything to get the show back on the road.

The driver of 2364 misjudged the angle of attack at Canklow Bridge in Rotherham, as a car approached in the opposite direction, in 1991. The resulting damage required removal of the roof and a new one fitted, which is seen in these two shots.

Bus 2451, had only recently been repainted into the Mainline livery, but has caught fire. Luckily, it had been extinguished quickly, but this rear shot shows the chimney arrangement that helped spread so many Dominator fires.

2420, seen right, wasn't so lucky and was withdrawn after this incident in 1993.

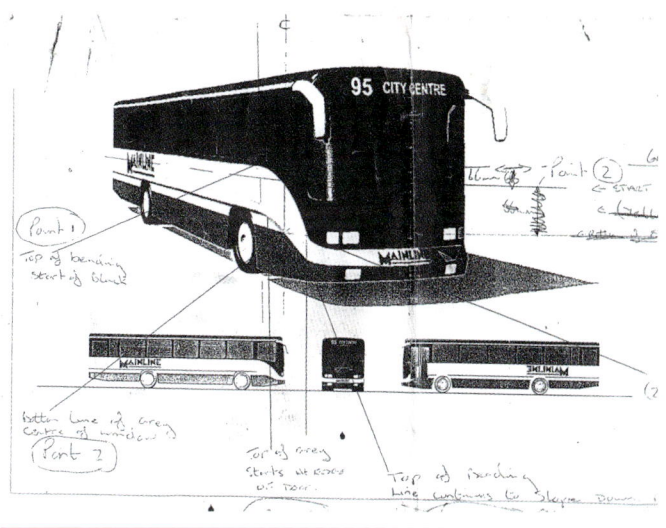

Clockwse from Top Left

If only running buses was easy. An errant Metrobus, 1950, has come to grief at Millhouses with a hub failure and 2477 has hit a cherry picker in Sheffield Interchange.

Generally garages get on with the job of day to day work. Here two shots of 2487 show it undergoing an axle change and then in later life, work on its demister motors. 2362 is seen on the pits in Doncaster, undergoing a routine exam.

Paintshop staff are generally issued with diagrams to work from. No apologies for their condition, but these show the working diagrams for the Silver Service livery and unrealised branding for service 60.

Chapter 16

The Fleet

The company inherited nearly 1000 vehicles from the PTE on deregulation day in October 1986. As well as the operational fleet, there was also a number of buses that were recorded on 'fleet strength', but would never operate a mile of service for the company.

The fleet summary intends to give an outline of the company's buses between deregulation day, and the end of 1998. Unfortunately, space precludes a more in depth look at the items such as chassis/body numbers, registration details and allocations. For those, the Omnibus Society and the Sheffield Omnibus Enthusiasts Society hold a vast array of materials for the ardent enthusiast.

Withdrawal dates are given by year. This is when the vehicle was 'struck off' the fleet. A vehicle may have been withdrawn some time previously and been retained on reserve, stored or placed on hire to another operator.

The information is conveyed in the normal style for body types and capacities

Body types an seating codes are shown as follows:

Before seating capacity

A - Articulated Bus

B - Single Deck Bus

C - Singe Deck Coach

DP - Dual Purpose Seats

H - Highbridge Double Deck Bus

O - Open Top Bus

After seating capacity

D - Dual Door

F - Front Entrance/Exit

L - Rear Tail lift fitted

R - Rear Entrance/Exit

T - Triple Door

t - Toilet Fitted

For example, H46/32F, refers to a highbridge bus, fitted with 46 seats upstairs, 32 seats downstairs, with a front entrance/exit door.

Below

By the end of 1997. the fleet was fairly standardised, with the double deck fleet predominately Dennis in manufacture.

Seen here are all three main variants of the body, with 2312 representing the Northern Counties batch, 2264, 2105 and 2255 representing Alexander and finally 2364 with an East Lancs version.

Exterior parking was cheaper than being undercover, and this can be seen to good effect at Doncaster garage.

Fleet Summary 1986

Opening Fleet for SYT Limited (including new and reinstatements for 1986)

	Chassis	Body	Fleetnumbers
10	Leyland National 10351 B/1R	Leyland B44F	5 - 14
6	Leyland Leopard PSU3G/4R	Duple DP53F	15 - 20
1	Leyland National 2 NL116L11/1R	Leyland B49F	21
2	Leyland National 2 NL116L11/1R	Leyland B22F*	22/3
8	Leyland National 2 NL116L11/1R	Leyland B52F	24 - 31
14	Dennis Domino SDA1202	Optare B33F	41 - 54
3	Ford Transit	Carlyle DP20F	61 - 63
1	Leyland Leopard PSU3C/4R	Alexander DP19F**	65
2	Leyland Leopard PSU3C/4R	Alexander DP49F	66/68
1	Leyland Tiger TRCTL11/3R	Plaxton C51F	70
1	Leyland Tiger TRCTL11/3R	Plaxton C49Ft	73
3	Dennis Dorchester SDA808	Plaxton C44Ft	75 - 77
4	Leyland Leopard PSU3E/4R	Duple DP53F	96 - 99
1	Leyland Olympian TL11/2RSP	ECW CH47/20Dt	100
1	Leyland Atlantean AN68/1R	Alexander O43/31F	287
2	Leyland Atlantean AN68A/1R	East Lancs H43/32F	322 - 323
45	MCW Metrobus DR102/3	MCW H46/27D	450 - 494
5	MCW Metrobus DR104/3	MCW H46/27D	495 - 499
2	Leyland Olympian ON6LXB/1R	Roe H47/29F	501 - 502
1	Dennis Dominator DD101A	East Lancs H45/28D	521
2	Dennis Dominator DD120B	East Lancs H45/29D	523 - 524
1	Daimler Fleetline CRG6LXB	Park Royal O47/31D	700
1	Leyland PD3/1	Roe H39/30R	904
1	Ford T152	Duple C31F	1020
1	Leyland Leopard PSU3F/5R	Duple C45F	1021
1	Leyland Leopard PSU3B/4R	Plaxton C51F	1026
1	Leyland National 1151/2R	Leyland DP20F ***	1029
3	Leyland National 1151/2R	Leyland B28F ***	1030 - 1032
4	Bristol LHS6L	ECW B35F	1050/1/2/4
1	Bedford YLQ	Duple C45F	1056
8	Leyland National 1035 1B/1R	Leyland B44F	1059 - 1066
5	Leyland National 2 NL106BL11/1R	Leyland B44F	1072 - 1076
3	Leyland Leopard PSU3C/4R	Plaxton C51F	1085 - 1087
2	Leyland Leopard PSU3E/4R	Plaxton C51F	1092 - 1093
1	Bedford YLQ	Plaxton C45F	1096
1	Leyland Atlantean AN68/1R	Roe H43/33F	1135
1	Leyland PD2/30	Roe H33/26RD	1156
8	Leyland Fleetline FE30/AGR	Roe H43/27D	1436 - 1441/4/5
5	Leyland Fleetline FE30/AGR	Roe H43/27D	1448/51 -53/55
6	Leyland Fleetline FE30/AGR	MCW H46/25D	1511/14 - 18
31	Leyland Fleetline FE30/AGR	Alexander H45/29D	1530 - 1560
15	Leyland Fleetline FE30/AGR	East Lancs H45/29D	1561 - 1575
14	Leyland Atlantean AN68A/1R	East Lancs H45/29D	1576 - 1587/89 - 90
74	Leyland Atlantean AN68A/1R	Roe H45/29D	1601 - 1674

Wheelchairs = *7, **8, ***5

	Chassis	Body	Fleetnumbers
6	Leyland Atlantean AN68A/1R	Alexander H45/29D	1675 - 1680
52	Leyland Atlantean AN68A/1RSPL	Alexander H45/29D	1681 - 1732
44	Leyland Atlantean AN68A/1RSPL	Roe H45/29D	1733 - 1776
30	Leyland Atlantean AN68B/1R	Alexander H45/29D	1777 - 1806
30	Leyland Atlantean AN68B/1R	Marshall H45/29D	1807 - 1836
60	MCW Metrobus DR102/6	MCW H46/31F	1837 - 1896
20	MCW Metrobus 2 DR104/11	MCW H47/33F	1901 - 1920
20	MCW Metrobus 2 DR104/12	MCW H47/33F	1921 - 1940
10	MCW Metrobus 2 DR102/50	MCW DPH42/28F	1941 - 1950
10	MCW Metrobus 2 DR102/53	MCW DPH42/28F	1951 - 1960
10	Leyland DAB 07 - 1735B-2220SY	Leyland DAB AB61T	2001 - 2010
3	Leyland DAB 07 - 1735L-2220SY	Leyland DAB ADP67D	2011 - 2013
174	Dennis Dominator DDA133	Alexander H46/32F	2101 - 2274
1	Dennis Dominator DDA165	Alexander H46/33F	2275
29	Dennis Dominator DDA165	Alexander H46/32F	2276 - 2304
10	Dennis Dominator DDA165	Northern Counties H47/33F	2311 - 2320
15	Dennis Dominator DDA901	East Lancs H46/32F	2351 - 2365
49	Dennis Dominator DDA901	Alexander H46/32F	2401 - 2449
20	Dennis Dominator DDA910	Alexander H46/32F	2451 - 2470
15	Dennis Dominator DDA1011	Alexander DPH45/33F	2471 - 2485
5	Dennis Dominator DDA1011	Alexander DPH45/24F	2486 - 2490

1987

New

	Chassis	Body	Fleetnumbers
26	Dodge S56	Reeve Burgess B25F	101 - 126
13	Dodge S56	Reeve Burgess DP25F	127 - 139
60	Dodge S56	Reeve Burgess B25F	140 - 189

Withdrawn during 1987

501/2, 1026, 1050/1/2/4, 1087, 1135, 1436 - 1441, 1444/5/8, 1451 - 1453, 1455, 1511, 1514 - 1518, 1536

1988

New & Acquired

	Chassis	Body	Fleetnumbers
30	Renault S56	Reeve Burgess B25F	190 - 219
2	Bedford YNT	Plaxton C53F	82/87
1	Leyland Leopard PSU3C/4R	Plaxton B53F	84
1	Leyland Leopard PSU3F/4R	Plaxton B64F	86
1	Ford R1014	Plaxton C35F	89

Withdrawn during 1988

9, 12, 13, 450 - 499, 1020, 1056, 1059, 1096, 1619, 1623, 1643, 1646, 1650.

Vehicles taken over from H. Wilson (trading as Premier) allocated fleetnumbers, but not taken on to fleet strength, have been omitted.

1989

New & Acquired

	Chassis	Body	Fleetnumbers
8	Renault S56	Northern Counties B23F	220 - 227
12	Renault S56	Northern Counties B25F	228 - 239
15	Renault S56	Reeve Burgess B25F	240 - 254
4	Ford Iveco Daily	Reeve Burgess B25F	255 - 258
2	Leyland National 10351/1R	Leyland B41F	3/4
4	Leyland Leopard PSU3E/4R	Duple C53F	92 - 95
1	Leyland Leopard PSU3D/4R	Plaxton B55F	69
1	Bova Futura FHD12-28D	Bova C49Ft	71
1	Volvo B58	Irizar C49F	72
2	Dennis Javelin	Duple C53F	78 - 79

Withdrawn during 1989

61 - 63, 66, 68, 72, 86, 322/3, 521, 523/4, 700, 1561 - 1575, 1601 - 1618, 1620 - 1622, 1624 - 1642, 1644/5, 1647 - 1649

1990

New & Acquired

	Chassis	Body	Fleetnumbers
50	Volvo B10M	Alexander B51F	601 - 650
50	Renault S56	Reeve Burgess B23F	301 - 350
4	Leyland Tiger	Duple C51F	62/3/7/8
1	Volvo B10M	Plaxton C46Ft	72

Withdrawn during 1990

11, 14, 15 - 18, 28, 30/1, 84, 89, 96/7, 99, 106, 1031/2, 1063, 1066, 1085/6, 1530 - 1535, 1537 - 1560, 1577, 1579, 1581, 1583 - 1587, 1653/4/7, 1661, 1663 - 1680, 1708, 1718, 1735, 1837 - 1845, 1851, 1880, 1883 - 1886, 1888 - 1896

1991

New

	Chassis	Body	Fleetnumbers
40	Volvo B10M	Alexander B51F	651 - 690
2	Volvo B10M	Plaxton C48Ft	1010/1
39	Renault S56	Reeve Burgess B23F	351 - 389

Withdrawn during 1991

3, 5 - 8, 41 - 52, 54, 92/3, 1029/30, 1065, 1072/3, 1092/3, 1576, 1578, 1580, 1582, 1589, 1590, 1651/2, 1655/6, 1658/9, 1660, 1662, 1705, 1776, 1846 - 1850, 1852/3, 1856/7, 1860, 1862 - 1864, 1867, 1869 - 1873, 1875, 1877 - 1879, 1881/2

Right

Bus 20 was transferred from Herries to Leadmill to operate the X32 to Leeds.

It's seen here on the pits, being prepared for service, which would include refitting of ticketing equipment, and restoration of the destination blinds.

1992

New

Chassis	Body	Fleetnumbers
25 Volvo B10M	Alexander B51F	691 - 715
1 Volvo B6R	Plaxton B34F	401
1 Dennis Dart 9SDL3	Northern Counties B35F	402

Withdrawn during 1992

21, 24, 65, 67/8, 70/1, 73, 75 - 77, 78/9, 82, 87, 94/5, 100, 101 - 105, 107 - 135, 138/9, 141/2, 146, 149, 152 - 159, 161/2, 167, 179, 185/6, 188, 1010/1 1060/1, 1074 - 1076, 1681 - 1685, 1687 - 1694, 1698/9, 1703/4, 1706/7, 1709 - 1717, 1719 - 1734, 1736 - 1749, 1751/3/4, 1757 - 1765, 1767, 1769, 1770, 1774/5, 1779, 1783, 1785 - 1799, 1804, 1809 - 1811, 1813, 1815 - 1817, 1822, 1835/6, 2422

Coachline fleet transferred to SUT/Sheafline in 1991, and officially withdrawn from main fleet at start of 1992.

1993

Acquired (SUT/Sheafline fleet, including Coachline)

Chassis	Body	Fleetnumbers
2 Leyland Atlantean AN68B/1R	Marshall H45/29D	800/1
2 Neoplan N416	Neoplan B50F	802/3
1 Leyland National 11351A/1R	Leyland DP45F	804
2 Leyland National Greenway	East Lancs B48F	805/6
1 Leyland National 11351/1R	Leyland DP48F	807
16 Leyland National 11351A/1R	Leyland B49F	808 - 823
20 Leyland National 11351A/1R	Leyland B50F	824 - 843
8 Leyland National 11351/1R	Leyland B52F	844 - 851
2 Leyland National 10351A/1R	Leyland B41F	852/3
5 Leyland National 10351B/1R	Leyland B44F	854 - 858
3 Leyland National 11351A/1R	Leyland B49F	859 - 861
8 Leyland National 11351A/1R	Leyland B50F	862 - 868
9 Leyland National 11351A/1R	Leyland B52F	869 - 877
7 Leyland National 2 NL116L11/1R	Leyland B52F	878 - 884
2 Leyland Tiger	Duple C51F	1001/2
3 Dennis Dorchester SDA808	Plaxton C44Ft	1005 - 1007
2 Dennis Javelin	Duple C53F	1008/9
2 Volvo B10M	Plaxton C48Ft	1010/1

Withdrawn during 1993

53, 136/7, 148, 150/1, 170, 173, 176, 178, 187, 834, 1768, 1780, 2269

Right

Until the call to the paintshop, buses had their previous SYT fleetname covered over with a Mainline vinyl, as shown by Halfway based 2483 seen in Sheffield Interchange.

1994

New

	Chassis	Body	Fleetnumbers
1	Volvo B10L	Saffle B40D	403
2	Volvo B6	Plaxton B40F	411/2

Withdrawn during 1994

4, 140, 143 - 145, 147, 160, 163/4, 166/8/9, 172/4, 180, 182 - 184, 411/2, 801, 807, 816, 824, 826, 829, 830, 837/8, 840/6, 850/1, 865, 869, 872, 876, 878, 1062, 1696, 1766, 1771, 1772, 1781, 1814, 1819, 1829, 2420, 2440/3/4

1995

New & Acquired (absorbtion of Don Valley Buses)

	Chassis	Body	Fleetnumbers
30	Volvo B6	Plaxton B40F	411 - 440
25	Volvo B10M	Alexander B49F	716 - 740
9	Volvo B6LE	Wright B36F	441 - 449
2	Volvo B6	Alexander B40F	103/4
1	Volvo B10M	Plaxton C49Ft	1000
1	Dodge S56	Reeve Burgess DP25F	129
2	Dodge S56	Reeve Burgess B25F	163/4
1	Mercedes Benz 811D	Dormobile B24F	60
1	Mercedes Benz 709D	Carlyle B29F	66
2	Mercedes Benz 709D	Robin Hood B29F	68/169
2	Mercedes Benz 811D	Alexander C33F	70/2
2	Ford Transit 190D	Dormobile B16F	105/6
1	Mercedes Benz 609D	NW Coach Craft C24F	75

Withdrawn during 1995

20, 175, 189, 200, 205, 206, 221, 258, 800, 804, 808 -812, 814/5/7/8, 820 - 823, 825, 828, 831 - 833, 835/6/9, 841 - 845, 847/8, 852 - 864, 866 - 868, 870/1, 873 - 877, 1821, 1824, 1826, 1827, 1832

1996

New & Acquired

	Chassis	Body	Fleetnumbers
8	Volvo B10M	Alexander DP49F	741 - 748
32	Volvo B10M	Alexander B49F	749 - 780
2	Volvo B6LE	Wright B32F	450/1
4	Volvo B6LE	Wright DP36F	452 - 455
11	Mercedes Benz 709D	Plaxton DP12FL	112 - 122
1	Freight Rover Sherpa	Carlyle B15FL	9

Withdrawn during 1996

10, 19, 23, 25 - 27, 29, 60, 68, 69, 75, 105/6, 129, 163 - 165, 169, 171, 177, 191, 223/5/8, 231/2, 234/5, 238/9, 255 - 257, 402, 403, 802/3, 805/6, 813, 819, 827, 849, 879, 880 - 884, 1000, 1002, 1005 - 1011, 1064, 1686, 1693/5/7, 1700 - 1702, 1750, 1752/5/6, 1773, 1777/8, 1780/2/4, 1800 - 1803, 1805 - 1808, 1812/8, 1820/3/5/8, 1830/1, 1833/4, 1868, 1913, 2128

1997

New & Acquired

	Chassis	Body	Fleetnumbers
1	Volvo B6LE	Wright B36F	400
8	Dennis Dart 9.8SDL	Plaxton B36F	4000 - 4007
10	Volvo B10BLE	Wright B44F	781 - 790
3	MCW Metrorider MF150	MCW B21F	3006/11/12

Withdrawn during 1997

22, 66, 70, 72, 193 - 195, 197, 199, 201/3/8, 210/1, 220/4/6, 251, 1001, 1905, 1920, 1925/6, 2101/4/6, 2110 - 2115, 2117, 2123/5, 2130/5/8/9, 2141/3/4, 2150/2/3, 2161, 2173, 2197, 2318

1998

New & Acquired (Northern Bus)

	Chassis	Body	Fleetnumbers
16	Mercedes Benz Vario	Plaxton B29F	123 - 138
31	Dennis Dart SPD	Plaxton B41F	508 - 538
23	Volvo B10BLE	Wright B41F	791 - 813
4	MCW Metrorider MF150	MCW B23F	3001 - 3004
10	Leyland National 11351A/1R	Leyland B49F	21 - 30

Withdrawn during 1998

21 - 30, 62/3, 98, 103/4, 190/2/8, 202/4/7/9, 212 - 219, 222/7/9, 230, 236/7, 240 - 242, 245, 252, 1858, 1918, 1927, 1930/1, 1944 - 1946, 1950, 1952 - 1955, 1958 - 1960, 2116, 2122, 2129, 2155/6, 2166, 2178, 2223, 2456, 3012

Right and Below

The more imaginative your marketing, the more likely you're going to do well.

Virgin Holidays used this to good example on Metrobus 1935.

Mainline was also adept at using billboards to great advantage. Mind you, cornering may have been difficult in this B10M.

Above

The fleet was always full of surprises, there never being a dull moment.

Bus 18 was painted out of Coachline livery into this not unpleasant white, red brown variant of SYT livery. 287 was latterly used in normal service at Christmas time to promote the company. 521 shows the unusual exit arrangement at Halfway garage, whilst 2188 has silver wheels in this early Mainline repaint.

Overall adverts were generally garish affairs. 2116 is extoling the virtues of Flamingo Land, 2222 advertises the arch enemy of all public transport, the car, in this advert for Sheaf Motors, whilst underneath the forest of contravision, Metrobus 1940 is prompting the general public to hope 'it's you' in this advertising campaign for the National Lottery.

The end......

Above

Remembering where you came from is always a good thing.

SYT/Mainline is now but a memory, but there are millions of people who fondly remember the company.

Now part of FirstBus, in 2018, the company painted one of its Volvo B7 single deck buses in the retro Mainline colours, turning heads around the region.

Just to prove things never stand still, this bus has also now been withdrawn, but is seen in happier times at Arundel Gate, Sheffield.

Back Cover

Rounding off our book, what better way, than a quick snapshot of the 14 years covered in it.

From top left: 2142 is seen at East Bank garage; 1811 in Rotherham; 2219 at Doncaster garage; 2407 at Firshill; 2421 & 2185 in Rotherham; 643 in High Street, Doncaster; 1755 in Sheffield; 852 at Rotherham Bus Station; 433 at South Elmsall; 65 showing off its wheelchair lift; Rotherham engineering workshops; 2487's new rear end; 610 at Greenland garage; 2106 at Walkley and finally, three Dennis Dominator rear ends, in the yard, at the town's garage.